The Infamous Cherry Sisters

The Infamous Cherry Sisters

The Worst Act in Vaudeville

DARRYL W. BULLOCK

McFarland & Company, Inc., Publishers
Jefferson, North Carolina

ISBN (print) 978-1-4766-7556-5
ISBN (ebook) 978-1-4766-3479-1

LIBRARY OF CONGRESS CATALOGUING DATA ARE AVAILABLE

BRITISH LIBRARY CATALOGUING DATA ARE AVAILABLE

© 2019 Darryl W. Bullock. All rights reserved

No part of this book may be reproduced or transmitted in any form or by any means, electronic or mechanical, including photocopying or recording, or by any information storage and retrieval system, without permission in writing from the publisher.

Front cover: Poster used to advertise the first performance by the Cherry Sisters, designed by Jessie Cherry, January 1893 (Orville Rennie and Jane Rennie Collection, 1875–1987. Ms178. Special Collections, State Historical Society of Iowa, Iowa City. Used by permission).

Printed in the United States of America

McFarland & Company, Inc., Publishers
Box 611, Jefferson, North Carolina 28640
www.mcfarlandpub.com

For Ella, Lizzie, Addie, Effie and Jessie...

Acknowledgments

First and foremost, I am forever indebted to Hang Nguyen for her invaluable help in sifting through the Orville and Jane Rennie Collection, the primary source for all things Cherry. Hang, without your generous assistance, patience and understanding this book would never have been written. I am also beholden to Darren A. Peace, for not only being a fine editor, but for being my friend for near enough all of my adult life.

Special thanks to Layla Milholen at McFarland & Company, to Lynette Brenzel and the team at the Marion Heritage Center and Museum, to Mary J. Bennett and the team at the State Historical Society of Iowa, and to Mark Stoffer Hunter and the team at the History Center, Cedar Rapids. Huge thanks to Diane Langton and Brian Morelli of the *Cedar Rapids Gazette*, to Jay Kacena of the Friends of Oak Shade Cemetery, and to Patsi Gann and her sisters for keeping the spirit of the Cherry Sisters alive in their hometown.

Thanks too to Dan O'Brien, author of *The Cherry Sisters Revisited* for his time and input, to theater historian Cezar del Valle for his insight in to the world of vaudeville and the American theater, and to Jack El-Hai for pointing me in the right direction in the first place. Finally, thank you, Niall, for your unending, unstinting faith and support.

Table of Contents

Acknowledgments   vi
Introduction   1

1. The Cherry Sisters Opera Company   5
2. Down on the Farm   17
3. Riot in Dubuque   27
4. Live, with (or without) a Net   40
5. Four Freaks from Iowa   48
6. And Then There Were Three   61
7. Riot at the Armory   75
8. The Cherry Sisters vs. the *Des Moines Leader*   84
9. The Cherry Sisters Held to Ransom   94
10. On the Comeback Trail   105
11. Can She Bake a Cherry Pie?   116
12. Effie for Mayor!   124
13. On the Comeback Trail (Again)   135
14. The End   148
15. Aftermath   155

Appendix 1: The Cherry Sisters in Concert   163
Appendix 2: A Cherry Sisters Timeline   166
Chapter Notes   193
Bibliography   203
Index   205

Introduction

Cherries red and Cherries ripe,
The Cherrys they are out of sight.
Cherries ripe and cherries red,
Cherry Sisters are still ahead.[1]

This is the story of how five untrained—and seemingly untalented—women, all from the same dirt-poor farming family, became huge stars and, for a brief period, joined the ranks of the best-paid performers on the American stage. In 1890s America, more than a century before the Internet and social media allowed an almost instantaneous sharing of stories, word spread like wildfire that the Cherry Sisters were the single most inept act then performing on the stage. It was said that they were "so bad they were good," and audiences, often armed with missiles, would happily travel miles and pay good money to see them fail. These "unsophisticated country girls who gained much notoriety by reason of the unique entertainments that they give"[2] became world famous for all the wrong reasons. "The Cherrys are four girls who think they can act. They are alone in this opinion."[3] No one who ever saw the Cherry Sisters perform would forget them. Neither would they forgive them.

The Sisters were possessed of an unshakable belief in the quality of their work, so much so "that a cyclone could scarcely throw them from their base,"[4] yet almost everything that has been written about them—outside of one or two scholarly studies—has reiterated the idea that their act was laughably bad. People have been repeating that line ever since they first took to the stage, when ridiculing the guileless women became something of a sport. It is rare to find a performer who has not suffered at the hands of critics, yet the vitriol levied at the Cherry Sisters went far beyond criticism and often descended into full-blown misogyny. Nothing was off limits: not only were they ridiculed for their lack of acting ability, they were also mocked for their looks, their beliefs, their political affiliations, their decision to remain unmarried, and more besides. After what was only their second performance in front of a paying audience they were being referred to in the press as "the Cherry freaks," and on many occasions unflattering comparisons were drawn between the Sisters' strict moral code and that of the hatchet-wielding radical prohibitionist Carrie Nation, the public's then-current *bête noire*. The Sisters reached the peak of their fame at a time when women were still being denied the right to vote, when a woman's place was very much supposed to be in the home, raising children and never questioning her position in life. Over the best part of half a century, while managing a stage career and several businesses of their own, these five women struggled to prove that they could be just as resourceful, adaptable and as capable as men.

The Cherry Sisters "probably caused more laughter than any other performers who appeared on the vaudeville stage,"[5] yet, as they gained notoriety, their audiences became more boisterous, and on several occasions Cherry Sisters performances descended in to full-blown riots. Artists who choose to stick their heads above the parapets stand the chance of getting their hats knocked off, and the Sisters soon became adept at dodging rotten fruit and vegetables, shoes, eggs, festering meat, dead animals and anything else that was hurled at them—including, on one infamous occasion, a metal wash tub.

Such scenes were nothing new in theaters. In 1856 a Washington newspaper reported that "last night a fellow, either crazy or drunk, we should think, threw a live cat upon the stage during the representation of 'She Stoops to Conquer.' He was promptly arrested, taken to the guard-house, where he was fined $5 and costs."[6] At a performance of Wagner's *Tannhäuser* in Paris in 1861, members of the audience were so incensed at the quality of the ballet that had been inserted into the first act that they blew whistles and fights broke out. The following night tradesmen set up stalls outside the opera house, selling whistles to ticket holders. Such was the commotion that the opera was pulled after just three performances. The later appearances of George Jones, a.k.a. Count Joannes, were so reviled that "scarcely a word said on the stage was audible, so loud and continuous were the cat-calls, laughter, and sarcastic comments and advice given by the spectators to the players."[7] Inevitably a barrage of vegetables accompanied these performances, and when the Cherry Sisters pitched up in New York, local tradesmen made a fortune from fruit and vegetable stalls located outside the main entrance of the theater. On 10 May 1849 a riot broke out at Manhattan's Astor Place Opera House, during a performance by the British Shakespearean actor William Charles Macready, that left around thirty people dead and more than 120 injured. Three days earlier, in the same theater, Macready's *Hamlet* had been brought to a halt by a shower of rotten eggs, potatoes, apples, lemons, shoes, bottles of urine, and ripped up seats aimed at the stage by supporters of his main rival, Edwin Forrest. At least no one died at a Cherry Sisters performance—unless they laughed themselves to death, that is.

There were plenty of bad actors before the Cherrys took to the boards. Robert Coates, the famous amateur, had them howling in the aisles in England at the beginning of the 19th century, and his eccentric take on Shakespeare's Romeo was the stuff of legend. So fond was he of the death scene that he would re-enact it over and over, often during the same performance. James Owen O'Connor was another actor to whom the Cherry Sisters were often compared, always in less than complimentary terms. That's probably because O'Connor's audience was also known to shower him with rotten fruit and vegetables, and he had reportedly played behind a screen to protect himself from the onslaught ... although the comparison may have come about because O'Connor, like the Cherrys, spent a good deal of his time in court. The fact that he died in an asylum was just frosting on the cake.

The musical theater was a slave to fashion, yet in more than 40 years on the stage the Sisters' act barely changed. As the clothes on their counterparts became more and more revealing, the Cherry Sisters remained swathed in floor-length gowns, and, as sex became the main commodity on offer at the music hall, the Sisters continued to use the stage as a pulpit to preach about abstinence, the dangers of alcohol, and the fiery pit that awaited the wicked if they did not change their immoral ways. Effie Cherry—always the most outspoken and intractable of the bunch—spent a lifetime railing against permissiveness, and she was convinced that the negative reviews and vicious reportage that followed them throughout their career was leveled at them because they refused to play the game: "Managers ... thought more of the actress who would drink with them. A young woman's lot on the stage is not an easy one if she is a refined Christian woman with no brother or men folks to protect her."[8] Further, she was adamant that "all the wicked, false and malicious articles written in the newspapers throughout the country concerning the Cherry Sisters were written by unscrupulous editors and reporters devoid of all honor, morals or even respectability."[9]

I have been obsessed with the story of the Cherry Sisters for several years now, and it has been a constant source of amazement to me that, at no point in the century and a quarter since they first trod the boards, has there been a full-length biography of this singular phenomenon. For their tale is truly amazing. Theirs is a story that begins in farce and ends in tragedy, with plenty of both comedy and drama along the way. It is a story of more than music and mayhem; it is the tale of how close family ties were broken over petty jealousies, and how one woman's drive to make something of her life left her—and her family—with nothing. The Cherry Sisters claimed to have come from good American stock: descended directly from the Pilgrim Fathers, one uncle, the women insisted, had been a congressman who had a town and a university named after him; another relative had been the first man to publish a Thanksgiving proclamation. Yet they died in penury, with two of them quite literally living in a hole in the ground. It's a soap opera worthy of the Victorian melodramas the Sisters often performed on stage. Yet documenting their story has not been easy. The majority of those who have attempted to write about them in the past have often chosen fun over fact, and although Effie Cherrie made several stabs at writing her family's biography, her inability to accept even the slightest criticism—and to play fast and loose with her own history—makes her an important but ultimately unreliable source. Even at their height, newspapers were seldom interested in the truth, forever confusing one sister with another, making up "quotes" from family members and allowing their reports to be colored by their own bias. Very few were going to let something as trivial as the truth get in the way of a good story.

For more than a century the world has labored under the impression that the five daughters of Thomas and Laura Cherry were little more than incompetents. But were they? Could they have been having us all on and, for a time at least, were they laughing all the way to the bank? Twenty-first century television is full of hit shows starring families with no discernible talent whatsoever and, had the Cherry Sisters been performing today, there is no doubt in my mind that they would be huge stars. The simple fact is that they were born at least 100 years too early. In a time when women had little, if any, voice, Ella, Lizzie, Addie, Effie and Jessie Cherry were pioneers ... and like many of the great American pioneers, none of the sisters were afraid to use a gun to protect their land, their family, or to make their point.

However good, or bad, the Cherry Sisters were, there can be no doubt that their act gave good value for money, and that they gave more pleasure to their audiences than many of their contemporaries. I hope that this book goes some way towards restoring their reputation as the Queens of Comedy, the brightest stars of the American stage.

* * *

Note: Throughout the text you will see reference to "the Cherry sisters," "the Cherry Sisters," "the Sisters" and so on. Where "Sisters" appears capitalized it refers specifically to the members of the acting troupe, in its various iterations.

1

The Cherry Sisters Opera Company

It was all Effie's idea.

One morning in January 1893, Effie Cherry called to deliver milk at Jennie Patterson's boarding house at 10 Twelfth Street North, Marion, Iowa. At the door her sister Addie, who had been helping Miss Patterson while she recovered from surgery, greeted her. "Addie," she announced, "I have made up my mind to give a concert at the opera house. What do you think of it?"[1] Addie, the elder of the two, was skeptical, reasoning that "there are some people in this town who would try and make it disagreeable for us," but the headstrong Effie, emboldened by her success in various school and church productions, quickly convinced her that this was indeed a brilliant suggestion. "That doesn't bother me in the least, Addie. I'm not afraid of them. I think we can get up a very nice entertainment with very little trouble. You might as well approve of my plans, for I am going right ahead with them."[2] With that she climbed on to her horse drawn buggy and was off. "You come over to the house tonight and we'll talk it over," she called out as she went on her way.

Their friends agreed with Effie that this was a pip of a proposal, and gladly offered to lend a hand. After Effie had approached the manager of the town's opera house to arrange for the hire of the building, Mary Braska, a local milliner who knew how much the girls enjoyed performing in front of their class at school, suggested that they try out their material by giving a recitation to some of the young men who were residing at Miss Patterson's. Eugene Parsons, a meat trader who would later become Marion's city clerk, and Carl Owen, a former classmate of the girls' eldest sister Ella, and now the owner of the town drug store, also encouraged them: it would not be long before the soda fountain at Carl Owen's was offering a Cherry Sisters sundae. Parsons lent Effie his coat, his case, and his silk top hat to use as a costume, and Owen and Miss Braska sold tickets. A splendid time, it seemed, was guaranteed for all, and the idea that the Cherry children were to put on an "entertainment" (the word the Sisters would forever use to describe their act) quickly became the number one topic of conversation in the town.

It has always been maintained that one of the reasons that the untrained and unprepared women went on stage was to raise money for a trip to Chicago to visit the World's Columbian Exposition, popularly known as the Chicago World's Fair. Over the years writers and reporters have also speculated that the sisters took to the stage in the hope of raising enough money to pay off the mortgage on the family farm. But the chance to gawk at the wonders of the modern world or keep the bank off their collective backs was only of secondary concern. The Cherrys believed that, once there, they would be able to find their itinerant brother Nathan—who was last heard of in Chicago—and persuade him to return to the family farm with them. Two of the sisters had already visited Illinois in a futile attempt to track him down, and their first ever press write up confirmed that "the concert given last evening was with the avowed purpose of finding a lost brother who has been absent about four years."[3] Although the thought that Nathan might have been an inhabitant of the Windy City provided Effie with the germ of an idea, the Cherry women would not journey to Chicago for a second time until several years after their concert debut, and they would never see their beloved brother again.

On 12 January 1893 the *Marion Sentinel* carried the following brief notice:

> "The Cherry Opera Co. is announced to appear at Daniels opera house, Friday evening, Jan. 20. Admission 35 and 50 cents. The costumes are in the latest styles. They will also play at Greene's opera house, Cedar Rapids. After that they will travel. Go and enjoy a rare musical treat. Don't forget the date."[4]

Amazingly, even though not one of them had appeared in front of a paying audience, the Sisters (or Effie, at least) were possessed of a huge amount of confidence, and were already thinking to a future at the footlights. "It was when we were in high school that we got the idea

Advertisement for the Sisters' debut performance, January 1893.

of going on the stage," she confided in a reporter more than thirty years later. "We wrote pieces and sang songs of our own."[5] Years later Harry Bell, an agent who worked in Los Angeles, claimed that he had given the Sisters their first break, ahead of their debut in Marion. He had been managing a troupe in Rock Island, Iowa, and they were about to appear in Cedar Rapids when several of his actors walked out. "They left me that afternoon," he explained. "This was naturally a bit discouraging at first but somebody told me that the Cherry family had three daughters and a mortgage on the farm and that the daughters were planning an amateur performance with a view of keeping the old homestead. I went to the young women and offered them three dollars apiece to fill the vacant spaces in my little band. That evening the Cherry Sisters made their professional debut. I was out in front when they went on and for a long time I couldn't make out what the sisters were endeavoring to do."[6]

Harry Bell's story was no more than a tall tale told by a peripatetic showman, and when he recounted the story of that debut performance five years later, the number of Cherrys he claimed to have employed had reduced from three to two. Comedian Frank Colton also claimed to have discovered the Cherrys, and in doing so "gave to the American stage the worst show ever witnessed,"[7] but his assertion that all five sisters came to see him perform and that they were so moved that they got up there and then and took to the stage between acts is also no more than a fantasy. Neither man would be the first or last to try and take credit for launching the Sisters on an unsuspecting world, although considering the mountain of bad press the women received over the years it is a wonder that anyone would wish to be acknowledged for having discovered them.

In truth, the five members of the grandly named Cherry Concert Company made their stage debut at Daniels Opera House in Marion on 20 January 1893. The troupe not only changed their name within days of announcing the date of their first concert, but also dropped the price of their tickets to 25 and 35 cents respectively. Promoted via self-designed posters that the enterprising women nailed up around the area that promised "Lovely Costumes, Rare and Sweet Music, Laughter by the Yard," the show featured the Cherry Sisters wearing homemade costumes and (legend has it) with gold paint—purchased from Carl Owen and left over from their posters—splashed liberally in their hair. "Marion society was all agog before the concert given by the Cherry Concert Company at the opera house last Friday night," the *Marion Sentinel* reported the following Thursday in a piece headlined "The Event of the Season." "It has been the main topic of conversation since when two or more people get together. It will be many a day before those who attended will forget the enjoyable time spent."[8]

Labeling the evening "a polished and recherché affair," the show began with a song from Effie, "Father, Steer for Me" (Effie later recalled that the opening song was composed by a cousin and titled "I Am Growing Blind"[9]) which received such a "roar of applause [that it] shook the opera house until the brilliant gas jets danced in amazement." Jessie then came on stage to play a solo on her mouth organ, which she followed by singing J.P. Skelly's turgid Victorian ballad "Why Did They Dig Ma's Grave So Deep?" Jessie was the hit of the night, and dressed as a flower girl she also sang "Buy My Flowers, Sweet Lady, Buy," a self-penned song that she had clearly based on Gilbert and Sullivan's "I'm Called Little Buttercup." Ella, who would not remain with the troupe for long, performed a self-penned attempt at a minstrel song entitled "Old Sam Patch" in blackface, dressed in her late father's coat and boots. Three of the sisters—Ella, Addie and Lizzie (although Effie later claimed that Lizzie did not perform on the night and instead merely sat in the audience)-capered around the stage swinging their arms in a vague approximation of a dance while Jessie played the mouth organ and Effie played piano. The Sisters were not alone on the stage: Professor John St. Clair and Will Prickett, of Cedar Rapids, who "played solos on the violin and mandolin,"[10] provided musical interludes. "The good people of this handsome, overgrown village on Indian Creek absolutely crowded and jammed, pushed and hauled, and literally walked over one another in their wild efforts to procure seats," the *Cedar Rapids Gazette* added, claiming that the roar of the audience was so loud that it shook the building. "The public wanted fun, the public got it; the young ladies wanted money, they got it."[11]

"I remember two things from that first performance," one of the sisters' neighbors recalled. "Ella made up as an old negro, slapping her knees and yelling 'I fell across a log and I thought it was a dog,' and Jessie with her long blonde hair down over her shoulders coming out barefooted carrying a basket of flowers to sing 'The Orphan Flower Girl.' 'When did you wash your feet last, Jessie?' the audience yelled. They didn't throw things but they whistled and stomped and sang."[12] Effie noted that the box office took "close to $200," and contemporary reports confirm that, after costs, the Cherrys were rewarded with $100 for one night's work—a huge sum in those days and more cash than the five women had ever seen before. That windfall—and the polite praise from the friends and neighbors who had purchased tickets for the show—convinced the women that it would be sound financial sense to repeat their performance on a bigger stage. They were, after all, unskilled and ill-educated, and had little to look forward to in life: no matter how hard they worked (and none of the Cherry women shirked their responsibilities in that respect), the farm would never be able to support them all. Effie's conviction that their future lay in show business was, it seemed, correct. A life on the road offered them a way out of penury, although Addie was not convinced that performing for a theater audience was the right decision. "That was where we made the mistake of our lives," she confided in reporters.

> There was a lot of roughs that brought cabbages and turnips and all that sort of thing to throw at the stage, and they made such a racket that we could scarcely hear ourselves talk. If only we'd begun with the YMCA we'd a-been all right. I tell you, it's the religious people you must get hold of if you want to make a success of an entertainment like ours.[13]

Having already boasted about their intention to play Greene's Opera House in nearby Cedar Rapids, and bolstered by the success of their debut, Addie and Effie went to see the manager to negotiate a deal. He was unconvinced of their ability to draw an audience, but, after some persuading, agreed to rent them the hall for $50. The following day, Addie and Lizzie took half of the money they had earned in Marion and booked the family act into Greene's for 17 February. While they were away, Effie was to visit the offices of the *Marion Register* to arrange for handbills and posters to be printed, but before departing, the ever-canny Lizzie had Effie write her an IOU for her share of the money. The document guaranteed Lizzie one fifth of any profits, and left Effie entirely responsible for any costs incurred should the Sisters bomb. Effie promised to give Lizzie two of her cows if she could not repay the debt, and awarded her the honorary role of manager for the night. Right at the very start of their career, Lizzie was displaying the financial acumen (or was it simply greed?) that would cause difficulties between her and her sisters for the rest of their lives.

That night the auditorium was packed. However, their hopes of being as well received there as they had been by their home crowd were quickly dashed. The audience, more sophisticated than the throng they had pleased in Marion, was rowdy, blowing tin horns and throwing missiles at the stage during their performance. The Cherrys, unaccustomed to such goings-on, assumed that the noise was a roar of approval for their efforts to entertain, and they continued with their show despite the pandemonium. They struggled valiantly on, performing the standards "The Curfew Shall Not Ring Tonight" and "My Bonnie Lies Over the Ocean"[14] alongside their own original material, but by the end of the evening it had become obvious, even to the seemingly oblivious sisters, that they were being mocked.

The reaction could not have come as a complete surprise, for Sam Daniels, the postmaster at Marion, had already cautioned Addie and Effie that "some of the Marion men ... are going down to break up your concert. I think a great deal of you girls, and I wouldn't want any harm to come to you, but I'm afraid these men mean business."[15] The normally stoic Effie must have regretted not paying heed to his words of warning.

Once the performance was over, Greene's stage manager told the tearful girls that, were they to make a second appearance beneath his proscenium arch, then he would have to erect a screen to protect them from the constant barrage of detritus,[16] but the reaction of the audience was no preparation for the opprobrium levied at them the following day. The threat of physical injury from the odd flying shoe was nothing compared to the shame that the sisters felt after reading the review in the *Cedar Rapids Gazette*, which reported that "such unlimited gall as was exhibited last night at Greene's opera house by the Cherry sisters is past the understanding of ordinary mortals."[17] The Sisters were crushed, but it is not difficult to comprehend the audience's disgust. The theater in the 1890s was a predominantly male domain, and the men went there in the hope of seeing voluptuous women with rouged cheeks showing some flesh. The other notable sister act of the day, the Barrison Sisters, were five siblings who teased and titillated audiences by asking "Do you want to see my pussy" before lifting their skirts to reveal a live kitten strapped to their crotches. The eldest Barrison Sister would then do a striptease before riding across the stage on a horse, apparently naked (she wasn't, but the body stocking, or "fleshings," she wore gave the appearance of nudity), and they were known as The Wickedest Girls in the World, or the Embarrassing Sisters. The Cherry Sisters offered no such display. Hardly voluptuous (Jessie was often described as dumpy or fat, Effie as being as thin as a rail), their homemade calico dresses, which the women always adorned with bunches of cherries, covered almost every inch of skin. The most the audience could hope for was a glimpse of Jessie's bare feet. No soubrettes these, either: the Cherry Sisters were more likely to castigate their audience than to flirt with them.

"They no doubt are respectable girls and probably educated in some few things, but their knowledge of the stage is worse than none at all," the report in the *Gazette* continued. "They surely could not realize last night that they were making such fools of themselves. If some indefinable instinct of modesty could not have warned them that they were acting the part of monkeys, it does seem like the overshoes thrown at them would have conveyed the idea in a more substantial manner. But nothing could drive them away and no combination of yells, whistles, barks and howls could subdue them." Adamant that the theater was filled not by "hoodlums," but by "the best people of the city," the unnamed reporter insisted that the Cherrys

> couldn't sing, speak, or act. They simply were awful. When one of them would appear on the stage, the commercial travelers around the orchestra rail would start to sing, the orchestra would play and the entire audience constituted the chorus. At one minute the

scene was like the incurable ward in an insane asylum, the next like a Methodist camp meeting. Cigars, cigarettes, rubbers, everything was thrown at them, yet they stood there, awkwardly bowing their acknowledgments and singing on. Possibly the most ridiculous thing of the entire performance was an essay—think of it, an essay—read by one of the poor girls, in which she plead for the uplifting of the stage and hoped that no one would be harmed by anything they may have witnessed during the evening.[18]

The women, it was reported, left the stage to howls from the audience and the strains of "Ta-ra-ra Boom-de-ay from the orchestra." Years later, when penning her memoirs, Effie would claim that "very little disturbance prevailed"[19] at the concert, and that the hoo-ha drummed up by the *Gazette* was done out of spite. She knew exactly who was to blame too: the agent from the *Marion Register* who turned up at their door just as they were to leave for Cedar Rapids, demanding they settle the bill for their printing. When they refused to pay then and there (but offered to do so from the box office that evening), the agent promised to "fix them" in the local papers and to ruin any chances they had of a successful career. Effie's rather lurid tale of a dastardly villain banging on the front door of the family home made it in to her unpublished memoirs, but—like much of her own version of their story—it feels somewhat revisionist, as does her insistence that a neighbor who read the review suggested that she "would give that editor a horse-whipping"[20] on the Sisters' behalf. For the rest of her life, Effie would blame a good deal of the bad publicity and poor reviews the Sisters received on troublemakers from Marion.

If the man from the *Register* had indeed intended to "fix" them, his actions had entirely the opposite effect. But the Cherry Sisters were not the only act to be treated so appallingly by the audience of the day; many vaudeville troupes suffered similar indignities. A "full chorus of pretty and shapely young ladies"[21] known as the Fanny Hill Company (named after the racy 18th century novel by John Cleland) which toured at the same time as the Cherrys was regularly assaulted with a barrage of tin cans, potatoes and the like. It must have seemed that, at a time when women at home were demanding emancipation, men were exercising their misogyny in the comfort of the theater instead. Audiences were rarely passive observers, and the atmosphere in these grandly named theaters was often more like that of a circus than of a refined opera house.

Incensed at their treatment in the press, the Sisters decided that they had to do something to protect their honor. The morning after that report appeared, a furious Addie—whose initial reaction had indeed been to horse-whip the reporter—turned up at the offices of the *Gazette* and demanded to see the man responsible for the review. When he refused to make himself known, she offered ten dollars to the first member of *Gazette* staff who would point him out to her. Insisting on a retraction, Addie handed in a handwritten letter that the newspaper dutifully reprinted "*ad literatum et punctuatim*":

> The Cherry Sisters Concert that appeared In the GAZETTE the other evening was intily a mistake and we take it back. The young ladies wer refined and modest in every respict and there intertanement was as good as any that has been given in the city by home people. The noise and tumult that was raised in the house was not done as was stated by the Cedar Rapids people but by a lot of toughs that came down from Marion with the intention of creating a disturbance which was very imbaressing to the young ladies and greately hindered there concert. But theay finished there Program under great disadvantage be it said in there favor with an unruly house and drunken Stage managers. Theas young ladies have left school to hold theas intanements to ade them in serching for an absent brother.[22][*sic*]

The day following the appearance of this barely intelligible retraction, whose publication only added to the Sisters' reputation as uneducated rubes, Addie marched to the courthouse in Cedar Rapids and demanded that the Justice of the Peace, Mr. I.N. Whittam, sign an order for the arrest of the writer of the original, scurrilous piece, city editor Fred P. Davis. The Cherrys were already accustomed to seeing their dirty laundry aired in public: Lizzie had enjoyed an ongoing feud with their neighbors, William Cook and his son Charles, and several of their run-ins ended up in the courthouse. The Cooks had buried dead and diseased cattle too close to their only source of water for the Cherry's comfort, and the ensuing battle of wills ended up with Charles Cook suing Lizzie for slander in January 1892. The charge against Davis stated that he did "make, compose and circulate defamatory and libelous matter of, and concerning, the Cherry Sisters' Opera Company, composed of five sisters who are refined, respectable and intelligent, and whose entertainments are highly appreciated."[23] Constable Patterson served a warrant for Davis's arrest the following morning. More than a dozen local newspapers covered this extraordinary turn of events, and before long papers in Boston, Chicago and other cities were also reporting on the proceedings. An unnamed writer on the *Boston Evening Transcript*, who had clearly never met the women, waxed lyrically about the "idyllic peace and rustic calm" of their farm, and how the work they had to do there to make ends meet "appears to have been informed with the spirit of poetry," but that the "volley of overshoes" that greeted them in Cedar Rapids "was an expression of disapproval that never could be lived down."[24] Ironically, as events would later prove, the *Des Moines Leader* was one of the few publications that waded in to the rescue: "[The] five young ladies ... are said to be good, hard working girls [who] yearned for fame of the undying sort which can only be won in the glare of the footlights and where the greasepaint lends a glory to the commonplace."[25]

The unnamed author of the piece was surprisingly prescient in his assertion that "the girls have pluck, even if it often leads them in to foolhardy enterprises."

With this one incident, the Cherry Sisters went from a local curiosity to being of national interest. The story was reported across the country with unbridled glee: the *Burlington Journal* informed its readers that Davis "wrote a racy roast on a gang of female barnstormers and now there's blood on the moon," adding that if he were found guilty he should be "bound hand and foot and be compelled to listen to the sisters sing."[26] With newspapers clamoring for interviews, and venues desperate to book this hottest of new acts, they succumbed to the advances of a professional manager, Mr. D.S.M. Fretwell of Preston, a man who specialized in presenting family friendly entertainment in small towns.[27] Davis, after being arrested by deputy sheriff Tom Brown and constable George Patterson, was released on $100 bail, and his newspaper immediately came up with a brilliant ruse: "Let the trial be held in the opera house and a fee charged. It would make the richest entertainment of the season. The sisters could sing and dance, and Fred is no poor timber in that line himself. The jury could join in the chorus and with the attorneys as end men there would be no lack of fun."[28] Over the years many have suggested that the Sisters were complicit in the subterfuge; if they were or not, the publicity surrounding this peculiar turn of events resulted in the Cherry Sisters being booked to appear in Des Moines and Quincy, Illinois, even before they had faced their attacker. An offer of $200 for the troupe to appear in Marion for the local Elks lodge had to be turned down, as it clashed with the date chosen for their return to Cedar Rapids. Lizzie, the most money-minded of the five sisters, would never have allowed that unless she had been convinced that they could earn more elsewhere.

Poster used to advertise the first performance by the Cherry Sisters, designed by Jessie Cherry, January 1893 (Orville Rennie and Jane Rennie Collection, 1875-1987. Ms. 178. Special Collections, State Historical Society of Iowa, Iowa City).

The confrontation took place on 14 March, again on the stage of Greene's Opera House. To mark the occasion, one of the office clerks at the Burlington, Cedar Rapids, and Northern Railway Company penned a poem, describing their previous performance.

> *There were five girls from Marion,*
> *Whose father died in his prime:*
> *He left them a farm to run,*
> *But not a single dime.*
> *One of them was an artist bold.*
> *Another an actress fine:*
> *The third was of a Venus mold,*
> *And the others right in line.*
>
> *So they organized a company.*
> *To travel the world around,*
> *And of all the combines on the road.*
> *Its equal can't be found.*
> *The songstress sang: "Who'll Buy My Flowers?"*
> *With all her vocal force.*
> *The audience laughed until it cried.*
> *And yelled till it was hoarse.*[29]

Davis's trial was to take place after a return performance by the schoolgirl Sisters, as Effie referred to them. Ella was 39, hardly a schoolgirl; even Little Jessie, the youngest of the girls, was 21 at the time, but for the rest of their lives, the Cherry Sisters would play fast and loose with the truth when it came to their ages. In 1908, in a letter penned by Addie and Effie to "the editors and reporters of the 'Waterloo Reporter' and 'Times Tribune,'" the women insisted that "when we first appeared in concert our ages arranged then from sixteen to twenty-two."[30] The Sisters arrived in the city a day before their performance, and entertained visitors in their rooms at the Arcade Hotel. One of their guests, the editor of Cedar Rapids' weekly *Saturday Chat* newspaper, approached them with an offer of a world tour if they would allow him to manage their interests.

This second concert boasted mostly new material—not that anyone present would have heard much, if any, of it. "Everybody was there, the butcher, the baker, the candlestick maker, and of all the crazy experiences Cedar Rapids was ever treated to, the one last night was the worst. It is all over now and it is to be devoutly hoped that never again will such an aggregation of pitiable, simpering gawks be permitted to array themselves on a stage for a frenzied audience to hoot at, to yell at and to throw at."[31] Needless to say, the house was "jammed full by Cedar Rapids' best to hear the girls sing, and a jury was appointed to sit in a box and pass on the libel. The audience—the biggest in Greene's history—had great fun with itself, joined in the singing, threw hats and umbrellas, blew whistles and tin horns, and didn't hear a word of the concert."[32]

At 8:10 pm the Cherry Sisters' new manager came in front of the curtain to address the audience, informing them that special policemen were patrolling the theater, and that "violent demonstrations of enthusiasm will not be tolerated for an instant."[33] The capacity audience of 1,200 began their barracking as soon as the curtain rose on Lizzie and Effie, whose opening song was drowned out by the noise: "every gesture brought out a howl, and each movement provoked a scream."[34] The flower girl skit was met with hoots of derision as Jessie tramped about the stage "with a basket of flowers and with less grace than an elephant would eat soup."[35] Entertaining themselves with choruses of favorites including "Little Annie Rooney," the audience was so boisterous that two further arrests were made that night.

After a short pantomime in which Davis was fetched, at gunpoint, to the theater to answer to the charges brought against him the jury—made up of twelve bald-headed locals—found the newspaperman guilty, and sentenced him to "in the absence of the Cherry Sisters from their farm, proceed at once to the said farm and manage the same, especially see to it that the pigs are fed at the proper time, that the cows do not go past their milking without due attention, that the ducks are regularly driven to water, and that the chickens are penned at night." Further, Davis was expected to "submit himself to the choice of the sisters, beginning with the eldest, and the first one who shall consent to such alliance, to that one then shall he be joined in the holy bonds of matrimony."[36] There's no evidence to show that Davis served any part of his sentence, and all five sisters remained unwed for the rest of their lives. The box office took an unprecedented $690, with the house retaining half, and the Sisters and their new manager taking a quarter each. Fretwell, a man known for his shrewd business sense, could not believe his luck as theater owners across the state scrambled to book this phenomenal new act, but the sisters themselves questioned if Effie were right about there being a future for them upon the stage. "You will ask why we continued in the entertainment field when we had such heavy odds to contend with," she wrote. "It was for this reason. We were alone in the world and had our own way to make. Our father had left no money at his death, and when we saw the crowds we could draw, and we knew we gave a very pretty and refined entertainment, why should we let them down us?"[37]

Despite the "court" finding in favor of the Sisters, the *Gazette* did not learn any lessons. The following day the paper wrote that "a stranger happening in the opera house last night and witnessing that performance would have come to the conclusion very quickly that a lunatic asylum had been washed away and that at least five of the inmates had been landed among driftwood upon the stage there."[38]

The Sisters had only given three performances in front of paying audiences, but they were already on their way to becoming national celebrities, making press headlines, and netting several hundred dollars as a result. To five single women who had firsthand experience of how financially unrewarding life on a farm was, it must have seemed to them that they had hit the big time.

2

Down on the Farm

Nothing remains today of the farm that the Cherry family once struggled so hard to maintain. If you are prepared to drive down a narrow, rutted lane, and then walk for about a mile or so over hills and through fields, you'll come to the hilltop that once housed a plot encircled by a ramshackle wire fence, and where the rapidly expanding family lived in what can only be described as impoverished circumstances. But there is no marker to signify the few acres of Iowan hillside in an area once known rather optimistically as Lakeside, where cows, colts and chickens once roamed, and no sign of the wooden shack, constructed by Thomas Cherry and his children, where a family once worked, played and prayed. Nothing. Yet it was here, among the trees that rise on the banks of Indian Creek, that Thomas and Laura Cherry raised their children, and it was here, in Linn County, Iowa, that the story of the infamous Cherry Sisters both began and ended.

Thomas C. Cherry took his wife and young daughter away from Marlborough, Massachusetts to build a new life in Linn County in 1856. Thomas was a painter by trade, taking on a wide variety of domestic work as well as painting signs for businesses. He served his apprenticeship in Boston, where his specialty was graining: painting cheap timber to look like much more expensive wood, a common practice among the bourgeoisie of the 19th century. His daughters would later boast about how he was "one of the most artistic painters and gainers of his day. Many were the beautiful pictures he painted and landscaped on the window shades for the housewives."[1] Thomas passed on his passion, if not his skill, for all things artistic to his daughters.

The youngest of three children, he told his rapt offspring that he had once been the gardener for an Earl in England, and that he had been forced to escape across the Atlantic after falling for his employer's daughter. His story was a fantasy—although he would later repeat it to visitors who tended him as he lay on his sick bed. His daughters loved fairy tales, and Effie would often return to the theme of star-crossed lovers facing epic journeys in search of their true destiny. Thomas had, in fact, been born in Rhode Island in 1821, the son of Nathaniel and Ann Cherry. Ten years younger than her husband, Laura Marinda Rawson was the youngest of the five children of Luther Rawson and Electa Hill. "One of Vermont's most beautiful daughters,"[2] Laura, who met and married Thomas in Boston, was a direct descendant of Edward Rawson, who had been born in Dorset, England but who had emigrated to Massachusetts before his twenty-third birthday. Edward Rawson was an intelligent and enterprising young man, quickly rising to the post of town clerk, then becoming both a notary public and registrar for the town of Newbury. In 1650 Rawson was elected Secretary of the Massachusetts Bay Colony—a post he would hold for more than thirty-five years. In 1676 the council of Charlestown instructed him to declare 29 June a day of giving praise for the good fortune that had seen their community established, and that had seen their safe delivery from the "present Warr [sic] with the Heathen Natives of this land." Unknowingly, Rawson became an indelible part of American history as the author of one of the country's earliest Thanksgiving Proclamations. Laura's children grew up believing that they were from good stock.

Moving west primarily because land there was cheap, Thomas, Laura, and their growing family became somewhat nomadic, first settling in Mount Vernon, Iowa before moving at the behest of friends to a new settlement in Clear Lake, then—after a flood wiped out their first crop—back to Mount

Postcard showing a section of Seventh Avenue, Marion, including Daniels Opera House (author's collection).

Vernon, off to Linn Grove, then briefly to Travis City, Michigan and Wheaton, Illinois. Thomas, it seems, had a touch of wanderlust about him. Some years after the Sisters first achieved fame on the stage, reports appeared in several newspapers that one or more of them worked in Morrison, Illinois as cook or housekeeper to the Reverend John Whipple. If that was the case, then Ella, being the eldest, seems to be the most likely candidate, and this must have happened before the family moved back to Iowa permanently. There, after a short time in Cedar Rapids, they finally settled on a rough, twenty-acre plot of land to the south of Marion.

The relatively new town of Marion began to take shape in 1839, on a semicircle of prairie land adjoining Indian Creek. Named after the Revolutionary War General Francis Marion, popularly known as the Swamp Fox, it soon became Linn's county seat. The entire population of this great metropolis numbered no more than 1,300: no wonder the local newspaper referred to the settlement as an "overgrown village." Eighty years later, in November 1919, a public vote was held and the nearby and much bigger Cedar Rapids, which could then boast a population of 45,000 as opposed to Marion's 4,000, became the county capital. When the Cherry family moved there, Marion was pretty and unspoiled, and the railroad had only recently arrived. At that time, land in the area sold for as little as $10 an acre, and unskilled laborers could expect to earn perhaps a dollar a day for a sixty-hour working week. The land Thomas took out a mortgage on was covered in trees, and timber was a saleable commodity. He would have paid a premium for land with a ready source of income.

Noted as "a city of schools and churches," where the "atmosphere has been fairly free from the fetid breath of vice and crime,"[3] Marion must have seemed like the perfect place to raise a good, God-fearing family. It was also felt his poor health would be better served by the clear, fresh air and mild climate. There is no word about what mysterious illness afflicted Thomas but, like his parents, he had never been exactly hale and hearty. Nathaniel Cherry had died when Thomas was just ten years old and his mother would also pass away before he was out of his teens. Slight and weak, life for Thomas was hard and unpredictable, and shortly after the family moved to their hillside smallholding—and before he had finished constructing their home with the timber he had hauled there from their previous home in Cedar Rapids— he was struck down with malaria (then known as "fever and ague"), leaving his wife and children to clear the land, dig out tree stumps and plant buckwheat while he recuperated. Luckily for him Laura was a stout, strong woman who seemed to thrive on hard work and piety ... and her daughters took after her.

Births generally took place at home: there was no money to pay for expensive hospital stays, the best the expectant mother could hope for would be the help of a local midwife, a female relative or perhaps a neighbor. With the invention of the telephone still many years away, there was no way to call for help in an emergency, and it was not unusual for a father to deliver his own children. Although it is usually held that all of the Cherry children apart from Ella, the eldest (born in 1854, although she would knock a full decade off her age in later years), were born on the farm, none of them were; census records show that the family moved to Marion sometime around 1872, after the births of their last children.

Elizabeth Viola (Lizzie) and Ada Roselma (Addie) had been born while the family was in Mount Vernon—Lizzie in 1857 and Addie two years later. The only surviving son, Nathan Albert, came along in 1863, while the burgeoning family was living in Linn Grove, Iowa. Another daughter, Inez (known to the family as Ina) followed two years after that. When Inez was eight years old, she too succumbed to malaria (at around the same time as her father), an illness from which she would never fully recover.

Effie Isabell Cherry came in to the world in 1867 (the date on her grave marker, 1876, is patently wrong. She is listed on the 1870 census as being three years old at the time, although confusingly she appears on the 1880 census as being 11 years old), and before she was two another girl, Anna, was born. This poor child would not last long: she shows up, as a one-year old, on the 1870 census along with all of her older siblings, but is never mentioned again, and does not appear in any of Effie's autobiographical writings. Unfortunately, infant mortality was high, and many children perished before adulthood. Jessie—the youngest Cherry Sister—and her twin brother Alfred were born in Cedar Rapids on 27 November 1871. Sadly, baby Freddie would not reach his first birthday; the twins came down with cholera and whooping cough when they were just ten months old and, although Jessie would recover, Freddie would not.

Work was dictated by the seasons. For a man like Thomas Cherry—when his health allowed—the winter meant chopping wood, fence mending, and general repair work around the farm, while in the springtime along with the older children he prepared and planted the fields. With no running water the children were expected to go down to the creek and return with a bucketful of water several times a day, no matter if it was blowing a gale outside or the land was covered in snow. The family struggled to be as self-sufficient as possible, with Laura and the older Cherry children making clothes, producing their own butter, soap, candles, and medicines (the family had their own recipes for cures for everything from snake bites to hemorrhoids), as well as milking the cows and collecting eggs. During the spring, the children had to hatch and care for chickens, while Laura planted vegetables in the garden and kept on top of her housekeeping duties: cooking, cleaning, and caring for the children. Thomas had planted apple, pear, cherry, plum and peach trees, and during the summer and fall Laura and her daughters canned vegetables and soft fruit, and apples, potatoes and other root crops were harvested and stored for winter use.

Most days the Cherry sisters would walk in to town, in homemade calico dresses and bare feet, to sell milk and eggs to their neighbors. If they were going to church, they would carry their shoes and stockings with them and put them on once they had crossed their land and reached civilization. To get to the main road that led in to Marion, they had to cut through their neighbor's farm, occasionally hitching a ride in to town with the farmer if he had business there. The eldest girls became adept at looking after the cows, and they also learned how to dress poultry, plucking the birds their father or brother had dispatched and selling those too. The family also bought in poultry to dress and sell on; a skill that Lizzie, in particular, excelled in. By the end of 1879 Lizzie had her own thriving little business, and was sending prepared birds to Albany, New York, more than 1,000 miles from the family farm (the Cherrys had cousins on Madison Avenue in Albany: presumably they helped promote their business). Local physician Doctor Crew recalled how the Cherry girls would turn up at his mother-in-law's door and ask: "How do you want your chicken? Dressed or undressed?"[4] The funny thing was, she could never recall having ordered any poultry from them.

The farm grew steadily: Thomas and his children built a barn for their cows, a hen coop, and dug out a cave on their land to store winter vegetables in. Nathan saved money he had earned cutting wood for a neighbor and bought a sheep. With plenty of work to keep them occupied, and a large family with whom to play with, study the Bible with, and to bash out a tune on the cheap piano that stood in the corner, the children showed little interest in associating with others of their age. When the weather was good, and when they had finished their chores, the Cherry children would walk the half a mile or so to the banks of Indian Creek, where they would fill their buckets with gooseberries, blackberries, hazelnuts, and black walnuts. Although there was no money for such trivial things as toys, Ella would often make her own out of scraps and off-cuts of wood, which she would give to the others at Christmas or on their birthdays. Recalling those days more than six decades later, Effie wrote that "Work to us was better than play, and when the day was done it was with pleasure that the older children would relate to our mother what they had accomplished through the day. So early in life our parents sowed the seeds of thrift in their children and taught us to despise no honorable work, be it ever so humble."[5]

School—although it was a three-mile walk from home—offered a welcome respite for the older children from their chores; their mother, who had been a teacher before her marriage, gave the younger ones lessons at home, using the *New England Primer*, the God-fearing puritan's favorite textbook, as her guide. None of the Cherry siblings stood out academically, but Ella often took part in school plays—fellow student Mary Dunham recalled how she "recited 'The Turkey and the Crow' at one of our literaries, to the mortal anguish of one of my classmates,"[6] and the whole family could be heard every Sunday singing at the top of their voices in church. Their mother instilled a fervent belief in God, one that stayed with the daughters of Laura Cherry for the rest of their lives.

> "I say!" screamed the Gobbler, as falling behind
> He saw his antagonist certain to win,
> "Look here! Did it ever occur to your mind
> "You're as black as the deuce and as ugly as sin?"[7]

One classmate, Carl Owen, remembered that, during a recital, "Ella gave something in which she was supposed to be a hunter. What did she do but throw a dummy pigeon of some sort in the air and then shoot at it. It scared everyone; including the teacher, half to death."[8] The Sisters would later regale audiences with their shooting prowess. "I remember that we boys used to go to the Cherry farm south of Marion to hunt squirrels," recalled another of their fellow students, F.P. Riddell. "When ever we'd shoot, we'd expect one of the Cherry girls to come out and try to chase us off their property."[9] Both Owen and Riddell would later be in the audience at the Sister's debut performance.

Effie, the most prolific writer in the family, was just 10 years old when she composed the prose poem "The First of May," and was chosen by her teacher to give the recitation on the day her class graduated. Jessie wrote sentimental lyrics, and all the girls occasionally wrote poetry, but throughout her life Effie would write short stories, one act plays and essays, as well as moralistic songs about religion, immorality and the dangers of alcohol.

In her late teens Ella left home in search of work elsewhere, and for a while was employed as a live-in servant by Harvey and Susan Grandle at their large house in Marion. Harvey and his brother Chrisley (who had been a teacher in Ohio before coming out to join his younger brother in Marion) owned several prime plots of Iowa farmland. Ella's work at the Grandle's was not too challenging and offered her a great deal of flexibility, allowing her to occasionally attend school. The eldest of the Cherry children were expected to pick up the slack by absorbing Ella's share of the workload as well as carry on attending the nearby school. It was not what you would call an easy life, and things became even harder when the thoroughly exhausted Laura died, after a four-day battle with pneumonia, in 1876.

The death of their mother, whom Effie described as having "large hazel brown eyes, dark brown hair and cheeks like a damask rose," was a body blow to the family. "Her death removed the light from the home ... she was [our] guardian angel."[10] Now, along with looking after the cows and poultry, Lizzie and Addie—aged nineteen and sixteen respectively—had to wash, sew, cook, and attend to the needs of their two youngest sisters; their barely teenaged brother worked the land. Ella left the Grandle's (Susan Grandle died in 1880 and Harvey remarried the following year) to return to the farm and keep house for their father, who had long since given up all pretense of being a painter. The family became even more insular, only being seen by their neighbors when buying or selling livestock or milk, at school, or in church. People in Marion began to think of them as a little peculiar.

In late 1884, with her health worsening, Ella and Addie took their sister Inez to St. Joseph to seek help. Unfortunately, the specialists they consulted could offer no aid, and Inez died on Christmas Eve that year; she was buried on the farm, next to her mother and baby Freddie (and, presumably, the infant Anna). Before the dawn of the New Year, Nathan took off for pastures new (his name is absent from the census taken on 1 January 1885), selling the tools and livestock that were his and telling his siblings that he had felt there would be more opportunities for him in Illinois. Nathan, now a man of twenty-two, was the one member of the Cherrys who seemed unhappy with life on the farm, and he rebelled against the family's moral path. Very much the black sheep of the family, while Addie and Effie had been in St. Joseph tending to Inez, he contacted them to ask for money. Lizzie got wind of this and wrote to the sisters, instructing them not to "send Nathan a cent of money until he promises to let lagger beer and tobacco alone. Now I don't like to be telling on him, but then I expect I should ... he takes his last cent and goes and byes cigars and when he hasn't any he takes mine. I don't think that is hardly fare, do you?"[11] [sic] It's safe to assume that Nathan was stealing money from his sister, rather than her smokes.

For Thomas this must have felt like history repeating itself, for he had lost contact with his own brother, John, when he was just a small boy. John Cherry was said to have gone off in search of his fortune in the West Indies, but he was never heard from again. Although the family would receive the occasional letter from Nathan, by the time that Thomas died, on 15 June 1888, all communication from his errant son had long since ceased. While their

The Cherry family home, photographed a few years after the last of the sisters left (courtesy Marion Historical Society, Iowa).

father lay on his death bed, Lizzie and Effie both made efforts to track Nathan down. Effie took out a small ad in *The Detective*, an eight-page newspaper that was published in Cedar Rapids, and which offered prospective bounty hunters information on criminals on the run from the law, as well as all manner of equipment for sale, from police whistles and handcuffs through to impressive, official-looking badges. She believed that he might have been using an alias: "Information wanted of Nathan Cherry, sometimes called Charley Reed. He left his home in Marion, Iowa two years ago. Last heard of he was in Chicago. A reward will be paid for information concerning his whereabouts, dead or alive."[12] Lizzie wrote to the chief of police in Chicago, entreating him to "help us find our lost or absent brother," but he—like the readers of *The Detective*—was unable to help.

The death of Thomas Cherry left his five surviving daughters "orphans to battle our way through life alone," as Effie put it. Although they would be forever referred to as orphans, all of the Cherry children, bar 15-year-old Jessie, were adults when their father passed away. Ella was now the titular head of the household and Jessie's legal guardian, charged with ensuring that the youngest of the Cherry clan kept up her attendance the nearby Lakeside School, and Addie moved out to try and add an extra wage packet to the family pot. She soon found a position working at Miss Patterson's Boarding House. Jennie Patterson had recently had surgery on her leg, so Addie took over the running of the house, cooking and cleaning for the guests while the proprietress of the establishment recuperated. With no training, little education and few prospects, the Cherry sisters had no option but to try and carry on with the only life they had known—selling milk, eggs, and poultry and growing fruit on the farm that had already killed five members of their tight-knit family. To save the six-mile round trip in to town every day, in the fall of 1892 Lizzie and Effie took on a smallholding in Marion and moved there with the six cows Lizzie owned to set up a small dairy. Ella was happy on the farm, was used to hard work and it seems that there was no job that a man would normally do that she was afraid to tackle. On one occasion she led a bull home from a sale, walking three miles back to the family homestead ankle-deep in mud, barefooted. Another, almost certainly apocryphal, tale has it that on one occasion several of the sisters were hauling a load of hay in to town when the rope fastened to a long pole which held the load in place broke. Two of the sisters decided that, as they did not have too much of a distance to go they could keep the load in place on the cart by straddling the pole, which they did until one of the wagon wheels struck a rut in the road, pitching the girls some fifty feet in to the air. Luckily the women landed in the creek, avoiding serious injury but receiving a thorough soaking.

Gauche but stubbornly independent, the five women were often the butt of some joke or other. In her unpublished autobiography Effie tells of how Ella was considered quite the beauty in her younger years, and that she was awarded a handsome bonnet after winning a local popularity contest. The truth was far more prosaic: Ella's name was put forward not because the local lads thought she was "the most popular and handsomest young lady in Marion,"[13] but because they thought of her as awkward and odd, and not the least bit comely. Her entry in to the competition, held as part of a Christmas fair organized by the B.F. Mentzer Hose Company (one of several brigades of volunteer firefighters) in December 1888, was a practical joke at her expense, a joke that none of the family were sharp enough to understand. Ella beat her nearest rival by seventy-one votes, and, "after mounting an elevated platform and donning the article of millinery for which she and her friends made so gallant a fight, she made a neat little speech which was received with deafening applause for about five minutes."[14]

Phlegmatically, the daughters of Thomas and Laura Cherry made a pact. As well as agreeing that they would never drink alcohol, they also decided that would never smoke cigarettes and they would never marry, their mother having instilled in them the adage that "those who marry do well, but those who stay single do better."[15] Although single young women were still, in law, considered as minors until their eighteenth birthday, it was not unusual for girls as young as fourteen enter in to marriage at that time in Iowa. Each of the five sisters held cards issued by Francis Murphy's National Christian Temperance Union, stating that "I, the undersigned, do pledge my word and honor, God helping me, to abstain from all intoxicating liquors as a beverage, and that I will, by all honorable means, encourage others to abstain." The Irish-born Murphy had come to America at sixteen. A heavy drinker and petty criminal who spent time in prison, he experienced an evangelical conversion and became a temperance activist, founding the National Christian Temperance Union, with its motto "with malice toward none, and charity for all," in Pittsburgh in 1877. The sisters would remain faithful to the temperance movement and would often use their fame to help promote its message.

"We don't drink liquor, or beer, or champagne or any of those things," Effie once revealed. "Once, by accident, I drank half a glass of beer and I would have liked to have died. It made me sick to my stomach."[16]

3

Riot in Dubuque

With the newspapers full of stories about their shows in Marion and Cedar Rapids, people were desperate to see (and book) the Cherrys, and the sisters and their new manager felt compelled to retain the services of an agent, a Mister E.C. Crandall. It appears that discovering using an agent would cost the Sisters far less than employing a full-time manager caused the thrifty women to immediately dispense with Fretwell, much to his annoyance. The Sisters insisted that any contract between them and Fretwell was null and void, as Ella had never signed the paper. Fretwell decided, perhaps wisely in hindsight, to cut his losses, although he insisted that any mail that arrived in Marion addressed to the Manager of the Cherry Sisters should not be passed on to the Cherrys themselves. Mr. Daniels, the local postmaster, displaying a flair for wit, returned such mail to its sender, but not until he had first written on the envelope that "they are unmanageable." Lizzie stepped in to the breach, and would act as the troupe's manager off and on for many years to come.

The Sisters were in demand, and the next few weeks whirled past at breakneck speed. At one of the first shows Crandall secured for the Sisters, in Iowa's Marshalltown, their performance was brought to an abrupt end when "an egg old enough to vote," struck Jessie "square in the mouth"[1] during their infamous sketch "The Gypsy's Warning," a self-penned melodrama based loosely on the folk song of the same name. Full of non-sequiturs, the laughable playlet usually featured Addie in a false moustache, hat, and waterproof coat, and Jessie as the soon-to-be-wronged young lady. While Little Jessie was being seduced by Addie's foul cavalier, the stage would suddenly be swathed in red light and Effie, as the titular Gypsy "swept out upon the stage like a tornado. She had on red shoes and stockings, a red flannel dress decorated with tinsel half-moons and dragon heads, and a hood of some costly material,"[2] and she would announce, menacingly:

> *Lady, in that green grave yonder*
> *Lies the Gypsy's only child.*
> *Listen to the Gypsy's warning,*

> *Gentle lady trust him not…*
> *He heeded not her weeping,*
> *Nor cared for her life to save.*
> *Soon she perished, now she's sleeping*
> *In the cold and silent grave.*

At a show in Clinton the Cherrys presented their newly written sketch, "Independent Polly," an effort so turgid that it was met with "a shower of bologna, corn cobs, cucumbers, and cabbage" that brought the entire show to a halt.[3] On 28 April, when the sisters played at the East Side Opera House in Waterloo, Iowa, the audience reaction was such that it was reported that "every number on the program received a hearty encore."[4] The report also questioned if "the sisters are considerably ignorant or very wise. If the former then they are conscientious in their performance; if the latter, they are giving this sort of performance to play upon the credulity of the people." This would not be the last time that critics would wonder if the Sisters' inelegance was no more than an act.

The audience that attended their show at Davenport's Burtis Opera House on 10 May were disappointed to discover only Effie and Jessie of the "famous World's Fair combination, five Cherry Sisters," as they were now being advertised (despite not one of them having attended the World's Fair), would appear. Lizzie and Addie had missed their train and Ella, the least star struck of the five, had already voluntarily left the troupe to stay at home to look after the farm. The show in Waterloo had been Ella's final performance with the Cherry Concert Company: she did not approve of their chosen career, and had been such an unwilling participant in their productions that her input had been mostly limited to helping her sisters on and off with their costumes. Her biggest contribution to the act had been the composition of several comedic black-faced minstrel songs, which invariably featured an approximation of an Uncle Tom patois that would now be considered embarrassing, offensive, and downright racist, although at the time black-faced minstrels were a stage staple. With no yearning for the footlights, Ella instead longed to be back with her beloved cows. In a rare act of fiscal solidarity, the five Cherry women agreed to continue to split their earnings five ways, recognizing that Ella's sacrifice allowed them to pursue their dreams. Addie, Lizzie, Effie and Jessie would continue on but Ella, by far the most sensible of the five, had no intention of joining her sisters on stage again … in fact, although she would, on a couple of rare occasions, join them, she would often berate the others about their choice to appear in front of an audience rather than work alongside her at the real family business.

No matter, for "pandemonium reigned supreme and vegetables rained in quantities"[5] upon Effie and Jessie from a capacity audience of 400 that had somehow managed to smuggle a bass drum, as well as a whole range of other instruments, up in to the gallery. "In spite of all that has been printed, read and said about the famous Cherry Sisters and their entertainment, nobody even in their wildest flights of imagination could have conceived the actual character of the show," the *Davenport Democrat and Leader* reported. Egged on by advance publicity—rival newspaper the *Davenport Daily Republican* warned its readers to "wear their everyday clothes as the air will be full of music and other things,"[6] and the *Davenport Weekly Leader* was at pains to point out that "nobody will be searched at the door before entering, but throwing bricks or rocks is barred"[7]–the audience was so noisy, and so much vegetation was aimed at the stage before the curtain had even gone up that the orchestra beat a hasty retreat. When the curtain was raised, the sight of Effie and Jessie standing in front of them, shaking with nerves, momentarily silenced the overexcited audience. "The look of them was killing and would have made a horse laugh. One of them was as tall as a rail and about of a similar build, while the younger was short and dumpy and dressed in a typical Mother Hubbard [*a long, loose-fitting gown with long sleeves and a high neck, intended to cover as much skin as is possible*], while the tall one with a face like a vinegar bottle wore a short skirt and bright red stockings." Their graceless cantering was compared to "a bovine going to pasture," and when Effie took the spotlight and attempted to sing, "the outburst of enthusiasm that greeted her was not confined to noise alone ... a potato struck the stage near to her with a biff. Then came a volley including every conceivable vegetable and fruit. In fact, she even got a cake with a sheet iron interior. But it didn't make any difference, she kept right on."

The hubbub continued, even when the Cherrys' support act, race comedian Jimmie Crow, took to the stage for what approximated a comic dance. After he too was assaulted by a volley of rotting fruit, pieces of timber and worse, Effie reappeared and told the audience that the show would come to an early end if they did not cease. Still the crowd jeered and laughed. When the manager of the house, Charles T. Kindt, came on to the stage he too was met with a "deluge of sticks, potatoes, even pieces of boards poured down upon him, and a tin horn struck him in the mouth." After Kindt was injured, the curtain was brought down, but even then, the entertainment was far from over. A crowd left the theater and went to the train station to greet Addie and Lizzie. The late arriving Cherry Sisters were escorted by police back to the Opera House, where they were reunited with Effie and Jessie, terrified and unable to leave because of the very real threat of a riot breaking out.

The *Democrat and Leader* dismissed the evening's entertainment as "without doubt the rankest attempt at stage work ever seen in Davenport. The Cherry Sisters, or the two that gave the howling séance last night, can neither sing, speak nor act, and are homely enough to scare a weak-minded man in to fits."[8] It would not be the last time the sisters had to rely on the local police to help them out of a tight spot: they would be very glad of their presence when their haphazard tour reached the city of Dubuque.

It doesn't take too much imagination, walking along the streets of Dubuque today, to be able to visualize the place as it was a century and a quarter ago. This picturesque city, on the banks of the Mississippi, has not changed that much in all of those years. Welcoming and well-kept, its historic cable car system and many Victorian buildings transport you back to a more genteel period, when mutton-chopped businessmen ran the town, and women managed the home. And on Eighth Street, you still can find the Grand Opera House. Opened in August 1890, some of the greatest names in entertainment have played at the Grand, including Al Jolson, Sarah Bernhardt, Henry Fonda, Paderewski, Billie Burke, Jack Benny and George M. Cohan, but the 1,100-seat theater had seen nothing like the Cherry Sisters.

Advertisement for the Sisters' appearance at the Grand Opera House, Dubuque, 1893.

News had already reached the town of the reception the Cherrys had been receiving at their shows, and the good folk of Dubuque were intent on upping the ante. The local newspaper, the *Dubuque Telegraph*, had been building anticipation for their appearance for some time, telling its readers that the reason the Sisters had taken to the stage was to pay off the $7,000 mortgage on their farm—a gross exaggeration of the actual sum owed—and that "judging from the houses they are drawing it won't be long before the mortgage will be paid."[9]

One of the many misnomers about the Cherry Sisters is that they settled on giving a performance despite having never seen a play themselves. This is simply not true, although their experience was certainly limited. On one occasion they went to see the popular comic operetta star Della Fox but, according to Jessie, "she wasn't acting the night we saw her show; we saw her sister instead." Fox (or her sister) must have been a big influence on the baby of the Cherry clan, as she appropriated the title of one of Fox's songs, "Fair Columbia," for her own patriotic composition, a song that Jessie would perform swathed in the American flag at almost every Cherry Sisters concert. In that same year that the Sisters made their stage debut, one New York critic wrote that "Miss Della Fox can neither act nor sing and is not pretty, but [she] rejoices in a marvelous popularity," a review that could have been written for the Cherrys themselves. Even before they had seen one or other of the Miss Foxes perform they had occasionally watched matinee performances at Daniels Opera House, situated on Seventh Avenue in Marion. The sisters supplied milk and, in a deliciously ironic twist of fate, fruit and vegetables to the venue's manager, Frank Simmons, and Simmons would often let them stay a while to enjoy the afternoon's entertainment. "Clara Morris and Sarah Bernhardt never came out our way, and it just happened that we never seen 'Uncle Tom's Cabin,'" Jessie explained. That changed once they began to perform themselves, the Sisters making a point of checking out their competition regularly. "We took in 'The Railroad Ticket' in Des Moines and 'The Smuggler' in Cedar Rapids. We seen Lillian Russell once. She was good, but she wore tights."[10] Russell, a fellow Iowan, was one of the most famous actresses and singers working in America during the late 19th and early 20th centuries, and for four decades the companion of Diamond Jim Brady.

Everyone, apart from the Cherrys themselves that is, seemed to know that something big was planned for their Dubuque debut, which took place on the night of 17 May. Advertised as "the event of the season," certainly the staff at the opera house, the local police and the council colluded with each other to ensure that this was going to be a night to remember. It started farcically when William Roehl, the manager of the Grand, sent an old, horse drawn open wagon, rather than a cab, to fetch the Sisters from the five o'clock train. He planned to have his big drawing card seen by as many people as possible as they were pulled through the city, and he had put up signs urging residents to come and greet the sisters when they arrived in town. The Sisters were none too pleased with this unplanned parade, and things became even more tense when they discovered that they had not been provided with any scenery for their act. After a tense standoff, with the sisters refusing to go on unless they had some sort of set, Roehl finally agreed to bring up some scenery from the basement storage area. Goodness knows what the Sisters would have said to Roehl had they been aware of the advance notices he had given to the press, warning audience members that no revolvers would be allowed inside the house, nor any rocks that could not pass through a two-inch diameter ring.

When it came time to take to the stage, the Grand Opera House was full of "fast young men and riff-raff" out for sport. They would not be disappointed. "Near the footlights sat a small group of hoodlums who had come with no other intention but to break up the show and to injure our business,"[11] Effie later recalled. Addie remembered that "there was a lot of toughs there with tin horns and all sorts of things. There was a lot of nice people too. There were ladies sittin' in the boxes in their silks an' satins: paid a dollar and a half for their seats."[12] "We had hardly started the act when one of the ruffians in the front row turned a fire extinguisher on the stage,"[13] Effie added. The audience "came armed with fire extinguishers, siphons, tin horns, decayed eggs, cabbages and other articles. The first girl to appear was struck with a cabbage and received a charge from a siphon. The next got a charge from a fire extinguisher full in the face."[14] Jessie, the sister who had been in receipt of the fire extinguisher facial, ran from the stage, her blue dress, white stockings, and buckled black slippers soaked trough. At that point an angry Effie returned with a shotgun, which she loaded in full view of the audience and brandished menacingly. As more cabbages came Effie, who was dressed in "a long blouse of blue jeans, beneath which were trousers of the same material," and a "cap with gold braid,"[15] was joined by her sisters, who were "bombarded without mercy."[16] The scene would later be immortalized in a full-plate illustration that ran in the infamous scandal sheet *The National Police Gazette*.

"It was supposed that the uncouth performance of the girls would occasion jeers and laughter," reported the *Dubuque Daily Herald*, "but instead they were treated with downright brutality."[17] The Sisters limped off the stage and were getting ready to leave the Grand when Crandall, their agent and *de facto* manager, came in to the dressing room and furiously demanded that they go on with their act. "Listen to me," Addie scolded. "If there is going to be any more show tonight, you'll give it yourself!"[18] When he reminded them that if the show closed early they would have to return ticket money, the Cherrys reluctantly agreed to return to the stage. Predictably, the audience was even more ferocious. A "wash boiler," or tin washing tub (one report downgrades the missile to a coal scuttle), was launched from one of the boxes and almost hit Jessie as she tried to play "Oh Where, Oh Where Has My Little Dog Gone?" on her mouth organ: "If it had struck her, there would in all probability have been one Cherry less in the bunch."[19] It was at this point that William Roehl came on stage to bring the night's proceedings to an end. He too was pelted with produce and, unable to make himself heard above the hubbub, bowed goodnight and brought down the curtain. At no point did the police, sent there to preserve order, or the theater staff attempt to quell the throng, even when "three links of sausages, tied up with pink and blue ribbons,"[20] struck one of the Cherrys in the face.

Two of the Sisters took cover in Roehl's office, while the other two and Crandall remained with their baggage at the side of the stage. Crandall tried to console the women, telling them that "we got their stuff and the damned fools got their fun,"[21] but all were visibly upset and crying. When the Sisters attempted to leave by the stage door they were once again greeted by a barrage of eggs, and crowds of rowdies gathered on street corners to launch further eggs as well as potatoes and stones at their carriage as it passed. When they arrived at the grandly named Hotel Paris, they were unable to leave the carriage, which had also had a can of yellow paint hurled at it, until several policemen turned up to escort them inside.

A visitor to the hotel that evening, Julius Geisler, described the scene:

> A howling mob followed them. As they stepped from the carriage some cowards threw eggs at them and followed them in to the hotel. This crowd was not made of boys, but young men, well-dressed and from outward appearances gentlemen, but it was a case of fine feathers. I talked to these people, but in a howling mob was only jeered and laughed at. These people forget that they have sisters at home, and whom they would not wish to have treated in such a manner. Your police, I am sorry to say, were nowhere to be seen or heard.[22]

"The outrageous treatment accorded the girls is denounced by all respectable citizens, and everyone who took part in it should have been arrested,"[23] *The Herald* thundered. An anonymous correspondent for the same paper took up a contrary position, reasoning that the sisters got what they deserved, and insisted that "the show is a fraud—in the parlance of the street, a fake. None know this better than the members of the company."[24] Fortunately, although their pride would have been severely wounded, none of the sisters were badly injured, although Jessie's eyes were inflamed from the fire extinguisher attack and Effie had "a cut on the side of her right hand made by something that had been thrown at her."[25] Lizzie told reporters that, although previous audiences had been loutish, "we never before ran the risk of being killed."

Once calm had been restored, Marshall Rice presented William Roehl with a bill for "$14 for preserving order."[26] Rice later insisted that he had done so "in a joking way and meant it as such."[27] The Dubuque riot made the national papers, and most noted that many of the young men who attacked the sisters were the well-dressed and well-educated scions of local bigwigs. "The feat all through was one of which all respectable people have good reason to feel ashamed. It was a manly thing to assault four unprotected girls who are endeavoring to raise a mortgage that encumbers a farm left them by their mother, who is now in her grave. The spirit of chivalry that ought to rush to the protection of women was not manifested."[28] In less than five months the sisters had come from local obscurity to become national celebrities ... for all the wrong reasons. The sisters threatened the local council with a $20,000 lawsuit, and told a reporter from the *Dubuque Daily Herald* that they had "never before been treated so outrageously," although they lied to the same reporter's face when they told him that "in no other city they visited had things been thrown on the stage," and exaggerated when they claimed that "the newspapers of the city were responsible for the treatment they have received," and that "their professional reputation had been ruined."[29] Several wits responded indignantly that the city should sue the Cherrys and their promoters for having perpetrated such an outrage in the first place. Effie, noting their agent's keenness to keep them on the stage despite the very real threat of injury, became convinced that he was colluding with the owners and managers of the houses they were playing to bilk the women: "This no doubt was the reason for the unlawful acts allowed in the theater at that time, for they knew if they got us worried and nervous they could handle things to suit themselves, which they did."[30]

The evening following the event—by which time the Sisters had already moved on to make an appearance in Bellevue—the Dubuque town council held an extraordinary meeting to discuss the Cherrys' claims, and those of the proprietors of the Hotel Paris, who also charged that the city owned them money for the damage done to their property by the mob. Surprisingly, despite the adage (often attributed to Phineas T. Barnum) that "there's no such thing as bad publicity," the infamy around the Dubuque incident seemed to harm rather than enhance ticket sales; only two people turned up to see the Sisters in Bellevue—and they had been given complimentary tickets.[31] At Muscatine the audience numbered just 25.[32]

Mayor Daugherty declared that the Cherry Sisters affair had been the most scandalous event that ever occurred in Dubuque; witnesses were summoned to give account of themselves and a committee headed by Alderman Powers made it known that, as far as they were concerned, Roehl, the policemen on duty that evening and the chief of police, Marshal Rice, were to blame for the fiasco. Roehl testified that, because of instances of audience violence had occurred during previous performances by the sisters, "Constable Mike

Coffee, and six men whom he selected were instructed to search everybody before [they were] allowed to enter," but that the "old wash boiler was handed through an open window from the fire escape."[33] He accused the marshal (who brought nine further men of his own, each given tickets by Roehl and stationed strategically around the Opera House by him) of attempting to extort money from the Sisters for protection, and stated that although he did not order Rice to stop the disturbance, neither did he instruct him "not to interfere unless the audience tore up the seats." He identified the men who wielded the fire extinguisher as "James Agnew and a man by the name of Grady."[34] Agnew admitted that he had indeed brought the extinguisher in, but he denied that it was he who had turned it on the Sisters. He refused, however, to name who it was that had.[35] Only after the washing tub was thrown upon the stage did the marshal make any attempt to stop the performance. Roehl concluded that, had Rice "arrested some of the ringleaders, it would have stopped the trouble."[36]

Rice, naturally, laid the blame for the fiasco squarely at Roehl's feet. He explained that his patrolmen understood that vegetable throwing and general rowdiness were expected by both the sisters and Roehl, and that his men were under orders not to interfere with any singing, yelling or horn blowing"[37] unless the crowd damaged the theater. Officers Tom Reilly and Bert Cain backed him up. Those that witnessed the wash boiler being launched at the stage simply assumed that it was part of the act,[38] not too difficult to believe, as the Sisters' "Irish Ballad" saw them use two washtubs. Any mention of money for police protection, Rice insisted, had been made strictly in a joking manner, and he pointed out that if Roehl had ordered him and his deputies to stop the performance, they would have done so at once.

The Sisters announced that they also intended to sue the Grand Opera House Company for damages, and the council made it clear that they would hold the management of the theater responsible for this blot on the town's good name. As the *Davenport Democrat and Leader* reported, "It would seem that it was about time, for the sake of humanity, for some one to capture these deluded Cherry Sisters, take them home, and if necessary chain them to something on the farm to keep them there. If they continue their starring tour much longer they are liable to be killed."[39] Inspired by the events following the Sisters' appearance at Greene's Opera House several young men, residents of the Dubuque YMCA, decided to hold a mock trial featuring themselves as the Cherry Sisters and a colleague as Roehl.[40]

After several days' deliberation, the committee found both Roehl and Rice culpable, with Roehl singled out as bearing most of the responsibility for the fiasco. "The manager of the opera house seems to be the one to blame.

He sent an old bill poster's wagon to take them from the depot, and in other ways subjected them to ridicule and insult."[41] Alderman Crawford, one of the investigating committee, felt that the report did not go far enough, and rebuked Marshall Rice and the police for allowing "one of the most outrageous affairs ever heard of. To think that Iowa ladies of irreproachable character—country girls if you please—and the daughters of a soldier should be treated in such a manner!"[42] Crawford's assumption that Thomas Cherry had been a soldier was understandable but erroneous; he would have been of the right age to have fought during the Civil War, but his health had prevented him from taking up arms.

While all of this was going on, back on the farm Ella was having problems of her own. The family had sub-let part of the land to a Mr. Houts for a twelve-month period from the beginning of March but, with the performing Sisters returning to the farm before embarking on tour in the fall, they decided to oust Houts from the land just three months in to his lease. Houts, naturally, was less than happy with this turn of events and took the women to court; the ensuing trial soon turned in to another local amusement starring the Cherry Sisters in the role of defamed and ingenuous innocents. With the initial jury unable to reach a decision and the proceedings rapidly descending in to farce, the hearing was abandoned and a second trial took place in the district court room in front of Justice Elsberry.[43] After hearing from both sides in the matter, Justice Elsberry dismissed the action, but not before a wag suggested that Houts might be encouraged to abandon his action against the Cherrys "if they would sit on the fence and sing to him."[44]

With no more engagements until the fall, Lizzie, Addie, Effie and Jessie returned to the family farm. This was a pattern that they would follow for several years, although, as theater historian Cesar del Valle points out, this was more through necessity than altruism. "Before air conditioning, most theaters closed for the summer," he explains, "With the season lasting from the end of August/beginning of September until the end of May or the beginning June." Effie, suffering with "nervous prostration,"[45] something that would be diagnosed today as a breakdown, took to her bed and did not leave it for several weeks. Somehow, in between court appearances, the sisters managed to pen a number of new songs and sketches during their summer vacation—although the period could hardly be described as a holiday, with all the women who were able to once again mucking in on the farm. One of the highlights of this new batch of material was "Eulogy on the Cherry Sisters," a song written by Effie and Jessie to the tune of "Ta-ra-ra Boom-de-ay." Originally a hit for English music hall star Lottie Collins, the Sisters' accompanists had first included an instrumental version of the song as part of their set at their second live appearance. They also attempted to organize a fundraising concert in aid of the local Baptist church, promising $1,000 from ticket sales, which would be matched dollar for dollar by a Cedar Rapids businessman if Mr. Simmons, the manager of Greene's Opera House, would give them use of the venue without charge.[46]

The members of the Cherry Sisters troupe readied themselves for a major tour beginning in September, with a return appearance booked for Greene's Opera House on the 11th, before commencing the tour proper. Reduced temporarily to a trio after Lizzie opted to stay on the farm to work alongside Ella, their cousin Isabell Rawson was pressed in to service. On at least one occasion (at Daniels Opera House in Marion on 31 March 1894), both Lizzie and Isabell appeared alongside Addie, Effie and Jessie. While in Marion, Lizzie effectively acted as her Sisters' manager once more, sending handwritten letters to theaters, opera houses and agents around the country in search of work. Lizzie's style left much to be desired, and her letters were brusque, boastful, and often threatening. On the reverse of a concert handbill, after bragging that the show would offer "side splitting laughter.... I would like to see P.T. Barnum get ahead of the Cherry Sisters in fun amusements, he can't do it," she scribbled "Notice: The Cherry Sisters hereby notify and warn all editors and individuals if any item appears in their papers detrimental concerning the Cherry Sisters or their concerts they will publish them in a way that will not be very satisfactory and wind up with a court hearing. We have got you spotted and we know who you are."[47]

Highlights of this new series of dates would include the new "parody on 'Ta-ra-ra Boom-de-ay,' a male impersonation by Miss Ella, the elocutionist, and a skirt dance by

Lottie Collins, as she appeared on promotional sheet music for "Ta-ra-ra Boom-de-ay," issued by the Emerson Drug Company, 1890s.

the company. But the hit of the play, according to the Cherry Sisters' homemade program, will be 'Barefoot Iona, the Orphan Flower Girl,' by Effie Cherry in her bare feet."[48] Not for the last time had the newspaper confused one sister for another: it was Effie who specialized in male impersonations, and Jessie who would portray the Orphan Flower Girl.

In an interview given to the *Cedar Rapids Weekly Gazette*, Effie bemoaned the way in which the sisters had been treated by the press. "I think that newspaper men are the meanest people I have ever met," she claimed. "They have treated us shamefully nearly everywhere." In a revealing article, Effie denied many of the scurrilous stories that had appeared in the press about them, and talked openly about their financial position. "We would have been rich if it had not been for the newspapers. They said we could not act and called us green gawks. Green gawks? Huh!"[49] Not long after, they were off to Clinton, not to repeat their earlier performance, but to seek representation for a "criminal and civil action against the *Daily Herald* of Clinton for libel alleged to have been contained in an article published a few days ago."[50]

Even though they had had a bad experience with their first manager (Fretwell), had had arguments with Lizzie over her attempts to manage the act and were already using the services of a booking agent whom they clearly did not trust, the Sisters were approached by, and accepted an offer from, yet another manager—a Mr. A.J. Wheeler. Wheeler was a man who knew when he was on to a good thing. Although they had already proved that they could make in excess of $100 a night, he signed Lizzie, Addie, Effie and Jessie to a contract that guaranteed them a flat $200 per month. That sum sounded wonderful, and far more than they could hope to earn from the farm, but the Sisters would be expected to perform night after night, and usually twice a day, for their money. Jessie had threatened to leave the act and return to school unless they engaged Wheeler, yet he was another man who could not be trusted, and he would not last long. "Lizzie," Jessie wrote, "I don't believe that Wheeler knows what he wants. I guess he's got a wheel in his head."[51] When the sisters played in Savannah, ticket sales were so poor that they were left $9 short of being able to pay the bill for their hotel,[52] and they were forced to travel on to Lyons without their baggage, which, along with their stage costumes, had been impounded. However, when the *Clinton Herald* asserted that the sisters were in financial trouble during a return visit to the city they promptly sued the newspaper for libel, seeking $1,000 in damages. Protest though they might, the truth of the matter was that the four performing Cherries were struggling with their finances, and back home in Marion Ella had run foul of the law yet again. When she was unable to pay "the sum of forty-nine dollars and accruing costs" levied by the District Court against

Ella, Effie and Addie for their action against Houts, the sheriff, Dan R. Kinley, seized a section of their land and offered it up for public auction. To compound the humiliation, the sale was to be held on the steps of the courthouse, in full view of everyone.

Clearly, that no matter what the sisters might have wanted the public to believe, as 1893 drew to an end the Cherry family were not as well-off as they claimed, and by the end of the following year the touring Sisters were in even worse financial straits. They may have been packing them in at the theater, but for some reason—bad management, transport and accommodation costs, their endless court costs and their own naivety included—they were not seeing a decent financial return. Costumes had to be paid for, musicians (and policemen) cost money, but whatever the Sisters were earning seemed to slip through their hands. In December 1894, while the Sisters were being accompanied by an unnamed, one-armed, novice manager without two cents to rub together, Addie was forced to write home to Lizzie for money:

> Our manager is almost done out because he could not go in to town and get it billed. He says we will lose one half of our crowd and we have not got even 25 cents to give him to telegraph. We was never run so short. If you will send $5 we will send you all we can spair next week. Send it by return mail so we can give him one dollar to pay his way he has got but one arm and so is not abel to work but seems quite a smart young man he don't act much like our other managers. But he can't work on nothing.... Now Lizzie if you don't send us 5.00 I am not so sure as we will send you any money next week but will keep it so we will not get broke again. But $5 is not much to ask of you. We do not want $15 [sic].[53]

Ella and Lizzie too had been looking for help with money worries, and Lizzie wrote to her cousin Helen Andrews in Albany, New York for assistance with the mortgage. In due course, Helen replied, telling Lizzie that she had "read in various papers that you are giving concerts, and I should think you would want to pay off some of the interest," adding that "some arrangement ought to be decided on and you should all abide by it."[54] It is understandable that their cousins believed the sisters were coining it in: the *Marion Sentinel*, reporting on a sold out Cherry Sisters performance in Mechanicsville, stated that "the Cherry Sisters cleared more money than any other company that has been here this past year."[55] Unfortunately, nothing could have been further from the truth.

4

Live, with (or without) a Net

In June 1895 an article appeared in the *Center Point Tribune* announcing the imminent arrival of the Cherry Sisters in the town. "The vegetables are just about the right size to toss on the stage very handily, the only draw back being the smallness of the cabbage heads," the editor, Charlie Floyd, wrote. "Johnny get your gun and the sword and the pistol!" Enraged by this very public incitement to take up arms, the sisters went in search of the editor and, upon discovering him in the street, set about him with horsewhips, much to the amusement of bystanders who, it was reported, "had a hard time pulling the infuriated 'actresses' off."[1] The sisters were arrested and fined $12 each plus costs for the assault. Charlie Floyd was one of those writers who attracted trouble. A proponent of *yellow press* journalism, his pencil was often employed to discredit women; in March 1897, the editor of the *Bedford Daily Times* was sued for $10,000 over an article Floyd had written in which he had slandered the wife of the editor of a rival newspaper.

They performed that evening as planned but, despite the free advertising, the show was a flop, with the box office taking just nine dollars. These money worries would dog the Sisters for the rest of their lives. Yet although they were struggling to make ends meet, the Sisters were remarkably generous when it came to their friends, exhibiting the Christian charity their mother had instilled in them by seldom turning down requests to play benefits for churches, the poor, or for their favorite causes. Ruth St. Denis, long since recognized as a pioneer of modern dance, put much of her success down to the Cherry Sisters. Addie and Effie had befriended her when they were all appearing in Somerville, New Jersey, and Miss St. Denis claimed that it was thanks to the Cherrys' encouragement that George W. Lederer, one of the earliest producers of musical revues in the U.S., took a chance on her and cast her in one of his shows.

The Sisters toured sporadically, playing dates throughout Iowa and Illinois. For weeks, occasionally months, at a time they returned to the farm in Marion to help Ella with the work and to wait for bookings. Addie, Effie and

Lizzie wrote many letters to theater managers to solicit work, and they took out adverts in the trade papers in the hope of finding new management. In a letter to veteran theater manager Al Onken, then in charge of the Orpheum in Portland, Oregon, they made it clear that they would not put up with any abuse directed towards them: "It has become necessary for us to say that we cannot finish our act on the stage as long as the audience is encouraged to throw missiles upon the stage which is nothing more or less than assault and battery. Such treatment would not be tolerated by any man, much less by a lady, and any man who would thus treat a woman without any cause or provocation is not worthy of the name of man. If there is not a stop put to this insult we shall certainly leave the stage the minute anything is thrown at us."[2]

Whenever they had opportunity they wrote new material for the act, and it was around this time that Addie was reported to have begun writing a long-form poem (the New York *Sun* claimed the finished version would feature no less than 77 verses):

Nine years ago I was called an old maid, but now I am skittish and fly;
Of all the old bachelors I was afraid, and was most uncommonly shy.
But all or a sudden, one nice day in June I found a young man to my mind.
When he tickled my chin I thought I would swoon, but love is only a blind.[3]

In La Porte, on 23 August 1895, the audience was so boisterous that all of the sisters left the stage and went down in to the audience, brandishing weapons. The hissing and howling had begun before the Sisters' commenced their performance, and "onions, cabbage and rotten watermelon rinds were showered upon the stage."[4] Jessie, swathed in the Stars and Stripes to perform "Fair Columbia," had "a pail of dirty black water thrown over her"[5] by an assailant who came from behind her on the stage, and she was arrested after she struck a young man by the name of Frank Fritz over the head with a poker. Following this altercation the sisters ended up barricaded inside the theater while an angry mob waited outside for them. Fritz, still nursing his wound, swore out a warrant for Jessie's arrest. All four were fined $5 each, plus costs, for assault and battery, the fines paid not by the Cherrys but by a collection arranged by audience members who felt that they were justified in their attack. The Sisters, naturally, had a different take on the evening's events. They told the *Marion Pilot* that they had "played to a $50 house, and but for the rowdyism of the young man Fritz all would have been calm, serene and unruffled." They added that "La Porte is a lovely little city, and its people cordial and very kindly disposed."[6] It must have pleased them no end to discover that the wicked Fritz was one of the people who had contributed to the fund to pay off their fine. The audience also brought the following performance, at the Grundy Center, to an abrupt and early end. This time the sisters, who came armed with clubs, descended upon the audience and cleared the hall within minutes. Several members of the audience were seen on the street the following day, their heads in bandages.

Ella, as if not to be outdone by her sisters, was making headlines of her own. In September she was arrested after threatening a Mr. J.A. Rose, an employee of her neighbor John Ross. Rose was cutting down trees on the boundary of the two properties and Ella took umbrage with him; the exact line that marked the division of their properties had been the subject of much angry debate between Ella and Ross over the years. After a heated argument she rushed off to the house and returned with a shotgun, announcing to the terrified Rose—who insisted that Ross had given him permission to chop down the trees—that the gun was loaded and if he did not stop immediately she would blow his head off. Constable Root was dispatched to the Cherry farm to arrest Ella and bring her before the court. The indignant elder sister insisted that she was perfectly within her rights to be carrying a gun on her own property, claiming that she was simply cleaning the weapon and that she neither loaded or aimed it, and furthermore she declared her arrest to be an outrage. Ella resented the idea that her word was worth less than a "low down villain and worm of the dust as that long-legged Rose," and told the presiding judge, Justice Whittam, that he should "go to Marion if you want to know anything about him. They will tell you there that his word is not of any account. He lies about me and I propose that somebody is going to suffer for it."[7] The case was eventually thrown out of court after an intoxicated Rose admitted to the judge that he continued to chop down the trees after he and Ella had their altercation and that, if so inclined, he would do the same again.

Ella Cherry, circa 1893 (Orville Rennie and Jane Rennie Collection, 1875-1987. Ms. 178. Special Collections, State Historical Society of Iowa, Iowa City).

A return visit to their hometown of Marion was a disaster. It's possible that the Sisters themselves sensed things were going to be tough for them, as they decided to change the name of their act to the Jubilee Concert Company, throwing a curve ball to any passing ruffians who may have been pulled in off the street by seeing the name The Cherry Sisters over the marquee. Evidently it was not just troublemakers who were put off attending, and the Sisters hastily printed hundreds of handbills, featuring the entire program as well as a heading making it clear that the performers were indeed "the Celebrated Northern Stars; Queens of Comedy and Song, the Renowned Cherry Sisters."

The Sisters, now working for their third manager, performed three evening shows over two weekends at Daniels Opera House, the scene of their first ever "entertainment," in November 1895 but this time the locals, once friendly to them, were out to cause mayhem. They had read of the way the Sisters had been received by other audiences and were smarting from the way their little town was being portrayed in the press. This was to be a series of grand homecoming shows; Lizzie hired the venue, making sure that the family would receive the lion's share of the box office, and the Sisters pulled out all the stops, with tableaux, songs, recitations and music, featuring old favorites and some exciting new material too. These three concerts would see the debut of "The Editor's Song," a new composition from Addie that satirized a number of prominent local newspapermen including Fred W. Faulks, the editor of the *Cedar Rapids Evening Gazette*. On top of all that, the shows would reunite all five sisters on the stage, with Ella coming in from the farm to recreate her "Autumn Scene" tableau, and Lizzie joining Effie and Jessie on stage for another tableau, "The Goddess of Liberty and Her Subjects."

Still, if they had expected a warm welcome from their home crowd then they were in for a rude awakening, and the third evening's performance descended in to a full-blown riot. As one witness to the debacle put it, "we saw it. To hear it was impossible."[8]

> It was the second appearance within a week of this combination of crude and strange histrionic characters and the opera house was packed with auditors, hundreds of whom came from Cedar Rapids. When one of the sisters made her appearance on the stage, clad in white to pose in a tableau in which red light played an important part, a bushel of decayed apples, oranges and lemons was fired on to the stage from scores of willing hands. She beat a hasty retreat to rid herself of the decayed fruit, which had spattered all over her and the curtain was rung down.[9]

Jessie had opened the concert with a tableau, "Clinging to the Cross," but almost as soon as the curtain went up a young boy in the audience took aim, and she was met with a piece of liver to her chest, the blood staining her white gown. Another newspaper reported that when the curtain went up "a section of the audience rose en masse, and threw cabbages, apples, live cats, chickens and sausages at the woman. She fled."[10] As the blood-soaked Jessie abandoned "Clinging to the Cross," Mr. Daniels, owner of the opera house, came to the footlights to appeal for calm from the audience, but he too took a piece of liver to the face. With Daniels' appeals ignored, the Sisters' new manager, J.E. Wells, was trotted out and he threatened to call a halt to the show unless the audience calmed itself, but as Effie came forward to sing her song "Chicago," she was met with a shower of "beans, potatoes, turnips, cabbages and stale pieces of meat from the butcher shops." It seems that, as well as tossing fruit and vegetables towards the stage, the local butchers and meat traders had been denuded of calves' liver, and a few enterprising young men had rigged up an apparatus—comprising of a series of baskets attached to a washing line on a pulley—to have rancid meat shipped surreptitiously through a window and in to the hall. When Effie was struck in the face by a piece of liver hurled by another young man, it was time for action.

> Exasperated at this reception Mr. Wells sprang out over the footlights and started for the boy, followed by Effie Cherry. He was soon surrounded by a gang, and when he attempted to hustle the boy out of the opera house a brother, Charles McCormick, swung a chair and reduced it to kindling wood over his head. The unfortunate manager was rendered unconscious by the blows and was carried back on to the stage bleeding profusely from a score of wounds on his head and face. Effie Cherry began to belabor William Beebe, a noisy man in the audience, with a rawhide. Beebe knocked the girl down and dragged her on the floor down the center aisle.[11]

Wells was lucky: Doctors Bailey and Moorhead, two physicians who happened to be in the audience that night, attended to him immediately. He managed to get away with a few stitches, but one of the doctors noted that "a little harder blow would have furnished a corpse and a murderer."[12] The show was finally brought to a close, and Daniels prepared himself for a lawsuit from the notoriously litigious Cherry Sisters. Considering the amount of violence that had taken place, it is a surprise that no arrests were made on the night, although the *Marion Register* labeled the disturbance "the most disgraceful affair ever witnessed in our city, and every one connected with it should be punished to the full extent of the law ... our fair city has been branded in the daily press as a border ruffian town in consequence."[13]

Filled with wrath at the treatment they had received in their home town, the Sisters refused to appear in Marion again until they received a formal apology. That finally came in 1908, as Addie and Effie were engaged to take part in the town's Fourth of July celebrations: "On the part of the people of Marion we would say that the Cherry Sisters in the past gave an entertainment in this city and were not afforded the proper protection from the police; neither did they receive the respect that ladies of the stage were entitled to. Now, therefore, we do as a committee, on the part of the citizens of Marion and the Mayor, offer to them our apology for the acts then committed, and fully sympathize with them as to their wounded feelings in receiving such treatment in their home town. We accord to them that respect that is due to all ladies, and we agree that it shall be our duty to see that such disgraceful conduct in the past from our people shall not be repeated if in our power to prevent."[14]

No doubt the Sisters, and their audience, would have benefited from the use of a screen that night. Although Effie Cherry would vehemently deny that they had ever performed behind a wire screen (or any kind of screen or net for that matter), reports about such a device first appeared after their second professional appearance, at Greene's Opera House in Cedar Rapids in February 1893, and followed them for the rest of their career. Indeed the *Cedar Rapids Evening Gazette* reported that using some sort of protection was the Sisters' own idea, and that "they propose to erect a screen that will cover the entire front of the stage to the ceiling, hoping that the stage-struck youths and smitten 'bald heads' cannot bestow so many bouquets and old rubber shoes on them as before."[15] Three full years later the same story was still making headlines: "The latest feature of the Cherry Sisters' entertainment is a large moveable wire screen, which is used by the girls as protection against eggs, cabbages etc."[16] Comedian Fred Allen insisted that they performed behind a net that "hung down from the flies and covered the entire stage, protecting the Cherry Sisters from impulsive members of the audience who had come to the theater laden with throwing tomatoes and sundry passé fruits."[17] Floyd Bell, press agent for the Ringling Brothers, was adamant that he saw them perform at the Dewey Theater in Minneapolis sometime around 1910 and that they "were given a barrage of vegetables and at each perform-

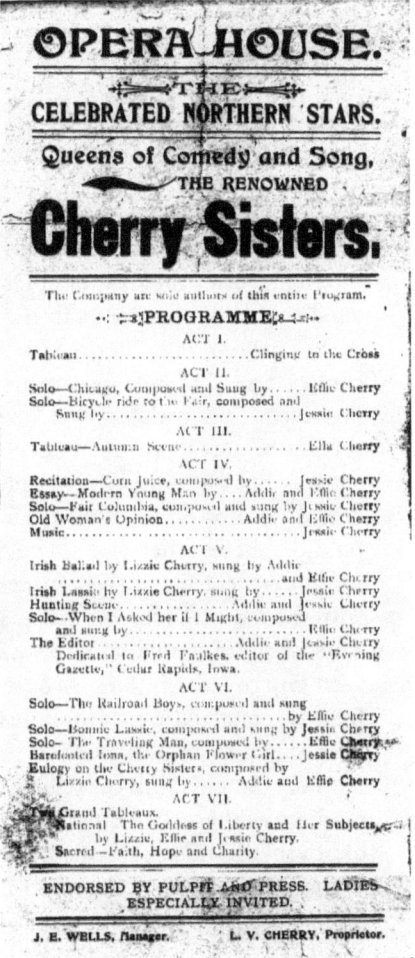

Handbill for the Sisters' concert at Daniels Opera House, 1895 (courtesy Marion Historical Society, Iowa).

ance [they] appeared behind a net. I saw them not once but half a dozen times appearing thus."[18] However, as Effie wrote, "the Cherry Sisters want it distinctly understood once and for all that never in our stage career have we played behind screens or nets in any form."[19]

Effie blamed this malicious falsehood entirely on the press. "The whole damnable screen and net story was written for no other purpose than to do us a great injury both to our financial business and our reputation. And it all started from that wicked low down newspaper representative whom we had the manager of the theater at Osage, Iowa put off the stage, and who threatened that he would fix us in the papers the next day."[20] Like so many of the stories around the Cherry Sisters, it is as impossible to be one hundred per cent certain that nets or screens were used as it is to be sure that they were not used. Effie insisted that "the Cherry Sisters *never never* played behind screens or nets in any form; never had any protection on any stage where our act was put on in our lives,"[21] but the reports of that fateful performance in Osage (and of many other performances over their career) would have the public believe otherwise. "The Sisters have at last succeeded in effecting a way to protect themselves from everything except pistol bullets. They carry with them a wire screen, such as is put up in front of base ball grand stands.... This is put up immediately back of the footlights and is securely held in place with guy ropes. Mr. S.G. Arnold says that the show went along without any further trouble, the girls looking like people giving a performance in a cage."[22] "At Osage a large audience was present to show their compliments of decayed fruit on the girls, but on seeing the wire netting they felt very small. A card reading 'cabbages solicited' was hung on the screen."[23] "The theater was full of boys with the usual collection of missiles. When the curtain rang up what was their surprise to find a wire screen strung across just behind the footlights."[24] One witness, a musician from Cedar Rapids by the name of J.A. MacLean, swore that he had been in the orchestra pit in Peoria in 1897 when the Cherry Sisters performed and that, that night, he saw with his own eyes the screen being used. "It was chicken wire of about an inch mesh, hung on a batten and covering the lower half of the proscenium,"[25] and it was, he believed, erected as a publicity stunt by the management of the theater.

Effie would spend her life battling against the way in which she, and the rest of the Cherry women, was portrayed in the press. She would cherry-pick the best reviews—or, more often than not, reword them to the Sisters' advantage—for their handbills and posters, and when she came to write her own, unpublished, "Autobiography of the Cherry Sisters" she liberally adapted the few lines of scant praise the act received as if they were glowing reviews. They may have billed themselves as the "queens of comedy," and "great Northern stars," but, in fact, most editors would agree with the write-up they received in the *Williamsburg Journal*, that stated:

> They advertise as queens of comedy and song; comedy is the picturing of the lighter passions and actions of humanity by comic presentation and intrigue. They present a Cherry, and have no more idea of comedy than a grasshopper has of astronomy. Effie and Addie have no musical talent and no conception of melody; their attempt at singing is on a par with the squealing of two old-time razorback pigs when the buttermilk can was in sight.[26]

Even those writers they thought of as friendly, such as Ella's old school acquaintance Mary Dunham, could not help themselves from having a laugh at the Sisters' expense, and Dunham's description of Effie's stage makeup is a case in point: "The colors were dashed on with a lavish hand. Dubs of red on the cheeks, liberal mourning emblems around the eyes, a mustache that would turn a budding youth green with envy. I watched her as she went on to the stage in her masculine attire, a tall hat on her head and a traveling bag in her hand. The audience howled as she appeared. She stood before the footlights a second in silence, and such an exhibition of absolute indifference I never saw."[27]

5

Four Freaks from Iowa

Oscar Hammerstein was a worried man; the creditors were at the door, accusing him of pulling a fast one by attempting to legally transfer all of his property to his wife. Less than twelve months after opening his huge new pleasure palace—the first ever theater in the area that would become known as Times Square—the impresario was facing huge debts, his long-held dream of providing New York with a world-class entertainment venue having turned in to a nightmare.

The Prussian-born Hammerstein, grandfather of the man who would write the lyrics to *Show Boat, South Pacific, The King and I* and *The Sound of Music*, had arrived in New York in 1864. He was just sixteen years old and still smarting from the final beating his overbearing father had given him, a thrashing that left a scar on his forehead that would stay with him for the rest of his life. Hammerstein senior was furious that the boy preferred music—a love instilled in him by his mother, Bertha Valentine Hammerstein—over Hebrew and mathematics, and that he had resolutely refused to settle down to his academic studies. The loving and cosseting Bertha had died when Oscar was barely fourteen, and without her to protect him the rebellious teenager felt that life in Civil War-torn America seemed more inviting than returning home for yet another thrashing at the brawny hands of his building contractor father.

After three months at sea, young Hammerstein arrived in New York and almost immediately landed a job, sweeping the floors of a cigar factory for $3 a week. Hammerstein found he had an affinity for the industry and quickly rose through the ranks, helping to industrialize the cigar-making process, improving working conditions and, in 1874, founding his own trade magazine, the *United States Tobacco Journal*. After a quarter of a century in the country he was a wealthy man, and the money he had made would allow him to finally pursue his true love—the musical theater.

Opera-mad Oscar, who for years had moonlighted as a manager for a succession of theaters, opened his first venue, the Harlem Opera House, in

1889—a luxurious affair replete with polished Italian marble and velvet curtains, adjacent to fifty dwellings that he had also invested in. A year later he opened his second house, the Columbus Theater, offering vaudeville and other less genteel forms of entertainment to those on show at his opulent Opera House. Yet although Harlem was now easily accessible, thanks to the arrival of the elevated railroad, the crowds did not flock to Hammerstein's venues and after his third effort, the Manhattan Opera House, also failed to draw the cultured audiences he craved, Hammerstein entered into a disastrous business partnership with vaudeville theater operators John Koster and Albert Bial. Frustrated, he sold up and moved downtown, vowing to "build a house the likes of which has never been seen in the whole world." The result was the magnificent Olympia Theater in Long Acre Square, a triple threat in that it housed a theater, a music hall and a concert venue behind its magnificent Indiana limestone façade, as well as a German-themed restaurant and a splendid roof garden. Costing, by Hammerstein's own estimate, somewhere "between two and three million dollars," and "occupying the entire block front, between Forty-fourth and Forty-fifth streets,"[1] the Olympia was the first such pleasure palace to be erected in a muddy street dominated by cheap hotels, stables and brothels that, in 1904, would be renamed after *The New York Times* moved its headquarters there.

Opening night saw a riot, with people desperate to get in to the new venue: "So great was the crowd and so eager were the people to get inside the building that one literally had to fight one's way in," the *New York Dramatic Mirror* relayed.[2] Hammerstein installed his eldest son, Willie, as manager but, before the place had celebrated its first anniversary, the family empire was again struggling. Not only had the building cost a fortune, it also had a huge wages bill, and patrons were not filling the seats. Audiences were already tiring of the high-brow European acts Hammerstein senior had been importing: "some were veritable gold bricks and the others, though they 'made good,' did not satisfy the public craving for originality and novelty on the stage. So he began to look about the United States for an attraction which would set the town talking."[3] His curiosity was piqued by a series of reports in the *New York Sun* concerning a troupe of women from Iowa who "had a great many things to learn, among them the proper method of protecting themselves from wash boilers, cannonballs, stove wood, cabbages, and unsavory hen fruit."[4] The women on the receiving end of the rotten eggs were, of course, the Cherry Sisters. A follow up article in the same newspaper ended with a warning: "The Cherry Sisters give a great show. It hath been truly said that there is nothing like it on earth. Strong men are driven to drink."[5]

Reasoning with his father that they had "tried the best, so why not try the worst?," Willie Hammerstein sent his loyal lieutenant, Alfred E. "Al" Aarons, westwards with strict instructions to secure the talents of the Charming Cherry Sisters and their famed revue. It took Aarons, formerly stage manager at the Manhattan Opera House and now fulfilling the same role at the Olympia, a while to find them: his first stop was Quincy, Illinois where he had heard that they were appearing, but by the time he arrived they had already moved on. From there he went to the Hopkins Theater in Chicago, where the owner put him in touch with George Peck, the current manager of Greene's Opera House in Cedar Rapids. Aarons arrived in Cedar Rapids on Thursday, 29 October. That same day a report appeared in the *Marion Sentinel* that must have caused him to question his mission:

> Addle Cherry … is a gushing young thing about 97 years old and wears hair left over from a last year's mattress. She is a good girl, though, and has a heart as big as a ham and as true as the Bessemer Steel Works. She is not a cherry, but a peach. When it comes to rainbows look out for Jessie Cherry. She is a whole quart of molasses by her lonesome, and when she did Trilby in a blonde wig as high as a hen house the audience arose and cried. Jessie Cherry is fruit and no mistake. Effie Cherry is a hand-painted darling. She is a gamesome, gladsome, voluptuous pet, with a wealth of feet. She was to have appeared as the goddess of liberty in the closing tableau last night, but the stepladder broke and this magnificent spectacle was abandoned. There is only one girl in the world like Effie Cherry—and that is Lizzie Cherry. Lizzie Cherry is a whole

The Olympia Theater, New York.

lunch. She has the gyratorical abandon of a yearling heifer and the liquid depths of her eyes would drown any man not over seven feet high. When the Cherry Sisters hold a reunion on the stage the world seems brighter, better, sunnier, and Elysium not so far away.[6]

Aarons returned to New York the following week with a contract signed by Lizzie on behalf of four of the Sisters. According to Effie's unpublished memoirs, only Lizzie had been at the homestead when Aarons came calling; the other sisters were away on tour, but for this trip Lizzie opted to rejoin the group and Ella once again chose to stay home and look after the farm, this time with the added luxury of help from two hired hands. Oscar Hammerstein would later tell reporters that "they were forwarded the usual first-class sleeping-car fares to bring them to New York. They made the long thirty-hours trip in a day coach and pocketed the difference. They came on here with only one street dress apiece. Their conceit is something phenomenal. They enjoy the jeers which they receive out West, as is proven by the stories in the papers there. They have been pelted with eggs, rubber overshoes, and umbrellas, and still they kept on for the sake of the money they hoarded. I will not permit that."[7]

The Sisters did not know what to make of the great metropolis; it was like nothing they had ever seen before. "'Why,' said Lizzie, 'I feel as if I had been down below and seen Satan grin!'"[8] "They arrived in New York last week, bringing their costumes and properties in carpetbags and haircloth trunks. They have been going around New York ever since, getting pains in their necks from looking up at the tall buildings."[9] As the city's theatergoers would soon discover, the Cherry Sisters were like something they had never seen either.

The Cherry Sisters made their New York debut on 11 November 1896; five days before the Hammersteins would reveal their new act to the paying public they invited "a few hardened veterans" (as the *Sun* put it) to meet the girls, witness their act and—hopefully—write about them in glowing terms. Unfortunately Hammerstein's hospitality was not enough to stem the poison that would flow from the pens of the city's critics, who had been alerted to the potential for fun by the sarcastic tone of Hammerstein's advance advertising, which made the most of the Cherrys' backwoods background.

After their performance Oscar stood in the magnificent marble lobby of his white elephant of a theater with his hands covering his face. "Did you ever see anything like it?"[10] he asked each person who passed him as they left the building, cursing the day he had allowed his eldest son to take over the reins of his beloved pleasure palace. Everybody admitted that the likes of Lizzie, Addie, Effie and Jessie Cherry had never been let loose on the New

York stage before. "The Cherry Sisters are four girls who think they can act. They are alone in that opinion."[11] Arthur Hammerstein, Willie's brother, later recalled that first appearance:

> We were utterly amazed by their performance. The four girls, all blonde and bony, trooped out on the stage with military precision and blank faces. One carried a bass drum, the second a clarinet, the third a cornet and the fourth was empty-handed—for a reason: she sang. The march finished, they ranged themselves stiffly in front of the footlights and bowed in unison. Then the leader called 'Go!', and they went. A bedlam of sound broke out which, roughly speaking, was based on 'Dolly Gray.' The effect was startling. The utter seriousness with which the girls were taking themselves created at first a puzzling restraint, but when human nature asserted itself the audience went into hysterics. The act was so terribly bad it was shriekingly funny.[12]

At an impromptu press conference held in Willie Hammerstein's office after their press showcase, the women were at pains to explain how they had been grossly misrepresented by the reports that had reached New York ahead of them. "They do scandalize us so," Jessie, described as wearing "a green dress with a turban of the same color and a limp red feather falling coquettishly over her left cheek," told the reporters present. "They tell such libels about us. The idea of saying we travel behind a net to keep people from throwing things at us. They said that about us in Iowy, and I wrote to the paper and made 'em take it back! We make more money doin' this, and we're going to stick to it until we've got enough money to buy a few more fruit farms. Then we're goin' to quit. We've got forty acres now, and Ella's home watchin' the two hired men."[13] The absent Ella was greatly missed by actor and lyricist James T. Powers (born James McGovern in New York in 1862), who penned the eulogy "To Ella Cherry of the Cherry Sisters":

> *I have lingered in the moonlight, I have wandered in the dell,*
> *Dreaming, thinking of a maiden I could kiss, but never tell.*
> *My thoughts have strayed to pearly streams and banks of mossy green,*
> *But the face of her I want to love, I've seen 'twas in a dream.*
>
> *Oh, how my mind has wandered, how my heart has cracked and ached*
> *After fits of troubled slumber my heated brain was baked,*
> *But a vision, lovely vision came to me last Monday night—*
> *When I saw the Cherry Sisters, my troubled heart grew light;*
>
> *For I saw in Sister Ella my vision in the dell.*
> *Oh, come to me, my Ella, we'll kiss and never tell*
> *Oh, my darling sunburnt Ella, through my brain young Cupid trips,*
> *Let me love you, Ella Cherry, let me kiss those cherry lips.*
>
> *Oh, tell me, Sisters Cherry, why have you stayed so long,*
> *In the woods of Cedar Rapids; oh, the Rapids they were strong,*
> *To keep you floating In the West and hide you from the East,*
> *Please meet me, lovely Ella—at the Waldorf we will feast.*[14]

With Ella not there to answer Jessie, egged on by a reporter from the *Sun*, penned a riposte:

*I ne'er lingered in the moonlight, or wandered in the Dell
And of course if I should kiss a man I'd run right off and tell.
My mind has never wandered; my heart has never ached,
So don't take me for a sucker, I'm from the Hawkeye State*

*You say you've seen a vision as lovely as could be;
No doubt but you were tipsy and had been out on a spree.
If you don't look out my Jimmie you'll be walking on your nose,
For you don't know what will happen where the corn juice flows.*

*Of all the cities in the east New York may be the best,
But you will think you are right in paradise when you strike the woolly west.
When you are weary of the east, Jim where you have dwelt so long
Seek the woods of Cedar Rapids, of Fifty thousand strong.*[15]

The local media went Cherry crazy, with the self-identified sophisticates writing for New York's newspapers awarding the troupe of female bumpkins with endless column inches. Hammerstein Junior could not believe his luck. Advertised to the public as "the Peerless Cherry Sisters! Warbling Wonders, Terpsichorean Triumphs. Robed in the choicest confections of Cedar Rapids modistes and displaying $20,000 worth of dazzling diamond studs," and with a suggestion that ticket buyers should "DOUBLE YOUR LIFE INSURANCE!" as "in Iowa, Illinois and Kansas they have often tickled audiences to death,"[16] their first night in front of a paying audience was a fiasco. The program announced that the Cherrys' act would consist of seven segments, "Eulogy on the Cherry Sisters," "in which the words have been written by Miss Lizzie to the music of a well remembered tune"; "Fair Columbia," "a song descriptive of our nation's glorious career; little Miss Jessie wrote both words and music to this, and also sings it in a glorious national costume"; "Irish Ballad," which was "composed by Miss Lizzie and sung with superb action by the Misses Addie and Lizzie"; "Bicycle Ride to the Fair," which Miss Jessie "sings all by herself and does a dainty little walk around with each chorus," plus favorites "The Gypsy's Warning," "The Orphan Flower Girl" ("Miss Jessie will make you weep in this") and the "Essay on the Modern Young Man," described as "the essence and pith of up-to-date wisdom, written and played by the Misses Addie and Effie." With the Cherrys afforded top billing over a half-dozen other acts (including "mirror dancer" Papinta and juggler Prince Kokin), and other halls within the vast building offering such delights as a game of polo with players on bicycles, it was nearing 10 p.m. before their spot came around. To hushed silence, shortly before the curtain went up, one of the women came before the audience to talk to them. "'This is our first appearance,' she said in her coarse, untrained voice, and with an awkward sweep of her bony arm. 'And I must say that the advertising we got in the papers was very funny.'"[17] Then the lights dimmed, the curtain raised, and the girls got their first glimpse of the capacity audience—according to the *Des Moines Register* fully four thousand people were sat there expectantly (the *New York Press* estimated a more believable 2,000). The four women stood there terrified. Jessie was able to hide most of her frame behind the big bass drum she carried; the others, in red dresses with satin sashes, decorated with bunches of cherries, were not so lucky.

"When the four were first revealed they wore turkey red calico frocks, and Jessie beat a drum while the quartet sang a description of their own merits to the tune of 'Ta-ra-ra Boom-de-ay.' They are homely, and the audience laughed wildly at their appearance and more boisterously at voices which cut the air in to jagged shreds." The catcalls started within seconds; when the girls sang "Cherrys ripe, boom-de-ay" someone in the auditorium called back "Cherrys are rotten!" and the rest of the audience soon joined in. The sisters left the stage, visibly shaken, before Jessie

> reappeared wearing a short skirt of red, white and blue calico. She has the family voice, and sang a national song of her own composition. She appeared twice again, once to sing about a bicycle ride to the World's Fair, and as the 'Orphan Flower Girl' wore no stockings. She carried a basket of flowers, and whatever the words of the song she sang may have been, nobody heard them. She would have been inaudible in the music hall if the audience had kept quiet, but already the spectators had begun to take an occasional and half-hearted share in the performance led by a coarse-voiced man in an upper box. There are soubrettes in the Bowery music halls funnier than Miss Jessie ever began to be, and the awkwardness of her gestures did not always appear to be genuine.

"Where are your stockings?" someone shouted. "Put on your socks," called out another. Jessie pulled up her skirt and looked down at her bare, brown feet mortified. She left the stage in tears; the audience was laughing so much that there was barely a dry eye in the house. As the *New York Press* reported the following day: "Words fail; language is inadequate; the pen falters and the descriptive writer throws up his job when it comes to telling how the Cherry Sisters look and act and sing."

> Dressed as Irish women Addie and Lizzie sang a song which nobody had even the heart to guy—it was just ordinarily bad. 'The Gypsy's Warning' was another effort that engaged the talents of three of the sisters, and an 'Essay on the Modern Young Man,' read by Miss Addie, was lost in the hubbub that accompanied it. As a Negro, Miss Effie attempted a few dance steps and sang a parody on 'After the Ball.' The dance was the one flash of what the audience had really expected throughout, and it responded vociferously. Probably the Cherries [sic] will be greeted tonight in silent wonder, not unmixed with pity ... they are bad, very bad.[18]

According to another reviewer, "the howling, catcalling etc. that greeted [The Gypsy's Warning] so paralyzed Lizzie that she broke down and wept and wandered off the stage trembling."[19] The *New York Times* had announced their arrival by branding the Sisters as "coarse, gawky and stupid," and the paper informed its readers that "while three of them are tall and angular, the fourth is very short and weighs 170 pounds."[20] That same august organ reviewed the evening's entertainment under the heading "Four Freaks from Iowa," and wondered if "the great crowd of people who watched it" were at all concerned that "the emotion they felt was pity for the four wretched women whose sorry antics had excited the derisive laughter of a few callous spectators, or whether it was shame at having to come to see what they had been told beforehand would be merely an exhibition of folly and weakness."[21] The *New York Mirror* noted that "a dozen sawmills at full speed could not have drowned Miss Effie's rasping voice," and that "Miss Jessie made everybody weep beyond a doubt, for they laughed until their sides ached, and the tears rolled down their cheeks."[22] Yet another reporter dismissed the night as a "disgraceful exhibition" put on by "four ignorant girls from a farm in the West ... so ridiculous that they are not even amusing."[23] James L. Ford, writing in the *New York Journal*, was convinced that the whole wretched performance was designed to be bad: "They sang in voices that were purposely out of key, and shrill enough to remind us of what we have suffered in English musical comedy. They made gestures in which they had been carefully drilled ... they suited themselves to the people they saw before them, and tried to be as freakish as possible."[24]

"Let me assure you that they are not at all to be pitied," Oscar told reporters. "The idea that they are guileless fools, brought here ignorant of the kind of reception they were sure to meet is entirely false. They have been playing now for four years, have met with this kind of reception everywhere, and while they may not thoroughly enjoy it, they do it for the cold, hard sake of making money. They have accumulated a lot of money, and are misers pure and simple."[25] The day after their official debut the *Chicago Daily Tribune* noted that "Addie, Lizzie, Jessie and Effie cannot sing, cannot act, and are gaunt and homely to the point of despair. They are so bad they are uproariously funny."[26]

What the audience did not see that first night was the sight of the Cherrys being pelted with rotten vegetables. In fact, although Willie Hammerstein seems to have encouraged his staff to stir up the audience, nothing outside of a few theater programs were launched towards the stage, and those were thrown by employees "obviously to incite the spectators to do the same thing." By the second night things had changed, as "turnips, onions, peanuts, apples and a conglomeration of miscellaneous articles"[27] including "two stuffed stockings" were hurled at the stage. The sisters broke down and refused to continue their performance; the audience, naturally, responded with catcalls, hoots and whistles. It was at that point that Willie had a brainwave. Recalling that report in *The Sun* earlier in the year which had first alerted him to the Cherry phenomenon, he remembered reading that they used to "carry with them a wire screen, such as is put up in front of baseball grandstands ... this screen is made in sections and can be made to accommodate a stage of almost any size."[28] Legend has it that he erected his own wire screen in front of the stage that would serve to both protect the sisters from harm and encourage the increasingly boisterous audience to vent their anger by launching any missiles in their possession stagewards. Buster Keaton wrote about the screen, and added that Willie Hammerstein passed out artificial fruit and vegetables to audience members who had not come equipped,[29] but Keaton was barely one year old when the Cherrys took up their residency at the Olympia; he did not begin performing as part of his family's vaudeville act until 1899.

Enterprising fruit and vegetable merchants set up trucks outside the main entrance to the Olympia, selling produce well past its best at premium prices to patrons as they entered the theater. Willie and Arthur Hammerstein were among the entrepreneurs. New flyers were printed which proclaimed "members of the company provided with screens," and that "cabbages and potatoes may be had at the door."[30] Fresh produce grew scarce in the city's greengrocers because of the demands of the Olympia audiences, as the *New York Clipper* reported: "Fruit and vegetable retailers have filed complaint that because truck raisers and commission men are selling direct to patrons of Hammerstein's theater, they are unable to meet the demands of their trade." Oscar was not entirely pleased at his son's activities, writing a letter to the *New York Herald* to state that "some boys in the gallery did misbehave ... but their actions were promptly stopped. I am presenting the Cherry Sisters as performers belonging to a class frequently met with in the border towns and mining camps of the West, and, though crude in their ways and in what they consider 'art,' they certainly give a clean and inoffensive performance."[31] Whatever his thoughts on Willie's enterprise, within a fortnight of their first appearance Oscar had made enough to pay off his creditors (he had debts of $84,000, according to the *New York Times,* all of which were settled), however the audience that had paid good money to see the Hammerstein-penned operetta *Santa Maria,* playing on the stage of the Olympia's grand theater while the Cherry Sisters packed them in at the building's music hall, must have wondered why they had bothered; the ruckus they caused permeated every brick in the building.

Despite the *New York Sun*'s insistence that "the four unfortunate Cherry Sisters are not likely to remain long on view,"[32] the Sisters were the hit of the season, and their success did not go unnoticed. Women in New York began to wear cherry-colored ribbons in their hair and to pin bunches of cherries to their clothing in place of corsages. Everywhere you went people were wearing Cherry Sisters button badges, depicting a spray of cherries in the center with the words "such a bunch—Cherry Sisters" around the edge. Everyone who was anyone—including future President of the United States Woodrow Wilson, then on the faculty at Princeton University—came to visit them. "He was a college professor then," Effie recalled proudly. "Came back stage to tell us he'd never seen an entertainment like ours." "Mrs. Astor gave us a $20 bill and said she'd never enjoyed a variety show so much," Addie added.[33] On Thanksgiving Day a parade of costumed cyclists drew roars of laughter from a crowd lining the sidewalk, principally for the "fine imitations of some sisters who hold forth at a well known music hall," as the *New York Tribune* put it. "A rotund, jolly wheelman, who bore all the characteristics of one of the star features of the horse-show, carried a banner that had the inscription 'we don't like fruit,' and was followed by four country maidens clad in red Mother Hubbard gowns, one of whom beat a large-sized drum."[34] Popular comedy duo Weber and Fields satirized them, as the Prune Sisters (they also satirized the Barrisons, as the Five Embarrassing Sisters), on the stage of their own Broadway music hall; if you could not get in to see the Sisters at the Olympia then you could find Duncan Clarke's Lady Minstrels lampooning the Cherrys on the stage of Broadway's Casino Theater instead. Popular comedian Marie Dressler—who would play on the same bill as the Cherrys just a couple of months later—burlesqued Jessie's bare-footed flower girl in her act to uproarious laughter.

Word of their triumph traveled far and wide, but not everyone was happy with the opprobrium cast towards them: "The men who go to their performances to ridicule their country methods simply degrade themselves," chastised New Orleans newspaper *The Times-Picayune*. "The sisters are women, and for that they are entitled to some sort of respect."[35] "The Cherry Sisters are four grotesquely incapable performers whom Manager Hammerstein engaged solely that they might serve as targets for jeers and missiles ... his idea was to give the patrons of the Olympia and excuse for indulgence in brutal rowdyism ... all of his advertisements were direct incitements to brutal ruffianism."[36] Oscar Hammerstein himself was castigated as "a sordid, brutal and low-lived person," with the writer hoping he would be driven out of business. A few dissenting voices agreed with James Ford's assessment, and refused to buy in to the conceit: "It is extremely probable that the Cherry Sisters are merely unusually artistic fakers, actresses so clever that they are able to play their parts off stage as well as on it," wrote the *Rochester Democrat and Chronicle*. "This probability is strengthened by the fact that the public is asked to believe that nothing in their three years' experience on the stage has in the least shifted the Cherry Sisters' point of view ... that they have never once 'tumbled to themselves.'"[37] The same newspaper later reported that "a well-known actress who saw the sisters, remarked when they first came out on stage: 'These women are not fools.'"[38]

Although they were earning in the region of $500 a week (some reports claimed that the Hammersteins were paying them $1,000), the Sisters themselves were far from ecstatic with their initial reception. "They ain't told nothing but a lot of lies about us since we came to New York," an exasperated Effie told a reporter from the *New York Press*. "We're as mad as hornets at that there press agent. He just laughs and says he ain't to blame. Our manager's comin' next week and he'd better look out, and the newspaper men too. He's just as fearless and as obstinate as we are, only he's a man. New York fellers don't pay no attention to what we say, 'cause they think we're just weak women that are just talking because we think it's fun to hear ourselves."[39] The manager they talked of was Will Manchester, a percussionist in the orchestra at Greene's Opera House back in Cedar Rapids, who the Sisters contracted to come out to New York and represent them. Manchester was aware that the Sisters were helping the Hammerstein's achieve up to $8,000 a night, and that interest in them was being shown from agents in other major cities, including Boston, Philadelphia and Washington. Manchester duly traveled to New York to assist them, and, like many before and after him, to add a healthy amount to the balance of his bank account. When Manchester returned to Cedar Rapids a week later he made no mention of obtaining a raise for his charges, but did report that a grateful Oscar had purchased new silk dresses for each of the Sisters.

The new dresses were a sop of sorts, and did much to lessen Effie's resentment at being portrayed as a rural rube. "They told us to bring all our oldest clothes and so we left our nicest things at home, and I s'pose folks'll think this is all we've got," she revealed. "We did bring the diamond necklace along. Perhaps you noticed it? Jessie wore it last night."[40] A photo of the Sisters appeared in *The New York World* purporting to show them "displaying $20,000 worth of dazzling diamond studs," and they were often photographed wearing black velvet chokers with ostentatiously large stones at their centers. Oscar Hammerstein told the press that the necklace the Sisters "so proudly talked about is in reality a collection of country fair Kohinoors, such as are sold at wholesale by the quart."[41] The man from the *New York Press* described it as "several pieces of glass sewed to a band of black velvet ribbon."[42]

5. Four Freaks from Iowa

Illustration of the Sisters' carriage ride around New York, 1896.

One evening, less than a week in to their residency, the roof garden of the Olympia was taken over by some "five thousand hilarious young men with plenty of money to spend and under the impression that they owned the earth." The men, Princeton and Yale students and their well-heeled friends, had paid a dollar apiece for the privilege of drinking after midnight within the confines of the theater's magnificent garden, entertained by a company of cancan dancers. When the ladies' French fancies failed to impress, the rowdy crowd—some of whom had witnessed the Sisters' act firsthand, others who had come from Koster and Bial's, where the bawdy Barrison Sisters were appearing—called for them to be brought up to the roof. "The Cherry Sisters were willing, but Hammerstein was weak. 'Better not go on the roof tonight,' he said. 'Very rough crowd up there.' 'But we want to go,' said the little sister, who came out in bare feet. 'We have been on the stage three years, and we have college boys in Iowa. We know 'em.'"[43] Willie insisted that the Sisters went back to their hotel, and they grudgingly obliged. After all, that night's performance had wiped them out: "It was the first time," said Lizzie, "that we ever had stage fright." Their appearance had been greeted with a blast of tin horns, kazoos and college catcalls. Effie, seemingly relishing the attention, played to the audience, changing one of the lines in her address to "of all the boys my choice would be a football man each time."[44] This nod to the crowd heralded a shower of coins, which Jessie gladly gathered up.

With none of the Sisters joining the rabble on the roof, pandemonium broke out; Captain Sheehan, the New York policeman in charge of the Tenderloin district, told Willie that his staff must stop serving alcohol unless it was accompanied by food. Hammerstein argued that the students and their friends had eaten everything they had in the building. Surprisingly there was only one arrest made that night: 21 year-old Yale student Bert Brainerd, fined $3 for being "so drunk he couldn't take care of himself."[45]

As rowdy as the audience had been that night, their attention marked a change for the Cherrys. Although they would still have to dodge cabbages and rotten fruit, they could also boast that "instead of old shoes and eggs, they have had flowers and money thrown at them."[46] A local artist presented them with a portrait, which Lizzie described as "a girl with a cherry in her mouth and her hair tied with a ribbon in the back,"[47] that they hung in the parlor of their rented rooms. The women sent the flowers to Cedar Rapids to be exhibited in Carl Owen's window, and although by the time the bouquets reached home they must have been a little bedraggled, the Cherry Window attracted much attention. Naturally the parsimonious family retained the money, although Lizzie explained that Jessie was fed up with chasing pennies across the stage and she "just lets the stage boys have most of it now."[48] After filling the Olympia to capacity for four full weeks, adapting their set to include their infamous version of the *Trilby* story (and incorporating their version of the song "Don't You Remember Sweet Alice, Ben Bolt?," yet another syrupy song about the death of a young woman), the sisters ended their stay in New York with a tour of the city. Whatever anger they once felt towards the Big Apple's newspapermen must have softened somewhat, as their tour guide was none other than James L. Ford, the correspondent for the *Journal* who had been convinced that the Sisters' innocence had all been an act. "I took them for a drive," he wrote, "and one of the young ladies while comparing the society of New York to that of Cedar Rapids remarked 'Those Vanderbilts don't seem to put on as much style as we expected. I saw Mr. Vanderbilt the other day and he wasn't a bit better dressed or half as stylish as Mr. Slocum of our town, who runs the Square Deal collar and cuff place on Main Street and is a great society man. Why I should think that Mr. Vanderbilt would dress up a little more fancy when he went out in the park of a morning!'"[49] Effie revealed to the newspaperman what she thought was the secret of their success: "our entertainment is always crowded, and I'll tell you why. There's nothing in it that anybody need feel ashamed to listen to, not even if he was a minister."[50]

With a return visit to the city (this time at Proctor's Music Hall) booked for the following February, the Cherry Sisters bid goodbye to New York on 12 December. The next day their bags were packed and they were off to Chicago, to fulfill a three-week long engagement at the city's Imperial Theater. The Sisters were mightily pleased with themselves, but nothing could have prepared the Windy City for what was about to hit it.

6

And Then There Were Three

In Chicago the troupe was paid $400 a week which, according to Effie's own recollection, was the same as they earned during the four weeks that they had headlined at the Olympia, but was significantly less than the $1,000 a week many newspapers claimed they had been getting. Sadly, although they would continue to perform for more than thirty years, they would never again earn as much money as they did during their weeks with the Hammersteins or in Chicago, and after these dates, although they often proved that they could still pack the houses, wages began their inexorable slide downwards. Some of the money that they earned was spent hiring a detective to seek out their errant brother Nathan, a search that once again proved fruitless, and within a few months Effie was telling reporters that "there are five of us girls. Mother and father are dead. That's all there is of our family."[1] It seemed as if they had given up all hope of ever finding Nathan alive.

They debuted at the Imperial on 15 December. Before the curtain went up, a large placard was placed on the stage, warning the more boisterous among the audience than anyone caught throwing anything at the performers would be evicted. No missiles were launched, but before the Sisters had finished the first verse of "Eulogy on the Cherry Sisters" "the audience was in such an uproar that the Iowa quartette was all but driven off the stage, and before the second number was ended a large share of the audience was moving for the doors."[2]

With no Cherry Sisters to fill his theater, the ever-enterprising Hammerstein employed what he was convinced was the next best thing. James Ballard, the Bard of Iowa, was a self-proclaimed poet who hailed from Red Oak, and who was said to be equally as awful as the Sisters. According to the *New York Journal*, Ballard "confesses that he has written more than 44,000 lines of alleged poetry during the last twenty years. No outburst of enthusiasm can drown his utterances, for he has a voice like a fog horn and an immaculate gall. Poetry is not profitable in Iowa, so Ballard runs a produce farm in connection with his literary mill. He daily drives through the town of Red Oak in a light vehicle on one side of which is painted the words 'Radishes and Poetry,' and on the other 'Lettuce and Lectures.'"[3] For a while he followed them on the circuit, often reciting his absurd doggerel in the same theaters and opera houses days or weeks after the Cherry Sisters had vacated. Advertised as "the only living rival to the Cherry Sisters," and known as the "Cherry Brother of Poetry," the Sisters were naturally indignant that their good name be besmirched by being acquainted with someone as useless as Jim Ballard; he (or his agent) seizing on the opportunity for publicity, challenged the Cherrys to a public contest to see which of them was the best (or worst). It was suggested that the superintendent of an asylum might consider acting as referee. Ballard was never going to be the box office draw that the Cherry Sisters had proved to be, and before long word got around that Hammerstein had asked the Sisters to return, offering "$2,400 a week, but they did not like that he made so much on their last engagement, and now they refuse to go on for less than $10,000. This is no fairy tale."[4]

While in Chicago, the Sisters took up residence at the Revere House Hotel on North Clark Street. The city proved a generous host, and they played a number of different theaters there. They liked the city well enough, but Effie was less taken with the public art on display. "The statues and monuments! Why, I went in to the art gallery in Chicago, an' I think the people ought to go there in a mob an' throw all them statues in the lake!"[5] In mid–January, after their week-long booking at the New Tivoli, on Wabash Avenue, proved such a draw the sisters were contracted to play for a further week, but first they had to fit in a trip to St. Louis, where they had been booked to appear beneath the glass-domed roof of the ornate Hagan Theater for a week. Mr. Hagan himself promised that he had "made every preparation to prevent violence being done them, and a special platoon of police has been assigned to the theater, and all persons will be thoroughly searched for hen relics and similar missiles." It was reported that "for a time he was disposed to stretch a wire screen across the front of the stage, but the Cherries [sic] told him to cheer up—that there was absolutely no danger. They are all expert dodgers, and if necessary will wear deodorizing masks."[6]

Playing on a bill that also featured contortionists the Pantzer Trio, trick cyclist Will Newhouse plus the usual mix of comedy duos, black-faced minstrels and the like, the Sisters' offered Jessie's "Fair Columbia," "The Gypsy's Warning," and a couple of *tableaux vivants*. During their second week at the New Tivoli they added the deathbed scene from Harriet Beecher Stowe's famous anti-slavery novel "Uncle Tom's Cabin" to their set, with Addie adding a blackface turn to her repertoire. The Sisters debuted plenty of new material, including Jessie's song "Alone on the Street" (originally titled "After the Play"), which was "declared to be no relation to 'After the Ball.' Notwithstanding this assurance it was evident to the naked ear that Miss Jessie's song bore many marks of family resemblance to Mr. Harris' famous ditty."[7]

> After the play is over
> After the closing song
> After the crowding people
> Have joined the city throng
> There in the open highway
> As he had been before
> There is a heart that is breaking
> After the play is o'er.[8]

Reporters from Chicago's *Times-Herald* refused to believe that the act was for real. "It is such an obvious great big fake. They never came from Marion, Iowa; they are the product of the heart of some great metropolis. They are not sisters, save as they are old and ungainly and shrewd, and strive to make themselves ungainlier and older ... this was a clever scheme of theirs and they have worked it. They wear queer clothes that just miss being absolutely ridiculous...."[9] The Cherrys were such a hit that they ended up playing the New Tivoli for a total of three weeks. Back in Des Moines, pencil portraits of two of the famous sisters were unveiled at the Iowa Society of Fine Arts' annual exhibition, and soda fountains across the country were offering "Cherry Sisters" flavor drinks.

Returning to New York, in February 1897 the Sisters appeared on the stage of Proctor's Pleasure Palace, a new theater on East Fifty-Eighth Street. Costing around $1 mil-

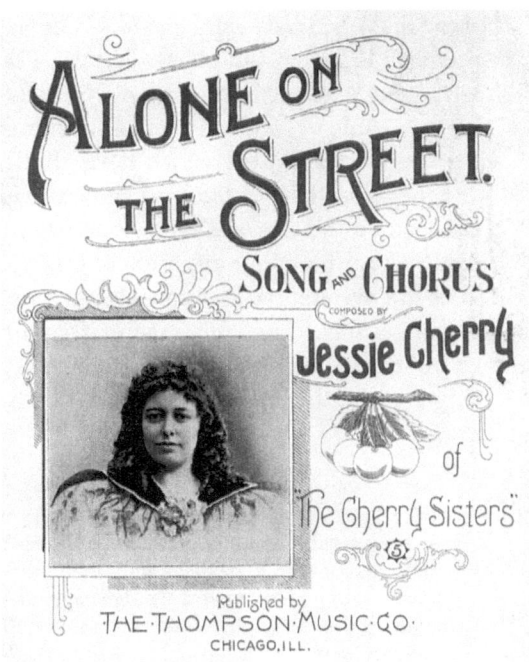

Sheet music for Jessie's "Alone in the Street," circa 1899.

lion to build, the Pleasure Palace was a huge and flamboyant building, with a commanding tower on the corner topped by a minaret. Like Hammerstein's Olympia, the Pleasure Palace also boasted a roof garden, an ornate opera house and a vaudeville theater, as well as a library, a reading and writing room, stands offering flowers, books, newspapers, coffee and other refreshments, a barbershop, a boot-black stand and even a swimming pool. When Epes Winthrop Sargent (later associate editor of *Variety*) covered the show in his own magazine *Chicot's Weekly*, he reported that the Sisters "had been given 'four golden horseshoes' in Chicago, and presented with a glass cane handsomely decorated with ribbons at St. Louis. If arrangements could be made, I should be glad to present them with a horseshoe attached to the business end of an able-bodied and hard-working jackass." They picked up yet another manager, this time a John Cort, who quickly got his new earner booked in to theaters in Chicago, a city which could not get enough of the Cherrys, Cincinnati (the Star) and other communities in the Eastern states. Their "Uncle Tom's Cabin" skit proved such a success with audiences that it was suggested the Sisters might go on tour in a play based on the novel.

The first week of March found the Sisters still at Proctor's, with a variety show that included such long-forgotten acts as Little Louise Truax the Phenomenal Whistler, and Master Witter J. Peabody, boy soprano. The show was a hit, and stars including Lillian Nordica, the pre-eminent opera singer of her day, came to see them there: "no amount of noise or guying can snuff out the sparks of ambition which nave kindled in the spaces under their hair, and they gave their whole freak show at every performance."[10] Also appearing at Proctor's, in her own show, was Marie Dressler, the comic actress who had made a huge hit of her imitation of Jessie Cherry. The sisters were not happy with the preferential treatment shown to Miss Dressler, an actor who had begun her stage career more than a decade before the Cherrys and who would go on to become a phenomenally successful movie star, and complained at length about the amount of money that had been spent on scenery for her act.

> They are very particular about having things just fixed to suit them on the stage. They have a strong weakness for using the best set of scenery in every house they play. Last week a beautiful new conservatory scene was put on at the Palace, having been made especially for Marie Dressler's act. When the fruit syndicate saw this they grew madly jealous, and remonstrated with the stage manager, demanding that the scene be set for them the rest of the week, reminding him that Miss Dressier was only one, and that they were a whole 'troop.' He had to think quickly, as they threatened to strike if their wishes were not complied with. He told them that the scene was Miss Dressler's own property, and that nobody else could use it. They had to be satisfied with this explanation; but they found fault with so many other things that every one connected

with the theater, from Manager Price down to the keg-tapper in the café, wore a worried look, which did not leave them until the Cherrys' baggage was safely landed on the sidewalk.[11]

Despite their grievances, the Cherry Sisters "drew many curiosity seekers who had lots of fun with the four merry maidens from the West."[12] In an effort to save face, the Sisters wrote to *Variety* castigating Price for trying to rip them off, by passing off ten pounds of sand as a mixture for stage lighting—many of the theaters the Cherrys were playing having not yet gone fully electric.[13]

Early 1897 was a busy time for the Cherrys. News of their New York triumph traveled fast, and adverts they placed in the trade press to solicit work for the "Celebrated Cherry Sisters Specialty Company," offering their "strictly refined" act to "first class houses only"[14] were paying off, bringing in offers from round the country. They also announced that they were going in to the living picture business (an early name for motion pictures), and although they do not appear to have produced or appeared in their own movies, their touring company would sporadically exhibit short films between acts for a number of years to come. The motion picture industry was still in its infancy, with films silent, black and white and lasting no more than a minute or so— but the Sisters had been entranced by seeing the films screened by the Lumière brothers at Proctors and, by accident rather than design, they became unwitting pioneers of the traveling cinema. A week-long engagement at the Empire Theater in Buffalo, advertised as "a sure cure for the blues," had to be extended by a further week, so great was the demand for tickets. The Empire's management promised "a bushel of laughs, brought direct from the balmy fields of the West at a large expense," and audiences certainly felt that they got their 10 cents worth. Stories soon spread that the sisters had made so much money that they were able to purchase not one but two fruit farms to add to the land Ella cultivated in Marion, and that they had also invested in a ten acre building plot, known as the Paddington Homestead, on Marion Boulevard, at a cost of $17,000. Cherry mania was at a peak, and when Ella called on a neighbor, Gertrude Kurtz, to deliver fruit, Mrs. Kurtz invited her to stay the night so that she might regale her houseguests with stories of her famous siblings.

In fact, so busy were they, a rumor spread around the vaudeville circuit that the Cherry Sisters appearing on the stage of Hyde and Behman's in Brooklyn were imposters, and that the real thing was back in Iowa, "remaining quietly under cover during a period for which they are paid for the use of their names."[15] The perpetrator of this ruse was said to be none other than Oscar Hammerstein himself, who soon discovered that Ballard the Bard, with his absurd clothes and pompous speeches, was nowhere near the drawing card that the Cherry Sisters had been for him.

The Sisters had no need to employ others to stand in for the real thing; however that did not prevent other acts from trying to cash in on their infamy. In early January they received word that another act, Duncan Clark's Lady Minstrels, were passing themselves off as the Cherry Sisters; Clark was promoting his show as featuring the "four ripe Cherry Sisters, direct from New York." Clark was used to trouble: several of his all-woman act were actually men in drag, and he had been arrested in Utica in 1887 for "conducting an immoral show." The real Sisters employed a lawyer, Harry Overton, to issue a writ against Clark, prohibiting him from using their name in any of his advertising. At the same time another act called the Cherry Sisters was treading the boards in Australia, advertising their own appalling act as having debuted in "English and American variety halls,"[16] flagrantly attempting to cash in on the worldwide notoriety of the original sisters. "The majority of the audience 'guyed' and hissed, or in other ways marked their disapproval. The display altogether was not an edifying one." There were five Cherrys in this bunch, and they made their debut on stage on 14 August 1897, when the real Sisters were at the height of their fame, although the Iowa sisters would have had an attack of the vapors if they had seen just how much bare flesh was on show at an Australian Cherry Sisters concert. There was also a British act going under the name of The Cherry Sisters; in the 1920s another Vaudeville double act employed the Cherry Sisters moniker while playing in Michigan, and in the middle of the 20th century a female vocal group using the same name made a number of recordings and appeared regularly on television in the United States.

Brooklyn, at that time, was a city independent of New York, and would not be incorporated into what we now know as New York City until January 1898. The Sisters played Hyde and Behman's as part of Reilly and Wood's touring company, providing the closing on a bill that featured up to 10 different acts. "Hyde and Behman, always in search of novelties to please their patrons, have engaged for next week, at a big salary, the latest novelty craze, the Cherry Sisters, from Cedar Rapids, Marion County, Iowa. These girls present a specialty which for originality has no equal on the vaudeville stage. The songs, recitations, etc., which comprise their act, being six in number, are of their own composition, and are set to the airs of popular melodies, and sung with a style which is unique, to say the least."[17] "The Cherry Sisters came to Brooklyn last night, and were uproariously received.... Hyde and Behman have done a public service in bringing them here ... they are unique. Their songs are as far from music as one could imagine, and are sung to such inspiring melodies as 'Father, Dear Father, Come Home With Me Now.' Not one of the three apparently has any musical talent."[18]

Wherever they played the audiences came out in droves. The Hyde and Behman shows were sold out, and they continued to break box office records despite the horrific and chauvinistic write-ups the newspapers afforded them. The *Oskaloosa Daily Times* reported that Effie "ought to be able to stun the sensibilities of the human heart. But she can't. The only way she could do it would be with a hatchet or club or some other means of quick motion. Then too, she might invest in a couple of dollars in teeth and thus fill a long felt want in the aperture of her face. Her mouth is not so bewitching as bewildering." The same report decided that Addie's skirt dance "would suffocate a cow," and that Jessie "swooned away like a cow when knocked on the head with an ax. She would make a lovely corpse."[19] In Baltimore the local daily reported that "never before has there been a group of four awkward, ugly, peculiarly dressed young women who have delighted in going through antique chestnuts of melody off the key, out of time and with gestures whose lack of grace was little short of ludicrous.... Their part of the bill, as near as could be guessed, was a travesty of the style of Sunday school entertainment, which delights the people of towns of the size and culture of Cedar Rapids."[20] After a performance at Buffalo's Court Street Theater it was noted that "singing off the key is decidedly their forte, and as for their elocutionary ability, it is enough to fit one for an insane asylum. In the beginning, the audience watched them with some degree of mingled surprise and merriment, but it did not last long, and the girls were then unmercifully guyed. It is said that they really believe they are already variety stars and that there is no fake about their gaucherie performances. If this is true, they are a novelty that will be short lived, but if all the lack of finish in what they say or do is assumed, they are decidedly four very clever women."[21]

For more than two months, the Sisters and the Reilly and Woods team got on well. They were happy to be advertised as "the greatest novelty act in America," and said nothing about audiences being encouraged to "come help pay off the mortgage on the farm,"[22] but when the company cashier failed to turn up and pay their $400 wages after their final performance (at Williams' Academy in Pittsburgh) the Cherrys—after a fruitless visit to the local police station—got the train back to Iowa. The *Marion Pilot* announced that "the Cherry Sisters' manager ran off with their last week's salary,"[23] but Harry Williams, owner of the Academy, told reporters that "Pat Reilly told me that he had to get even with the Cherry Sisters for failing to keep an engagement at the London Theater, New York. It seems the theater was not up to the ideal of the sisters, so they refused to do their act. Reilly had to replace the Cherry

Sisters with other vaudeville talent and naturally was put to some expense. Reilly said the Sisters had broken their contract with him, and he felt justified in doing what he did."[24] As you would expect, the Sisters soon instigated a suit against Reilly.

Sore and, as they saw it, out of pocket, the Sisters pressed on under their own aegis. At a performance in Waterloo the local paper noted that nothing was thrown at the stage—such a rare occurrence that the reporter was moved to write a poem about the event:

> *Not an egg was thrown,*
> *Not a cabbage fell*
> *On the stage where the sisters were clinging.*
> *There was many a groan,*
> *And the people thought—"Well.*
> *Did you ever hear such singing?"*[25]

At the Bijou Theater in Washington, D. C., the sisters were engaged for a week as support to the Irish comedian Dan McCarthy. McCarthy did not find out about the addition to the billing until the night of the performance, and he was none too happy about sharing a stage with the Cherrys. "I hollered. I told Burns that I was a comedian, and that I thought too much of my reputation to play on the same stage with a collection of insane farmhands. Why, it was awful. People throw things at them on the stage and all the decent people left the theater. I was ashamed to go on the stage or on the street, either, and I wasn't glad to meet any of my friends for fear they would guy me."[26] The critics thought similarly, branding the Sisters' act "a grotesque performance ... they refrain from doing anything well and the ability with which they sing off the key and out of time, without a single lapse in to harmony, represents something akin to genius."[27] The audience did not agree, and the Sister's debut in the capital was met with "a fusillade of nickels, pennies, and dimes that rained about them with startling persistency," although when a barefoot Jessie appeared "a cabbage thrown from an upper box, occupied by a party of well-known society men, fell before her followed by a rain of cigarettes, paper balls and cigarette boxes."[28] Robert Whitesell, the manager of the Bijou, requested that the Sisters stay an extra week. Ella's former classmate Mary Dunham, now writing for the *Marion Register*, visited the Sisters backstage at the Bijou and wrote that she had "nothing but respect for the Cherry Sisters. It is a hard way to earn a living ... but if they wish to do it, they have a right to choose their own way."[29]

In early June, stories began to appear in the press that the Cherry Sisters had been reduced to a trio. "Jessie Cherry has left the company. The other Cherrys declare she lacks the true artistic instinct."[30] Happily the stories were

The Celebrated Cherry Sisters, from left: Effie, Jessie and Addie, circa 1897.

incorrect: like so many both before and after, the reporters had simply confused one sister for the other, and it was Lizzie that was off.

During a week's engagement in Des Moines, Addie, Effie and Jessie had discovered that the eldest of the touring Sisters was secreting money away, and that she was boasting of being the most talented of the four. She was even telling people that it was she who had originated the act. Lizzie had become unhappy with touring, and the schism had been coming for a while. While in New York, as well as complaining about Marie Dressler, she had demanded that E.D. Price, the manager of the Pleasure Palace, buy her a new silk dress before she would join her sisters on stage. The Sisters may have been earning $400 a week as an act, but Lizzie had was adamant that they were each paid $100 individually—and her sisters soon realized why. When traveling, she refused to buy her own train tickets or pay for her lodging, expecting those expenses to come out of joint funds even though she insisted on having her own bank account and paying her wages in to the same. Things became so impossibly strained between the Sisters that Lizzie's role on stage was reduced to singing her own "Irish Ballad" (in a duet with Addie), and taking part in the *tableaux vivants* "Rock of Ages" and "Goddess of Liberty."

The woman who had done the most to try and manage the family business was out.

William Haas, the agent who landed the sisters the Reilly and Wood's engagement and the man who would become their next manager, explained that Lizzie had simply had enough. After one performance "they thought they were slighted. Lizzie went home, and thinking she could make the other three give up the road actually escaped in the night with all the beautiful red satin cherry embroidered gowns." At their next appearance, at a religious revival, "the trio went on in street clothes and were even a greater hit than ever,"[31] however it seems that things came to a head on 5 June after arguing over money, and the others refused to let Lizzie appear after "harsh language was used."[32] In retaliation Lizzie threatened to start out on her own, either as a solo artiste or as part of a new Lizzie Cherry troupe.

With dates still to fill, the other sisters sent word for Ella, "who is the poetess of the aggregation, and said to be sufficiently atrocious on the stage to make her a good member of the troupe,"[33] to join them which, despite making her opinion of their lifestyle well known, she dutifully did. Sadly, upon leaving Des Moines, the sisters forgot to pay the orchestra that had accompanied their performances, and a writ was issued against them. Constable Patterson, of the Des Moines police, caught up with them several weeks later and put an attachment on their box office earnings, taking $85 from their nights' income. The Sisters retaliated by issuing their own suit against Patterson.

Vaudeville star Della Pringle and her husband George Adams saw four Cherry Sisters perform in Knoxville on 9 June, and Pringle was so upset by the sight of the women being pelted by rotten fruit that she went back stage to commiserate with them. She was surprised to find the Sisters unfazed by the reaction of their audience. "Do you suppose they think they are clever, or do they know they are rotten," Della asked her husband on the journey home. "I'm damned if I know," he replied.[34] Ella did not remain with the act long, and by the time they reached Dubuque on 17 June the Cherry Sisters had officially become a trio. Lizzie failed to see through her threat of forming a splinter act, and instead continued to work alongside Ella on the family farm, investing some of her money in horses and, a few weeks after leaving the act, $300 on another plot of land. The girls would eventually make up, Cherry blood being thicker than water after all, but for now Lizzie was out of the act and would no longer be allowed to assume the role of manager.

With or without Lizzie in their ranks, by now their name had become synonymous with appalling. Other terrible acts were compared to the Cherry Sisters, and the St. Louis Browns (the former name of the St. Louis Cardinals), then languishing at the bottom of the league, became known as the "Cherry Sisters of baseball." Yet despite this—or precisely because of this—the audiences still flocked to see them. In Keokuk, a show that was originally to take place on the stage of the local opera house had to be transferred to the municipal park, where (according to a letter signed by the sisters and sent to the *New York Dramatic Mirror*) between matinee and evening performances they played to "fifteen thousand people, the largest audience that ever gathered in the largest place of amusement in Iowa, and [we] had the satisfaction of being complimented by the best people of the city for giving the best entertainment that ever visited Keokuk. We netted the manager of the Park $7,500."[35] The Sisters, now accompanied on the road by William Haas (known to his charges as Uncle Billy), announced that they were "the greatest novelty of the age. Cannot be imitated. The greatest box-office winner of the twentieth century," and that they possessed "the most elaborate wardrobe on the American stage." Such was the demand for tickets for their next engagement, at the Hotel Orleans in the resort of Spirit Lake, that the management of the hotel had to arrange for extra transport to bring people to the site. "We are putting in our greatest season," Effie told a reporter from the *Rock Island Argus*. "We are now in great demand. The people seem to be beginning to appreciate our entertainments—that is the educated, refined people. We are having a splendid success, making lots of money. Since we started out we have made between $45,000 and $50,000. But my, the ones who have made money are the theater managers."[36]

With so many bookings coming in, and with the row with Lizzie still fresh in everyone's mind, the Sisters decided to continue touring through the summer rather than take a break on the farm. But although audiences were good—"every town they go to the house is crowded to overflowing"[37]—well-behaved crowds like those they encountered at Keokuk and Spirit Lake were the exception, rather than the rule. Their appearance at Call's Opera House in Algona was interrupted when someone in the front row threw a dead cat on stage, and at the Opera House in Estherville, Iowa, the Sisters had to abandon their show after a barrage of potatoes and onions prevented the Cherrys from continuing. "If there is any more disturbance the curtain will go down and the naughty crowd can go right straight home," an exasperated Effie announced, although the Sisters' protests "were answered with cheers and another shower of vegetable bouquets."[38] The Opera House in Fort Dodge was packed, but the frenzied audience, partly made up of soldiers from the local camp, forced the Sisters' pianist to beat a hasty exit before replacing him with one of their own; soldiers got up on stage to dance and one of the sisters was hit in the head with an onion.

Sherman Brown, manager of the Davidson Theater in Milwaukee, recalled that the Sisters "were nuts, and as beautifully isolated from art as a burr on the tail of Mary's lamb. Except for unplucked eyebrows, there wasn't a curve in the three of them, and all as past reshaping as the oranges Cezanne paints."[39] The Sisters were contracted to play for Brown as the chief feature of the Schiller Vaudeville Company, but they "were hooted off the stage, and the performance proved of such poor quality that the management wisely canceled the engagement," and the Davidson remained closed for the rest of the week.[40] N.C. Field, the editor of the *Glenwood Opinion-Tribune*, described Effie as "a tall, angular individual ... homely enough to stop a clock," Jessie as "plump ... with just a trace or two of comeliness," and Addie as "about half way between the other two in form, feature and various other respects."[41] When they performed in Rockford, Iowa the Sisters stayed at the Beebe House Hotel. Bessie, the seventeen year-old daughter of the hotel's manager, recalled that "they were very ladylike. They rehearsed and worked on their costumes in their rooms. My older brother came home telling us what a silly thing the show was. He told how they threw vegetables on stage. Some folks thought those girls knew what they were doing."[42]

With their reputation at stake, the trio dispensed with the Haas Brothers and took on yet another new manager, C.B. Sears, whom they met in Rock Island. They would soon come to regret signing with him. Sears decided to take a pre-emptive measure, and had a press hand-out prepared which included not just a biography, but also personal recommendations from a selection of fine and upstanding folk including clergymen, judges and a former governor of New York. "The Cherry Sisters are honorable young ladies and there is nothing bad about them or their entertainment," the Reverend A. Garton, pastor of the First Baptist Church of Burlington, Iowa attested.[43] In an effort to attract more women to the show—and presumably, by their presence, reduce the rowdiness—they gave out Cherry Sisters buttons and photographs of the trio to selected audience members, but a show in Dubuque—the scene of the 1893 riot—was brought to an abrupt end when the onslaught of rotting vegetables was accompanied by deceased (and, presumably, diseased) rats.

In Kansas City it was not dead rats but dead cats the Sisters had to dodge, and Effie was hit by a fusillade of rotten fruit during her "Traveling Man" skit. They asked the local police to provide protection and two officers were positioned at the theater, although they do not appear to have prevented the local theatergoers from having their fun. Sears had taken on local theatrical agent Chet Crawford to help promote the Cherrys, but as he revealed,

They gave the worst performance that I ever saw. I hired a lot of boys to go up in the gallery and throw beans and vegetables. It was unnecessary; the people had come prepared. They threw everything upon the stage except the seats. It was such a bad performance that it was good and we packed the house every night.[44]

When they came to the end of their run the Sisters fired Sears, blaming him for not having looked after them. In retaliation, Sears refused to pay their bill at the Ashland Hotel, and had their luggage impounded until his claim, for breach of contract plus $14 owed to him, was honored. "The Brute," Effie wailed. "How could he treat ladies so after we have raised him from obscurity? Because he did not do what we employed him to do we discharged him, as we had a perfect right to do. But here he comes and has our trunk carried away by an officer. It is outrageous!"[45] With Sears gone the Sisters attempted to re-engage "Uncle Billy" Haas: he and his brother refused to go out on the road with them again although they agreed to continue to find them bookings, but before the year was over they bid goodbye to the Haas brothers once again and struck out on their own. In December, with a week-long booking at Clifford's Gaiety in Chicago to fulfill, they were fronting what was being advertised as their own burlesque company, featuring a ragbag cast that included the Sammis Twins, eight year-old boxing prodigies, and James E. Black, the legless dancer, as well as the Cherrys in a playlet called "A Voyage to Paris." Although this appearance was hailed as "positively their last appearance in Chicago," after a few other dates they returned to play Clifford's Savoy for a further week commencing 26 December, this time with the one act farce "A Little Monte Cristo" added to their repertoire. They would remain a popular draw in Chicago, and 5,000 tickets were sold in advance of the Sisters' week-long engagement at Howard's Theater the following December. The sisters may have been nominally in charge, but they were clearly struggling to manage on their own: on the last night of a three-night booking in St. Joseph, they appeared on stage in their street clothes. Apparently aware that an officer of the law was waiting in the audience with a warrant allowing him to take possession of their wardrobe to settle an outstanding bill, the Sisters had craftily shipped their luggage off to Quincy that morning. With nothing but the clothes on their backs to offer, the officer was unable to impound anything to help settle the debt.

Dealing with money had always been Lizzie's task, and neither Addie, Effie, nor Jessie showed much interest or acumen when it came to managing their finances. Despite the added responsibility of paying for the rest of the acts in their entourage, the sisters made it known that they intended to travel to Europe, and that they were intent on performing in London and elsewhere. None of the women followed up on this threat, nor did they later launch an attack on Cuba, regardless of the reports that appeared in January 1899, when the news broke that the Sisters were to visit Havana to enact what one newspaper described as an "awful revenge"[46] on the Cubans. The Sisters were back in Chicago at the time, playing a two shows a day for a fortnight at the Drexel Theater, as part of a 10-act revue that also included acrobats Wertz and Adair, and contortionist Paul Brachard.

Coming less than a year after the end of the Cuban War of Independence, the revelation that they were intent on going to the country gave newspapermen plenty to joke about, and the Sisters took delight in threatening to sue yet another columnist after he wrote that

> The Cubans have endured much, but when they awaken to the fact that their island is to be made an asylum for such freaks it wouldn't be a surprise to us if they arose en masse and took up arms again. Even the American soldiers would be excusable if they disregarded orders and joined with the indignant natives. The Cubans have endured about all human beings can be expected to endure. We are better able to tolerate this affliction than they are. As a nation we should make martyrs of ourselves for the sake of humanity and force the Cherries to remain under the home tree.[47]

The Sisters themselves took the war very seriously, penning a collective letter which called President McKinley "a theaf and a robber" [sic] for threatening to "take away the inderpendence of the Cubans," [sic] an action which, they stated, would "rest a stain forever on our beloved flag," and that would place "our beloved country on a level with England in her treatment of Ireland."[48] The Cuban situation weighed heavily on Effie in particular. Inspired by her belief that no good Yankee would stand for the treatment McKinley had meted out to the Cubans, she wrote a number of patriotic pieces for the Sisters' act, and they added a new tableaux, "America Crowning Cuba" to their set. Her McKinley bashing seemed to delight the Sisters' audience, but did not go down well with everyone they met. When playing in Danville, Illinois, the Sisters were shaken at the reception they were given by the theater's backstage staff, who "conducted themselves in a most boisterous manner." The Sisters agreed that "in all their travels they never received the treatment that was accorded them" there, with one man insisting that "they were Democrats and ought to be dead."[49] They had become accustomed to being insulted for their looks, their dress, even for their material ... but to be branded Democrats was one insult too many.

7

Riot at the Armory

On their return to Iowa, the Sisters boasted of how they had earned $10,000 from their recent trip east, and that they intended to buy a fine house in Cedar Rapids as well as extend their land in Marion. The claims, no doubt dreamed up by their agent, were far from the truth, but when word reached Ella that the trio was branching out in to property on their own, by purchasing a parcel of land between Marion and Cedar Rapids, she was somewhat less than thrilled. It was of no interest to her or Lizzie what the others did, she insisted. "That's theirs. They made the money in their concerts." Relations between the five sisters had been frosty since Lizzie was pushed out of the act, and Ella talked of renting out the family farm and moving, with Lizzie, to another plot the family had recently purchased, near the Cedar Rapids suburb of Kenwood Park. Lizzie, she explained, had "acted the dramas and the tragedies. Effie was the singer, she had the mouth for it. I suppose I might have gone and made as much as staying on the farm, but I was a little afraid to risk it."[1] The good folk of Cedar Rapids were less keen on having the Cherry Sisters call the city home and, as it transpired, Ella would remain on the family farm, and Lizzie would divide her time between looking after her own adjacent plot and staying in the house Addie, Effie and Jessie took near Cedar Rapids, while she also maintained her own cows and horses on the smallholding in Kenwood Park. This suited Lizzie just fine: she had a whole house to herself while the younger trio were working away, she was able to find them concert engagements or occasionally join the act, and she could spend as little time as necessary with Ella, who the more worldly wise Lizzie thought miserly and dour.

On 17 January 1898 the three Sisters, now with yet another new manager, J.J. Kirby, former editor of the *Boone News*, played Smith's Armory in Iowa City. Kirby would go the way of all the others who had attempted to manage the unmanageable, and within a few months they were looking to engage his replacement, H.G. Chapman of Sioux City. Even for an act as used to disorderly conduct as the Cherrys, the date of the Armory performance would go down as one they would rather forget.

> Word from Iowa City says that a riot raged there for several hours over a theatrical performance given by the Cherry Sisters. There are five of the young women, and they are known throughout the west for their total lack of dramatic ability. They were first put on the stage as a joke, but their dismal attempts to entertain were so ludicrous as to make them a 'drawing card.' Then they toured the big cities of the central and eastern states. A number of State University students who attended the show became so disgusted that they started a riot. The Cherry sisters escaped through the rear door of the theater, being escorted to their hotel by the police. The students jeered and hissed them, and the tumult became so great that several arrests were made. But even then the police failed to quell the disturbance and a fire department company was summoned. Two lines of hose were turned on the rioters. The chill of this drenching finally discouraged the mob, which, however, was not dispersed for hours. Several persons were slightly injured.[2]

Claims that more than 1,000 students from the University were involved seem somewhat exaggerated, but what is true is that the Armory—which could hold 1,200–was full to capacity a good hour before the Cherry Sisters were due to commence their entertainment, and that the eggs and rotting vegetation they brought with them was already flying about the hall before the curtain went up. Orlando Grinnell, music teacher and singer, along with his wife and daughter, came on stage to sing a few songs and remonstrated with the baying crowd. Any hope of quelling the audience was soon lost: the family was met with a hail of rotten fruit, vegetables, and tin cans. Had the audience realized that the Grinnells and the Cherrys were lifelong friends (some reports state that they were, in fact, cousins) then their reception could easily have been worse.

The audience was informed that the Cherrys would not appear unless they settled down, and an uneasy hush descended. Nevertheless, no sooner had the sisters started their show—with Jessie banging the big bass drum while Addie and Effie puffed themselves up, readying to sing "Eulogy on the Cherry Sisters"–that vegetables and tin cans rained down upon them too. The curtain was immediately closed and Mr. Grinnell came on to appeal for calm. Once the noise had abated the curtains parted again to reveal Effie standing there, fairly quaking in her boots. She had barely opened her mouth to sing when an egg hit her in the face and she fell to the floor.

The Sisters refused to continue, with one of them declaring that they "would not act before such a crowd for a round million dollars."[3] At this point the students rushed the stage and the three women were hurried out of the building. The crowd demanded their money back, but when Mr. Coldren, the manager of the Armory, refused to refund a single cent, several of the students began to rip up the seating in the auditorium. When a large number of the young men realized that the Sisters were heading back to their lodgings, at the Hotel Kirkwood, they decided to follow them. An enormous mob, far greater than the number of people who had been in the Armory, gathered outside the hotel and began singing songs and letting off fireworks. In at least one report, one of the sisters is said to have opened the window in their room and emptied a chamber pot onto the crowd below.[4] Several windows were broken, and some of the young men managed to get inside the hotel, where they headed for the room in which the Sisters cowered and began beating on the door. While they tried to gain access the police were called, but even though they fired blanks to try and stem the riot they had no effect. In desperation, the fire department was called out, and two hoses were turned on the mob. A number of arrests were made, and five men spent the night in police cells as a result, but by midnight order had been restored. The mayor of Iowa City revoked the license held by the Armory, ensuring that the Sisters would not be able to play there a second night,[5] and the Sisters left Iowa City the following day on the one o'clock train. "The Cherry Sisters expressed their regret for the unfortunate occurrence and say that they were never treated so roughly before, and dear little Jessie stated emphatically that they would never come to Iowa City again unless they could show in some leading church."[6]

In spite of this, or perhaps because of events like this, they continued to pack them in. A concert that same month, at Evan's Theater, Red Oak (the home of their rival, James Ballard), the management reported that not only had the sisters enjoyed "a large house," but that their show was the "best performance of the kind ever given in the house."[7]

With so much success, it seems a somewhat bizarre move by Addie, just a few weeks after the Iowa City incident, to put pen to paper to inform the editor of the weekly entertainment newspaper the *New York Clipper* that "the notices that have appeared in the press throughout the country stating that the students of Iowa City broke into the Cherry Sisters' entertainment was a most malicious falsehood." Addie claimed that the stories were invented to injure their reputation, and she stated that

Again
THE CHERRY FAMILY
POSITIVELY THE LAST APPEARANCE OF "THE CHERRY FAMILY" IN THIS PLACE.

TO-NIGHT
I. O. O. F. HALL

Doors open at 7:30 p. m.
Curtains drawn at 8 p. m.

ADMISSION 10C
ADULTS AND CHILDREN SAME PRICE. MANY INTERESTING FEATURES ADDED

COME!

A handbill advertising the Sisters' show at the International Order of Odd Fellows Hall, 1897.

it was another troupe—the Grinnells—that gave the concert, and therefore it was not the Cherry Sisters that caused the riot that brought the town to a standstill. The letter also informed the editor that they had never performed in Iowa City, which at first might have seemed a bold-faced and rather ridiculous lie, but as their performance at the Armory had been brought to a close before any of them had actually sung a note, in the strictest sense of the word Addie was telling the truth. If the Sisters had hoped that news of the incident would not travel, or perhaps that their outright denial would be enough to stop the story from spreading they were sadly mistaken, and reports of the riot appeared in newspapers around the United States, and even as far away as Australia. Goodness knows what the Grinnells must have thought of the Sisters trying to blame the outrage on them.

On 1 February 1898, the evening that the Sisters were to appear on stage in Glenwood, they broke a personal rule about the kind of people they would socialize with, and had dinner with the editor of the *Tribune* in the dining room of the Commercial Hotel. The group chatted about politics (the Sisters were all staunch Republicans, much to the newspaperman's regret) and religion, but when asked if their act owed its success to the huge amount of free publicity they had received in the nation's newspapers, Addie replied that their success had been achieved in spite of the newspapers, rather than with their assistance, and although they were used to being lied about, some editors "were just as nice as they could be."[8] Two days later they had to be escorted back to their hotel in Atlantic, Iowa after a barrage of catcalls caused half of the audience to walk out and the indignant Cherrys brought the curtain down early once again.

February was a busy month, with a series of one-night stands across Iowa. Once again, money was tight, and when the Sisters pulled out of a performance in Correctionville the manager of the opera house took out a lien against them to cover his lost earnings. The reception their entertainment received in most of the places they played was, as they had by now come to expect, rather boisterous, so there was no reason why their show in Sac City (on 10 February) would stand out as anything out of the ordinary. The show, like many others, was brought to an early end by the audience, which was so noisy that, just four numbers in to their program, the girls refused to continue. Yet when the manager of the theater, Mr. Schaller, brought the curtain down, the audience refused to leave, and they continued to hurl abuse and missiles at the stage for over an hour. Finally, as one contemporary report told it, the Sisters "got out the back door and were taken to the hotel in a bus, but several dozen eggs were smashed on the vehicle en route. The sisters were furious, and came near clawing the face of Manager Schaller, whom they accused of putting up a jot on them."[9]

7. Riot at the Armory

The sisters stayed in Sac City until the Saturday morning as guests of the Hendrickson household. Before leaving for their next engagement, they purchased a knife and a revolver, telling anyone who would listen that they would not hesitate to use them should they encounter another audience as unruly. They had already moved on when the *Odebolt Chronicle* printed the following scathing front-page review, under the title *The Cherries Were Here*:

> When the curtain went up on Wednesday evening of last week the Cherries saw a good-natured audience, large enough to fatten their exchequer to the extent of $35, net. The audience saw three creatures surpassing the witches in Macbeth in general hideousness. Effie is an old jade of 50 summers, Jessie a frisky filly of 40, and Addie, the flower of the family, a capering monstrosity of 35. Their long, skinny arms, equipped with talons at the extremities, swung mechanically, and soon were waved frantically at the suffering spectators. The mouths of their rancid features opened like caverns and sounds like the wailings of damned souls issued therefrom. They pranced around the stage with a motion that suggested a cross between the *danse du ventre* and a fox trot, strange creatures with painted faces and hideous mien. Effie is spavined, Addie is knock-kneed and stringhalt, and Jessie, the only one who showed her stockings, has legs without calves, as classic in their outlines as the curves of a broom handle. The misguided fellows who came to see a leg show got their money's worth, for they never saw such limbs before and never will again—outside of a boneyard.
>
> The first glimpse of the Cherries was worth the price of admission. One shriek of laughter swept over the house. Not even in the woods around Sac City, nor in the wilds of Monona County, could three such raw and rank specimens of womanhood be found. The men howled and the women shook with merriment. There were no vegetables thrown, but there was lots of talk. It would take the sisters six weeks to answer the questions that were fired at them. At intervals Effie and Addie would jaw back and threaten to stop the show, but the boys never let up. When Jessie came out in her bare feet many solicitous inquiries were made about the condition of her corns, and she was freely advised to trim her toenails. And such feet! No instep, flat ... and Z wide. Jessie, however, is not sensitive. She calmly went on with her part, evidently considering her feet her strong suit. Finally the program came to an end and the audience left, well satisfied, as a rule, although some who had never heard of the Cherries before were angry because the noise prevented them from hearing the girls.
>
> The Cherries honestly believe that they are giving an entertainment surpassing anything on the stage, and that their audiences hoot them because they can't appreciate true merit. They have been systematically stiffed by every manager who has engaged them with the notion that they are away up. If they were not stuck on themselves no money could induce them to stand the jeering they get. But having salted down $60,000 in the bank and purchased several large farms with the proceeds of their foolishness they are willing to keep it up as long as they can make it pay. Their personal characters are above reproach; they are virtuous both from necessity and choice, as any one will conclude at sight of them. The most skilful impersonator would find it impossible to burlesque the Cherry girls. They are nature's own raw material, unique and inimitable.[10]

Penned by the *Chronicle*'s editor, Billy Hamilton, it was, even for them, the most scurrilous piece published so far. Yet it would have been overlooked had it not been for the fact that many other newspapers reprinted the article almost verbatim. When it reappeared in the *Des Moines Leader*, the women decided enough was enough. It was time to take action and, on 20 April a petition was filed against Samuel Strauss and Allan Dawson, publishers of the *Leader*. Their case, brought by Addie, Effie and Lizzie jointly, came to court in June 1898, and the complaint—for $15,000 in damages—was heard by Judge Holmes. After hearing evidence on both sides, with the defense insisting that the claim against the newspaper be dismissed as the sisters had been unable to prove that the editorial had in any way harmed their ability to earn money, the judge decided in favor of the *Leader* and informed the sisters that they might stand a better chance of gaining satisfaction if they brought separate cases, demonstrating how they had been libeled individually. This the three sisters did, with each of them taking out suits against the *Des Moines Leader* for $15,000 apiece.

In July they were contracted to give six shows over three days at an amusement park in Rock Island, appearing with touring variety troupe Semon's Extravaganza. Watch Tower Park was the first and largest amusement park west of Chicago, built at the end of a streetcar line to encourage patrons to use the new-fangled transportation system. Admission to the park—and a ticket for the show at the open-air amphitheater—was included in the cost of the streetcar fare, and the demand was so great that the Sisters had to add a third show on their final day. Advertised as the "biggest show ever given here,"[11] not everyone enjoyed the Sisters' performances, with one newspaper reporting that "no one seemed to want to throw any cabbages or eggs, though one ear of corn did travel toward the stage, but the desire to yell, in a sort of chorus, possessed all hands and this rhythmical eruption was about as musical as the songs from the stage, and may be accounted a triumph of sound." The *Rock Island Argus* reviewed the first night of the show, and wrote that "Effie still looks as fierce as the day she threw the milking stool at the obstinate cow. Addie is not less reckless than she was when she cleaned out a 40-acre field and drove the army of hands to the neighboring hill tops in Linn County. Jessie is as innocent as when she first saw an electric car, and therein cultivated the swoon which she introduces in her Trilby act." Effie gave an interview to the same reporter following the show: it's safe to assume that she had no inclination of how the newspaper intended to roast them. "We are putting in our greatest season," she revealed, although in the Cherrys' world it pretty much every season was their "greatest season." "The people seem to be beginning to appreciate our entertainments—that is the educated, refined people. We are having good crowds here. We have had great receptions in all parts of the country, and in the east we were the heroines of the hour. We've made an awful lot of money, more'n we could ever make on the farm."[12] If that was true, where was it all going?

Audiences were still clearly enjoying what the Sisters were delivering. "The voices were strident and off-key, but they acted as if they were entirely sophisticated and were ready to dodge anything from a carrot to a wash boiler. People roared and slapped each other and leaned over their seats and cried."[13] In late 1898, with a series of dates to fulfill in the two States, Addie, Effie and Jessie (who the Sisters were still insisting was "a child, only fourteen years old,"[14] or "some fifteen years old,"[15] despite her being close on twenty-seven, and "considered the youngest composer in America and one of the best,") relocated to Rockford, near to the Illinois and Wisconsin border. They spent their first night in the city sharing a bed at a boarding house belonging to Mrs. John Lewis, at 224 South Church Street: "Jessie has cold feet," Addie revealed to their hostess. "She can sleep between us and we'll keep dear little sister warm."[16] It was suggested, in an interview with the *Belvedere Standard*, that they may make the move a permanent one, although Effie seemed baffled by local audiences: "People come and look at us as though we were freaks. I suppose they expect to see cherries growing right out of our heads!"[17] While playing small towns, and appearing at a couple of benefits, the "aggregation of raw-boned, lantern-jawed females ... that puts on a perfectly worthless show and makes money at the same time,"[18] decided to have another go at organizing their own touring show, advertising in the pages of the *New York Clipper* for "first class vaudeville artists and singers. People who have played the Keith and Orpheum circuit preferred," adding a caveat that "salaries must be reasonable."[19] Hedging their bets, they also wrote to agents, including New York manager Horace Grant, to offer their services, informing them that "if you wish to have the greatest drawing attraction in America and one that pleases the best people in the

The Cherry Sisters, from left: Addie, Jessie and Effie, circa 1897.

land and the finest act put on any stage, you could not do better than to contract with us. Salary is no object."[20]

The Cherry Sisters Vaudeville Company debuted with a week-long booking at Howard's Theater in Chicago on 4 December. Playing both matinees and evenings, the Sisters were accompanied by comedian Harry Fitzgerald, "travesty artists" Cushing and Merrill (who, earlier that year, had appeared at Smith's Opera House with Harry Houdini), Provo the juggler, and the A. F. Company. The first night was oversold, leaving hundreds of people turned away at the door, and among those that managed to get a seat was a crowd of local hooligans who tried to drive the Sisters from the stage by throwing objects at them during the performance. The following day the *Inter-Ocean* warned any like-minded ticket holders that "the management states that this will not be tolerated, and the act will be given in its completeness tonight if a net and a cordon of policemen are required."[21]

Having spent five years in the spotlight, the Sisters felt it was about time to share their story with the world. Fed up with constantly having to explain themselves, and embattled and embittered with the ongoing action against the *Des Moines Leader*, the Sisters contracted a writer, J.T. Lanigan of Clinton, Iowa, to pen their biography. John Lanigan had begun his professional career teaching in the schools of Center Township, Clinton County, before going to work as a correspondent for the *Clinton Advertiser*. A Catholic and a Democrat, Lanigan seemed an odd choice for the job, especially given their obvious distrust of newspaper men (Addie told a reporter from the *Belvedere Standard* that she regarded "reporters as a set of ruffians"[22]), but he completed his task and delivered his finished manuscript to Addie, Effie and Jessie in December 1898. Perhaps unsurprisingly, the three Cherry women were unhappy with the results and refused to pay him, leaving Lanigan little option but to take out a suit against them for $225.

The New Year began well, with successful engagements in Chicago and Buffalo, but the running of their own show was proving too difficult, and by February they were once again in dire financial straits. Perhaps in the hope of raising some capital, the Sisters launched yet another legal action, this time issuing a libel suit against O.J. Smith, the editor of the *Ackley Phonograph* newspaper, for a scathing review of their performance at Martins' Opera House in October. They may have stood a better chance of winning a libel suit had they chosen to sue the editor of the *Ackley World*, who wrote that "Their entertainment was the rankest of the rank and how they have been able to bleed the public continuously—and been permitted to live—is a mystery to all who witnessed their performance. From their opening song, 'tarra-boom-de-ay' [sic] until the closing tableau of Jessie climbing the golden stairs it was one continuous howl, with whistles blowing, ringing of bells and a hundred other contrivances for making a noise, all going at once, made the performance one to be remembered. The Cherrys evidently have hit upon an easy way of making themselves rich, and the ones who are the fools are the people who are gullible enough to pay their good money to see the performance."[23]

Having left the rest of the Cherry Sisters vaudeville Company behind, the Sisters accepted a booking at the Bijou Theater in Toronto. Initially set for a week, this would be the first time they had visited Canada, but the trip turned in to a disaster after poor ticket sales left W.S. Robinson, the manager of the Bijou, unable to pay them. The Sisters applied to the United States Consul for $35 to pay for tickets to enable them to reach Philadelphia, but their request was refused. The Sisters limped home and immediately sued Robinson for $37 apiece plus costs, charging that the theater's manager had refused to pay the wages they were due.[24] Pride would not allow them to re-engage Lizzie in any kind of permanent managerial role, and that was proving a costly mistake.

8

The Cherry Sisters vs. the *Des Moines Leader*

Billy Hamilton's review of the Sisters' performance seemed to annoy Addie the most. "I don't see how anybody's brain could conjure all that stuff. Why, this Cedar Rapids fellow said that we were spavined. Then he said that no one but Jessie wore their skirts above their ankles. Now, how did he know we were spavined? That's what I'd like to know. I don't mind a little joshing, but I won't stand a thing like that!"[1]

On 20 April 1899, the case of the Cherry Sisters vs. Samuel Strauss & Allan Dawson, publishers of the *Des Moines Leader*, came to court. With each of the three performing siblings due to appear, the trial drew a large and unruly crowd, and what should have been a solemn occasion descended quickly into farce. Addie, Effie and Jessie had made an extra effort to impress, wearing their finest clothes and even using a little makeup to try and show that they were neither as old nor as homely as Billy Hamilton had described them in his article. All three were eager to be involved, and throughout the hearing offered advice to their attorney, Mr. Crosby. Effie was particularly keen that the court insert the word "knock-kneed" into the claim, as this was a specific insult leveled at her by the *Odebolt Chronicle* that had cause her "much mental suffering."

The representatives of the *Des Moines Leader* stated that the three sisters "were engaged in giving public performances, holding themselves out to the public as singers, dancers, reciters, and comedians; that their performances were coarse and farcical, wholly without merit, and ridiculous." They also maintained that "the article appeared as a criticism of the performance given by the plaintiff, and to expose the character of the entertainment; that it was written in a facetious and satirical style, and without malice or ill will towards the plaintiff or her sisters." Hamilton, appearing on behalf of the *Des Moines Leader*, stated that his critique "was realistic and I wrote up the show in the way it impressed me. I certainly had no idea it would cause half the trouble it has. Now the sisters have never, so far, attempted to sue me. It would have furnished considerable amusement up in our neck of the woods.... I simply wrote the item from the standpoint of modern realism—gave my impressions. It was the oddest thing I ever witnessed."[2]

Addie, Effie, and Jessie were all called to give evidence. Each perjured herself immediately, with the twenty-seven-year old Jessie trying to pass herself off as a teenager and both Addie and Effie attempting to shave at least a decade each off their real ages. Addie told the court that Hamilton's article had received such a wide circulation (the *Chronicle* itself claimed that the report had been reprinted in more than one hundred newspapers) that it interfered with their ability to secure engagements, and therefore had a deleterious effect on their income. She also had the gall to tell the court that there were "no disturbances and no wild demonstrations accompanying"[3] any Cherry Sisters performances.

Called to the stand, Addie attempted to describe the average Cherry Sisters performance to the court:

> These entertainments are concerts, literary entertainments. I don't sing much; the others do. I give recitations and readings; recite and read in costume. In feminine costumes. Dresses as long as I have on, or shorter. I don't wear short dresses. Sometimes I have worn men's clothes. I never dance. I recite essays and events that have happened, I have written up of my own. I have none of them with me. One is 'The Modern Young Man,' the other 'An Event That Happened in the City of Chicago.' I sing an Irish song—an Irish ballad—also a eulogy on ourselves. It is a kind of a ballad composed by ourselves. I help the others sing it. I have forgotten it.

"An Event That Happened in the City of Chicago," also known as "The Modern Young Woman," or "A Tragedy Seen on the Streets of Chicago," was the tale of a girl who rushes in to a drug store to purchase make up; an embarrassing attempt by Addie at writing comedy. She was, it seems, aware enough of how their material might play in court to have conveniently forgotten her own words. She told Judge Bishop about her essay on newspaper editors, and she described her outfit for "The Gypsy's Warning" in great detail. "A Cavalier is a Spaniard, I believe. I represent a Spaniard. I wear my bicycle bloomer rig. They reach to my knees and are divided like leggings—black leggings with buttons on them. I wear a blue blouse—a blue velvet blouse. Sometimes red and sometimes green. I have many suits; wear them in turn. The leggings are always black." At this point it appears that Addie broke out into a little trot, to explain to the court how "in the chorus I walked a little around the stage; kind of fast walk or a little run." She also described how, during Jessie's performance of "Ben Bolt" she would "come and hypnotize her in a farce way. I would tell the audience that I would hypnotize her while she would sing. I didn't appear at any show without stockings. My little sister was barefooted in one act—in very long dresses to her ankles. She also appears in a long robe in a tableau clinging to the cross." In his defense, Billy Hamilton told the court that the Cherrys' entertainment was the most ridiculous performance he had ever seen.

> There was no orchestra there. The pianist left after the thing was half over. She could not stand the racket and left. There was no other music, except vocal music from the Cherrys. They read essays and sang choruses and gave recitations, interspersed with the remarks that, if the boys didn't stop, the curtain would go down. One young man brought a pair of beer bottles, which he used as a pair of glasses. They threatened to stop the performance unless he was put out, but he was not put out, and they didn't stop. When Jessie was on the stage she appeared in the Trilby act in bare feet and short dresses. She was asked to trim her toenails, and such irreverent remarks as that. She appeared more pleased than anything else. There was a song 'I want to be an Editor,' ...the song was so jumbled up one could hardly make anything out of it, except 'I want to be an editor, I want to be an editor,' whereupon the audience rose up as one man and called on me to stand up. I did not stand up. My wife was there. The audience was talking to the women and they would talk back. They would say, 'You don't know anything. You have not been raised well or you would not interrupt a nice, respectable show.' Nobody left during the performance except the pianist.[4]

Legend maintains that the Sisters performed for the jury, but this is not the case. Not only did they not perform in court, but there was no jury present. Addie certainly seems to have given some idea of her stage move-

TO - NIGHT!

The World Renowned
Cherry Sister Trio

**Authors and Composers of
...SONGS AND MUSIC...**

The most Talented Artists in America. Just returned from a successful trip through California

The Widest Advertised Professional People in the World

Buffalo (N. Y.) Courier: The Cherry Sisters entertainment is the best ever seen upon our local stage.

PROGRAM

1 "Eulogy on the Cherry Sisters."
　　　　By Addie, Effie, and Jessie Cherry
2 "Fair Columbia."
　　　　Words and Music by Jessie Cherry
3 "Irish Ballad, (The true biddie just from the Emerald Isle)
　　　　Words by Addie and Effie Cherry
4 "My Bicycle Ride."
　　　　Words and Music by Jessie Cherry
5 "The Traveling man," (A personation true to life)
　　　　Words and Music by Effie Cherry
6 "Essay," (A tragedy seen on the streets of Chicago)
　　　　By Addie Cherry
7 "My First Cigar." Words by Jessie Cherry
8 "Before and After." Words by Effie Cherry
　　　　INTERMISSION.

GIPSY'S WARNING.
CAST OF CHARACTERS.

9 Gipsy,................................Effie Cherry
　Cavalier,............................Addie Cherry
　Lady,................................Jessie Cherry
10 Recitation, "Corn Juice." By Jessie Cherry
11 Recitation, "The Hero of Manila."
　　　　Written by Effie Cherry
12 "The Hypnotizing of Trilby." (After being put under the powers of Hypnotism Miss Jessie will sing Ben Bolt)
　　　　By Addie and Jessie Cherry
13 "The Orphan Flower Girl."
　　　　Words and Music by Jessie Cherry

TABLEAUX.
1 AMERICA CROWNING CUBA.
2 GOOD NIGHT.

A Reserved Seat Ticket will Entitle the Holder to a Beautiful Photograph of the Cherry Sisters.

A handbill for a typical Cherry Sisters performance, 1901.

ments when she described the Sisters' act, but at no point did the three Cherry Sisters play to the crowd. However Charles A. Bishop, the presiding judge, told the court that he had seen the Sisters perform previously and that he was in the perfect position to deliver his verdict, which he did but only against Addie. In Bishop's opinion, *The Leader* showed no malice. Incensed, Addie arose from her seat "in a dramatic manner and asked the permission of the court to make a few remarks. Her countenance was flushed and her manner indicated that she was in a rage." Judge Bishop, perhaps wisely, refused to allow her to speak, and her lawyer pulled her back into her chair. The three sisters stormed out of the court in a huff, with Effie and Jessie—apparently bruised by the battle—choosing not to continue with their suit. Their appearance in court gave newspapers across the country the perfect excuse to reprint Hamilton's editorial, and reports about the case appeared as far away as Hong Kong.

On with the show. The three touring Sisters had dates to fill, and Ella and Lizzie had land deals to occupy them, and butter and eggs to sell to the good people of Marion. Most days the two elder Cherrys could be seen walking in to town, carrying baskets full of produce and, conspicuously, a revolver for their personal protection. The Sisters announced that they had invested in a 40 acre plot in the rapidly expanding suburb of Kenwood Park, Jessie took the opportunity to sign over a plot of land in her name to Lizzie (valued at $1,000) and a second, on the outskirts of Cedar Rapids (then valued at $300), to Ella, but neither Lizzie nor Ella were going to confirm just how much they had made (or lost) on each of these deals. However Ella was not as tight lipped when it came to discussing her three younger sisters, telling a reporter from the *Marion Pilot* that believed that the women "were great and successful actors, drawing big houses wherever they appeared, but that they were not good managers," and that she and Lizzie "could have saved them lots of money." She also tried to convince the unnamed journalist that any reports of differences between the five Cherry women was "all a hoax, gotten up by the lawyers and newspaper men to make them grief and trouble."[5] Lizzie too was adamant that any arguments between them would stay private. "You will never see the day when Lizzie Cherry will go to court in controversy with her sisters," she wrote to the editor of the *Marion Register*, reacting to a well-reported story that insisted Addie, Effie and Jessie were suing her for $630 in a dispute over money and property. "Father and mother taught me better, though my sisters may have forgotten it."[6] The elder Cherrys at least were adamant that their financial situation would remain a private affair.

The Sisters had been booked to tour the West, with dates in California and Utah, having discovered that they could continue to work through the long, hot summer months by playing outdoor pavilions and leisure parks. Chief amongst this series of bookings was a two-week stint at the Chutes pleasure park in San Francisco, on a bill that included head-to-head balancers the Romalo Brothers, female baritone Marion Blake and "knockabout comedians" Conlon and Ryder for the first week, and Miss Ann Fletcher (a female impersonator) and Mademoiselle Mabel Atlantis, a dancer who also juggled clubs and balls while balancing on a revolving globe, in the second, plus daily movie screenings and regular hot air balloon ascensions. "The Cherry Sisters will prosecute all persons purloining or imitating their act," the program declared. "The Cherry Sisters are known throughout America and Europe— how favorably, it is for the public to judge. They have appeared in every large city of the American Union. This is their first appearance in California, and, of course, everyone here is curious to know something about them. Probably no professionals ever lived that are more in earnest than the Cherry Sisters." The warning of a potential lawsuit was lost on the editors of the *San Francisco Music and Drama*, who reported that "The Cherry Sisters invaded the office of *Music and Drama* a few days ago with their war paint on and stated that if an apology was not immediately forthcoming for the very fair and just criticisms which had appeared in the paper concerning their freak act they would lock the office doors and sing. The fighting editor promptly capitulated."[7] An acerbic review of their six-week residency ("in their own pavilion," according to the advertisements) in Salt Lake City caused them to write to the editor of the *Salt Lake Herald*, complaining that "the article ... was false in the extreme. We know of no reason why we should be thus attacked unless it was done to injure our business and reflect upon our good name and reputation, which stands without a blemish before the world. We do not expect to please the depraved and debauched. Our program was written for those who appreciate talent and a pure, clean performance."[8]

Despite handing out hundreds of flyers that proudly trumpeted that the Sisters were "the widest advertised professional people in the world. Ten weeks in New York City, playing to over 300,000 people; ten weeks in Chicago, playing to over 250,000 people, and all other large cities in the United States, turning thousands of people away every night,"[9] money continued to cause them problems. The Salt Lake shows had drawn decent crowds, but the administration costs (which included hiring their own tent, paying for security, staff, and other actors) left them with little to show for more than a month of near-sell out performances. Their attempts to deal with Ella and Lizzie on an equitable basis meant that the Sisters were, quite simply, living beyond their means. Appearance fees and their share of box office returns were not enough to cover the bills. They landed the occasional week-long booking, but more and more now the Sisters were reduced to playing far less profitable one-night stands, with their only guaranteed income a share of the profits—if there were any.

In November 1900 John W. Geiger, one of the few people from Marion who would freely admit to being intimate with the Sisters' affairs, informed the editor of the *Ackley World* that the women were "practically dead broke again." Geiger told the *World* of how they had acquired one of the finest properties in all of Linn County and filled it with luxurious furniture, but that it had slipped through their hands. "Their only remaining farm consisting of the clay farm in the hazel brush in which they commenced their meteoric career," he revealed. "This has been due to their guilelessness and gullibility. They have been fleeced by this manager and that, and this confidence man and that, until little remains of the glory. They seem to have been susceptible to any cunningly planned appeal to their vanity, and fell easy victims to fortune hunters. They simply couldn't stand prosperity."[10] It would certainly help to explain what had happened to some of the money the Sisters had earned over the previous seven years; without doubt some had been used to pay off the mortgage on the family farm, and more still on other land and property. A good deal of the rest must have been spent on hiring policemen (at their own expense), a necessity for many of their performances, and in pursuing spurious legal battles to protect their name. Lawyers still had to be paid, no matter if the Cherrys won or lost their court cases and, more often than not, lose they did. But it seems that, for the most part, poor management was to blame. Jessie's diary entries for the first half of 1901 tell a sorry tale of one-night stands and poor door receipts: "January 10, Fulton, Ill. Took in $16; January 11, Morrison, Ill. Took in $22 ... January 24 we played at Warren, Ill. Took in $16; January 25, Shannon, Ill. Took in $17." Things did not get any easier as the year progressed: her diary entries record struggles with avaricious lawyers and, on several occasions, the Sisters being forced to leave Effie's jewelry behind as security against unpaid hotel bills. "On 11 June we played Colimes Iowa took in no $." The following day she records that "we left Colimes for Lisbon Iowa. Left our board bill unpaid." On 31 October, following a poor house in Oakland, Iowa, she wrote that "the opera manager had to advance us the tickets to get us there ... we couldn't get any musician and it was best that we couldn't. Our share after the entertainment was $3. The Anita opera man attached our baggage. We had just $1 left after expenses were settled."

Although Addie lost her court case in Des Moines, she was fully entitled to appeal to the Supreme Court, and the Sisters' attorney, James Patterson, intended to do just that. Jessie and Effie had, through their abandoning of the earlier action, effectively decided that enough was enough. However Addie had no intention of letting the matter go, and the case of Addie Cherry versus the *Des Moines Leader* was put forward to the Supreme Court of Iowa. The verdict in the case was delivered on May 28, 1901.

"If ever there was a case justifying ridicule and sarcasm, it is the one now before us. According to the record, the performance given by the plaintiffs was not only childish but ridiculous in the extreme. A dramatic critic should be allowed suitable license in such a case. The public should be informed of the character of the entertainment, and the publication should be held privileged."[11] That one short paragraph changed the libel laws in the United States forever. The case is still quoted from in law text books today, and its' infamy ensured that, no matter what else they achieved, the Cherry Sisters were from that point on an indelible part of U.S. culture. The Supreme Court ruling, signed by Mr. Justice Deeming, stated that

> An editor of a newspaper may freely criticize any or every kind of performance providing that, in so doing, he is not actuated by malice. Surely if one makes himself ridiculous in his public performances he may be ridiculed by those whose duty or right it is to inform the public regarding character of the performance. Ridicule is often the strongest weapon in the hands of a public writer; and if it be fairly used, the presumption of malice which would otherwise arise, is rebutted and it becomes necessary to introduce evidence of actual malice or of some indirect motive or wish to ratify private spirit. Unless there is true liberty of speech and of the press, liberty guaranteed by the constitution is nothing more than a name.[12]

The landmark decision was widely reported, however not everyone got the gist; several newspapers, including the *El Dorado Daily Republican* and the *Galena Evening Times* (both based in Kansas), erroneously reported that it was the Cherrys who had won the case: "Win Famous Libel Suit. Cherry Sisters, who have gained notoriety on the stage, get judgment against Des Moines Leader."[13]

While the court case and appeal to the Supreme Court had trundled on, Addie, Effie and Jessie continued to tour. Jessie, who Effie thought the star of the show, was not entirely happy, and wrote home to Ella and Lizzie on several occasions, telling the pair that "it seems to me like we have been away about twenty years,"[14] and entreating them to write back: "we have not heard from you in quite a while and we get homesick when we don't hear from you girls once in a while."[15] Ella and Lizzie, who were facing their own legal battles over unpaid taxes, were probably too busy to write. That same year, having refused—or been unable—to pay the $43 due, the court issued a warrant against part of their land to settle the debt. A further tax debt of just under $7, on land in Marion registered to Lizzie (the plot that had previously belonged to Jessie), was also left owing. If the Sisters were earning a fortune, clearly very little of it was finding its way to Ella and Lizzie, despite promises to share income from their live performances equally amongst the five of them.

With finances strained, the most sensible thing to do would have been to gain employment with a touring company, or perhaps try and find a theater or opera house that would offer them a residency—anything that would guarantee the Sisters a regular income. They made no secret of their admiration for Carrie Nation, the preacher's wife who had gained notoriety for using a hatchet to demolish barrooms. The most celebrated and controversial temperance advocate of the time she, like Effie, championed the idea of votes for women and it was suggested on more than one occasion that the Sisters and Mrs. Nation team up for a lecture tour—an enterprise that would guarantee them a sympathetic audience and a decent income. Perversely, they decided instead to try once again to set up their own company. "We're running our own show this summer—have no manager," Jessie told reporters. "Last winter we spent on the Pacific coast, mostly in California, and we did very well—made money. Since the summer season opened we've been playing mostly in Iowa and Illinois towns." When asked if they were heading back to the family farm any time soon Jessie revealed that "We haven't any farm near Marion, only a little fruit farm and our two other sisters are running that. They're not married and they're older than me. How long am I going to remain in the show business? Well, I don't know—till I get tired of it I suppose."[16] The Sisters also revealed that they were considering running their own newspaper, which they intended to call *The Theatrical and Society Compendium*.[17]

In August 1901 the Sisters were contracted by the Knights of the Globe, a fraternal organization based in Illinois, to perform at a public picnic in Theiler's Park, Joliet. Advance ticket sales had been poor, and on the day the audience con-

A cartoon satirizing the Cherry Sisters, 1901.

sisted of no more than thirty people. The stage manager, disappointed in the quality of their entertainment and the poor crowd, decided to bring their performance to an early end and the picnic's organizing committee decided to renege on their commitment to the Sisters, refusing to pay their appearance fee. Unable to settle their bill at the St. Nicholas Hotel, the Sisters' luggage was impounded by Constable Rainville; the stage manager of the abandoned event also demanded that the Sisters' manager, Cal Harris (employed by them after they abandoned their plans to manage themselves once more), cough up for renting the stage. Harris settled the bill, but Joliet had not heard the last of the matter, and the Cherrys sued the Knights of the Globe for $200. The case came before Justice Bradford on 4 September, while the Sisters were appearing in Wichita, with both parties claiming that the other had broken their contract. In this rare instance the Sisters won, and were awarded $120 for breach of contract. In September they performed in Clinton, Iowa and advertised that only women would be admitted. After the show the Sisters announced that, in future, they would only ever perform for female-only audiences, a warning they did not follow through with, although they would play select matinees to women-only audiences, including one at Miaco's Trocadero, Omaha in December during a week-long residency there.

After their ladies-only matinee the Sisters held a reception for the many hundreds of women who attended. "They think they give a high class entertainment," one of the members of the audience told a correspondent from the *Omaha Daily Bee*. "One of them told me that their place was not in vaudeville, but rather in some lecture course, where they could play to intellectual audiences. The hisses they get from the Trocadero crowds they construe as attesting to the rowdyism of people too feeble in intellect to understand their art. They are impervious to satire. For eight years they have put up with the inconvenience of having to dodge vegetables and things because there is money in it."[18] Not long after Addie, usually the strongest of the three, came down with a bad attack of measles and, as Jessie noted ion her diary, "Effie had the doctor come and he left some medicine. It tasted like slippery elm."[19]

The Trocadero gig was a good one, with the Sisters making $247.25 (from a box office of $823.65) for a week's work; not exactly the kind of money they had earned in New York and Chicago, but not too bad at all. However their time in Omaha did not go off without incident: the audience for their opening night brought "dead cats concealed under their coats ... liver, eggs and vegetables had been smuggled in to the theater as popcorn, but they depended on a detail of ten police to suppress a riot."[20] The police presence meant that no missiles save from a few corks and cigar butts were thrown, but one critic suggested that their performance "calls for the coining of a new word, something like 'rottenissimo.' With voices like the trill of a file serenading a saw and gestures like the Delsarte of a Dutch windmill, theirs is a genius that is born, not made."[21] The police certainly made themselves known: Frank Parker, attending the same performance, threw his rolled up program towards the stage and was promptly arrested and charged with disorderly conduct. "I never saw such an exhibition in my life," Parker told the court. "I'll throw a brickbat next time."[22]

9

The Cherry Sisters Held to Ransom

Although it was widely held that the Sisters had made a fortune, and that they had invested much of that money in land, the truth of the matter is that the women were barely scraping by. When boarding at the Midland Hotel in St. Louis in 1902 ("the cheapest place we could get ... we pay $7 apiece a week; our piano player and his wife pay their own food bill,") Jessie wrote to Lizzie, telling her that box office returns were starting to pick up, and that they "took in $59 yesterday ... our receipts are getting a little larger each day."[1] Even if they were keeping half of the box office they were still hardly living in the lap of luxury. News of the Sisters' money woes soon got back to the newspapers, with the *Peoria Journal* reporting that they "were supposed to be broke," but that they "have made good investments of the money they made in the past and they are getting ready to go out on the road again."[2] Clearly, though, the extravagant amount of money they had spent on land had not proved as sensible an investment as the sisters wanted everyone to believe; unscrupulous managers and agents had taken advantage of the Sisters' naivety, and had taken much of their earnings. A parade of charlatans and shysters—including, no doubt, the one who had sold them their glass "diamonds"—had made off with much of the rest.

The 1902 season saw a marked downturn in demand for the Sisters. They were still able to find dates, but those that were coming in were for smaller and less salubrious venues, and often for just one or two nights rather than more lucrative residencies. The winter saw them moving from town to town in Nebraska, Kansas and Texas, playing mostly one-night stands, the only respite from the incessant moving around coming at the end of February, when they secured a fortnight-long engagement in Fort Worth. Basing themselves in an apartment on Cass Street in Omaha, regardless of the challenging experiences they had already endured, the Sisters once again discussed the idea of setting up their own touring vaudeville troupe, which they announced

> **The Toler Auditorium**
> H. G. TOLER & SON, Owners.
>
> **COMING**
> Tuesday,
> Feb. 4th
>
> **CHERRY SISTERS**
> In their own original entertainment........
>
> **...ADMISSION...**
> **25, 35 and 50c**
>
> Reserved seat sale opens Saturday, Feb. 1st at 9 o'clock a. m. at theater box office.
>
> Every lady holding a reserved seat will be presented with a photo of these talented young ladies.

An advertisement for their concert at the Toler Auditorium, 1902.

would be called the Crescent Concert Company.[3] The Cherrys were seemingly ignorant of the fact that a touring company with the same name already existed, but it made little difference anyway, as they would not carry their plans through.

Bookings were drying up. In Wellington, Kansas, very few people turned out to see them, and even fewer saw their performance through to the end. It seemed like the joke had become a bit stale. Perversely Marion, the scene of so many disasters, chose now to advertise itself as "the home of the World Renowned Cherry Sisters." Newspapers were still having fun at their expense, with one local critic comparing Addie's legs to "clothes props stuck in a meat block," and declaring that "a more decayed bunch of fruit never appeared before in Wellington in one shipment,"[4] but dates were regularly cancelled because of combination of bad weather and poor ticket sales, and the Sisters' financial situation continued to worsen. If Addie, Effie and Jessie were blind to the fact that their days as a viable touring unit were coming to an end, sister Lizzie was not. Always the most business-minded of the five, she implored her sisters to give up the road and come home.

> Please don't go to Omaha or anywhere else but pull right home. Didn't you have a lesson last year? Don't wait for a worse one. I had rather you would come home without any money than to come home without arms and legs. You will never stop until something happens to you. I suppose that was why Nathan kept putting it off about coming home, because he did not have any money to bring home, that is if he ever got out of Chicago. Wouldn't we have rather had him home with only the clothes on his back than to cause us the deep worry that he had caused us? And now girls you must not do the same thing.[5]

In the same letter she threatened to marry the first man that came along and "run away where you will never see me again. Come home or this may be that last that I shall ever write you." The one bright spot was a six week summer season at the Delmar Gardens in St. Louis, although the women were none too enamored with the city, and penned a letter to the editor of the *St. Louis Post-Dispatch* to tell him so:

> The drunkenness and immorality seen in St. Louis is appalling to the respectable man or woman who is obliged to come in contact with it. Sin seems to run riot, and but little effort is made to stop it. The Christian men and women of St. Louis should be about 'their Master's business' and should rise up *en mass* against these social evils, and with a strong hand put a stop to the young men and women who are rushing on in their mad career to their own destruction. We hear a great deal about the necessity of sending missionaries to foreign lands.... America is in more need of missionary work today than any heathen country on the face of the earth.[6]

As 1903 began it must have appeared to the Sisters that, after a full decade of treading the boards, their years in the spotlight were at an end. Outside of a return visit to San Francisco's Chutes Park for a weekend to mark Washington's Birthday, few paying dates were forthcoming. With the farm providing barely enough income for Ella and Lizzie, the three performing sisters decided to turn their hands to running a business, taking over the operation of a guest house in Hot Springs, Arkansas. The choice of venue was an odd one, as the sisters had been all but run out of the town just a few months earlier and had stated publicly that they "would not play there again if they were each presented with a private residence and bathhouse,"[7] but as they often demonstrated the promise of financial security—and a permanent roof over their collective heads—was more important that bruised pride. Effie, who referred to her home state as "abominable," found Arkansas much more attractive, and the spa town of Hot Springs, extensively rebuilt and remodeled after the ravages of the Civil War, with busy bathhouses, smart hotels and a thriving tourist trade, was particularly appealing.

Addie, Effie and Jessie threw themselves in to running the dining room of the Sumpter Hotel, which they re-christened the Iowa Pure Food House, and while in the City they kept to their word and did not perform—although it is hard to imagine that one or more of the trio did not put on the occasional impromptu act for their customers.

> A Chicago man spent two weeks at the hotel during the last winter. The chief factotum around the hotel was a red headed boy, who had plainly just blown in from the back woods. One of the boy's tasks was to keep the box in each room filled with wood, the house being heated with wood stoves. Feeling in a generous mood one afternoon the Chicago man handed the boy a tip of a quarter after he had finished piling the box high with hard maple. It was evidently the first tip the youth had ever received. He held the coin in his open palm and looked up in astonishment at the donor. "What's this for?" he asked. "Why, that's for putting in the wood," answered the Chicago man carelessly and forgot all about it. There were some twenty other lodgers in the hotel kept by the Cherry sisters, next morning each of them found pinned to his or her bed a small piece of paper. On it the red headed boy had painfully writhed the following

note: "You owe me 25 cents for putting in the wood. Pay up at once." One of the guests complained to the Cherry sisters and they, with that absence of all sense of humor which made them such an attraction on the stage, immediately called in the youthful and red haired financier and discharged him. The Chicago man whose tip had been responsible for it all did not hear of the climax until the boy had left the house and entirely disappeared. And he now has an uncomfortable feeling that he is personally, though unintentionally, responsible for the boy.[8]

An impressive building in its heyday, and once the largest hotel in town, the Sumpter had made the national press three decades earlier when a stagecoach on its way there had been held up and its passengers robbed by Jesse James and his gang. Since that time, however, many more impressive tourist hotels had opened, and the Sumpter family, brothers William and John and their mother, who ran the hotel's letting rooms had lost interest in their own side of the business. The Sisters maintained hope that they would soon be allowed to take over the running of the entire operation. Lizzie suggested that they should carry guns or knives to protect themselves, and even keep a little dog to watch over their room while they were working, but before too long they were off anyway, having fallen out with the Sumpters and, in doing so, found themselves embroiled in yet another lawsuit.

While that case was pending, the Sisters were offered the chance to run an entire boarding house—restaurant, letting rooms and all—called the Reservation Inn. Hot Springs had a huge number of hotels and boarding houses, and despite all of their hard work and long hours, there was little the Cherrys could do to encourage boarders or diners to patronize their business. Letters home had to wait, even if Ella and Lizzie were becoming sick with worry and bickering with each other about what to do with their errant siblings. When a miserly Ella refused to shell out a few cents to send a telegram to Hot Springs, Lizzie lost her temper.

> I told her I would not ever trust her again, she seemed to value a little money more than human life ... it made me so provoked at her I could have given her a licking to hear her say 'oh how I do worry' and then wouldn't send a 30 cent telegram. It made me so mad to hear her say 'I expect something has happened, suppose some of them are sick or perhaps dead so they won't write.' I told her to go to the Old Nick, she was the biggest miser on earth.... I wish Par or Mar was here to tan her once in a while ... or twice in a while.[9]

Ella's words had been prescient. Jessie was not doing well, and by the August reports began to appear in the press that the youngest of the Cherry Sisters was a very poorly woman. She and Effie were both struck down by typhoid, a common disease often spread by contaminated water that affected tens of thousands of Americans in the early years of the 20th century. Effie was seriously ill, and Jessie had contracted the disease while attempting to nurse her. An anxious Lizzie went out to join her sisters and help Addie look after the two younger women. All of the Cherrys recognized that Effie was not as strong as she would have her public think, and Ella worried that she may have been nearing the end: "I am afraid that there might be danger of her heart giving out when the fever breaks unless she has a heart stimulant," she wrote. "Speak to the doctor about this."[10] Ella was genuinely concerned, and admonished her other sisters, telling them that, instead of sending for Lizzie to join them, they all should have come home. "Why did you not say that Effie is real sick and you have got to give up work to attend her? Then we would have sent you money to come home right away." That last comment, coming from the same woman who refused to spend thirty cents on a telegram, must have irked the Sisters somewhat. A further letter rebuked them for not coming back to Iowa to take advantage of the carnival season: "It does seem as though if you could get some one to book you and pay your fair you might come home and not cost you a thing … though I hate to advis you to ever do any thing of the kind again" [sic]. This recommendation, from the one sister who had always showed the least enthusiasm for performing and who often counseled against a life on the stage, was quickly followed by a sound reprimand: "I have got no letter from you today, why do you not write? I cannot work unless I hear how Effie is. Surely among you all you can find time to write as often as I do?"[11]

Against all odds, Effie quickly improved, and she wrote Ella to tell her "you don't know how glad I'll be when I get home. I'm getting well fast."[12] Jessie too rallied briefly, but soon was struck down once again and, on 30 September, Jessie died at 535, Quapaw Avenue, Hot Springs. When registering her passing, Addie and Effie listed her occupation as "singer and composer," and her age as twenty-three. There was no explanation as to how their mother managed to give birth to Little Jessie four years after she herself had passed away.

For the rest of her life, Effie would blame herself for her youngest sister's death. A reporter for the *Cedar Rapids Daily Republican* wrote of how "as she spoke of Jessie's last illness, contracted through faithful watching during her own illness, Effie walked over to the window and looked down in to the street below, the hot tears trembling on her cheek as she wandered down the path of memory to the golden days before their sister was called away."[13] Effie may have taken it personally, but Ella made it perfectly clear that she held all of them responsible for not having sent the youngest member of the family home. "Well, it's just as I expected," she wrote on hearing of Jessie's death. "You should have written for that money a month ago and sent Jessie home long ago. I do not see why we are so blind. Mary Braska said send Jessie home two months ago."[14] The sisters accompanied her body back to Cedar Rapids, arriving in the city on the morning of 4 October. Jessie's funeral service was held two days later at the First Christian Church, Fourth Avenue and Fifth Street, and she was buried at Linwood Cemetery. The local Elks lodge sent a floral tribute.

Jessie's passing devastated the four remaining sisters. Always the baby of the family, and often referred to as the most attractive of the five, she had been the star of the act. "All the joy in our life was gone with the death of our little sister," Effie wrote of their loss, "for she was one of God's most perfect flowers. He had gathered her from the fields of earth to bloom in the Paradise of God. All who had ever met and talked with her will say she was a most beautiful and lovable girl."[15] Jessie's death forced the family act in to retirement, and Addie and Effie gave up any thought of running a business in Hot Springs and returned to Marion, to seek solace in the embrace of their sisters. "We broke the lease," Effie later admitted, "and the landlord talked about suing us, but he didn't. The matter was settled without a suit,"[16] a rarity in itself for the notoriously litigious Cherry Sisters.

Trouble, of course, quickly followed. No sooner had Addie and Effie gone that D.N. Hitchcock, the owner of the Reservation Inn, was assaulted and seriously injured by two men. The sisters had employed both of the men; one as a dishwasher and the other as a waiter and the pair had gone unpaid when they left town.[17] Hitchcock, who also ran the Medicated Light and Bath Sanatorium, was something of a charlatan and known to pass himself off as a physician. Addie and Effie consoled themselves by reasoning that he had got his just desserts.

Addie and Effie did not stay long on the farm; although most reports had it that the women were still living as one happy family in Marion that was hardly the case. Ella did not approve of their peripatetic lifestyle, and relations with Lizzie were still fraught, so Addie and Effie soon let the two older women and returned to their own house in Cedar Rapids. "Marion," Effie revealed, haughtily, "is not our home. It is the home of sisters Lizzie and Ella. They are farmers and we are actresses. We live in Cedar Rapids in our own home there. Lizzie and Ella ... know nothing of theatrical life. They are not built for the stage, anyway, like we are, and I am inclined to believe that they would make a rather poor showing before the footlights."[18] After a few months at home Effie got itchy feet once more and decided that she wanted to go back out on the road. Addie was a little more reluctant than her younger sister, but after some persuading she came along too. It made sense, she reasoned: the farm was never going to make enough money to support them all, and the livestock they had on their own land belonged not to them, but to

Lizzie. The Cherry Sisters as a duo (occasionally enlarged to a trio by Lizzie) were on tour again by the summer of 1904, with week-long engagements in both Bay City and Saginaw, in a package that also included horizontal bar act Manning and Du Crow, and novelty aerial acrobats Orville and Frank. During winter 1904–05 they appeared in for a week at the People's Theater in Cedar Rapids, with the acts this time augmented by the Selig Polyscope, an early moving picture enterprise, and Indianapolis (their debut in that city), performing two shows a day at the small, family run Unique Theater.

While they were away from home, news reached Addie and Effie that a newspaper reporter in Portsmouth, Ohio had in his possession three recordings featuring Jessie and, although he had been informed that they could be worth as much as $500, he was prepared to sell them to the Sisters for just $100 (still a sizable sum, and equivalent to approximately $2,500 in 2018). The story made a number of newspapers, as well as the November edition of trade magazine the *Edison Phonograph Monthly*:

> The question of what value can be placed upon a Phonographic record of a dead sister's voice will be the question to be decided by the Cherry Sisters, whose notoriously rank show has made a success solely for the reason that it is the most ludicrous attempt at acting ever put before the American people in sincerity. Manager Higley, of the Grand Theater, received a communication from the Cherry Sisters, now at Cedar Rapids, Iowa, inquiring as to the identity of the party here who took the record of their little sister Jessie's voice. Manager Higley has learned that the party is a former attaché of the Grand and now in the newspaper work here.
>
> The records of little Jessie's voice are probably worthless to the present holder as far as their use is concerned, but to the Cherry Sisters, who desire to hear once more the voice now stilled in death, they would be invaluable, hence the feeling on the part of the owner that they are worth at least $100. If the Cherry sisters have laid aside any of the good coin handed over by those who have laughed themselves sore at a performance intended to be serious, they may be in a position to meet the demands of the individual monopoly. While the mere mention of the name of the Cherry sisters and 'Little Jessie' brings a smile to regular patrons of the theater, there is an element of pathos in the desire to hear a dead sister's voice that cannot be ignored, and it is to be hoped that the milk of human kindness will not be soured in the progress of negotiations for the Phonographic records.
>
> The holder of these records says he has no desire to gouge the sisters, even though they have been doing that for the public for a number of years.[19]

It is understandable that they would want the recordings back, even if one critic did unkindly refer to Jessie's voice as no more than "a little squeak, like an injured guinea pig,"[20] and another commented that "she had the worst voice that was ever inflicted on an audience. There was a peculiar, grating tone to it that enraged all who heard it."[21] However, being inordinately parsimonious, Effie decided that instead of paying the money over immediately she would first try and discover if there were other copies of the records and—if they existed—obtain copies from cheaper sources. Addie and Effie understood that William H. Jennish, a dealer in talking machines from Waterloo, Iowa, made the original recordings, and the pair wrote to him: "Are you the same gentleman who came to Cedar Rapids some five years ago and opened a phonograph parlor here, and we sang for you? Now, if you are not the same man, do you know who the party was who has the Cherry Sisters' voices? Out little sister Jessie is dead and for this reason we wish very much to secure her voice. We will consider it a great kindness if you can find the records for us. The song which she sang was called 'Fair Columbia.'"[22]

> Glory forever, the stripes and the stars,
> Glory forever: freedom is ours.
> Joyfully spreading its' light o'er the sea,
> Glory forever, Land of the Free![23]

Jennish stated that he had never operated out of Cedar Rapids. He informed the Sisters that it was not he, but a colleague by the name of Frank Thayer, who had been working there at that time. Frank D. Thayer had begun his phonographic business in Waterloo a few years before William Jennish appeared on the scene. He set up a second store in Webster City, but in April 1987 moved his business headquarters to Chicago, although he continued to also operate in Waterloo until at least the following January. Thayer had since passed away, but Jennish said that he would try and to put the Sisters in touch with his widow. It is unclear if the recordings were on discs or cylinders, but Thayer specialized in selling phonographs which, in the strictest sense, at that time meant machines that used Edison's cylinder system: his store in Waterloo boasted that it held "Edison Grand Concert phonographs. One thousand records, and five machines with operators who understand how to run them."[24] Jennish's Waterloo store also specialized in Edison's system, but by the time Addie and Effie contacted him he was out of the business, and was now employed by the City of Waterloo as a plumbing inspector.

It is also unknown if the three records contained three different recordings, or if they were three copies of the same performance. Rumors have persisted that a recording of Jessie performing "Fair Columbia" exists, but again, no such recording has ever been found, and the only confirmation of it ever having existed comes from contemporary press reports. Addie and Effie stated in their letter to Jennish that all of the performing sisters had recorded in Cedar Rapids, which leaves the tantalizing prospect that someone, somewhere, may well own recordings by Addie, Effie and Jessie, either solo or together. There is no mention of any of this in Effie's papers, and the fact that the records have not surfaced since means that they're probably gone for good. Records by other acts called the Cherry Sisters (including the female vocal group that recorded for Bluebird Records in the 1940s) have only muddied the waters.

As early as February 1906 it was revealed that Addie and Effie had spent some of the preceding twelve months "writing a book of their lives. They certainly were eventful ones, full of vegetables and old eggs, as those who have had the pleasure (?) of seeing them will vouch for, and if the book is correspondingly as interesting, it ought to sell like hot cakes."[25] Apparently their earlier experience, with J.T. Lanigan, had not dissuaded them from the idea of providing the world with a true and accurate account of their fantastic lives. Jake Rosenthal, an agent for the Bijou chain of theaters, booked the Sisters on a spring tour of the western states. Rosenthal got them plenty of work, but at a fraction of the money they had been commanding just a few years beforehand. The Sisters casually let it be known that, after this series of dates, they would be bidding farewell to touring for good. Effie, it seemed, had great faith in her written efforts proving to be the family's financial savior and in Decatur, when not insulting the locals ("It is the most unappreciative town we were ever in. These people here don't know good actresses when they see them"), Effie laid out her plans for their retirement. "We quit the road at the death of our sister Jessie, a little more than a year ago. Since that time we have been busy writing our life story, which is almost complete and which we will submit to a Chicago printing firm for publication. We expect to realize a large sum of money from its sale and we propose to spend it for special instruction in dramatic art." Effie was surprisingly candid when it came to talking about the Sisters' financial position. "We never failed to draw big houses and we should be worth some money, but we are not. Our managers usually got the lion's share of the box office receipts. But that condition will not exist in the future."[26] The planned book failed to appear, but Effie did

Jessie Cherry, circa 1899 (author's collection).

not abandon her literary ambitions; she would work on a manuscript for her *Autobiography of the Cherry Sisters* on and off for the next three decades. In 1910, when Lizzie was asked to contribute to a new book, *The History of Linn County, Iowa,* Addie and Effie penned a furious missive to the publisher, telling him that "we do not want anything whatever written in your book concerning any member of our family member,"[27] thereby protecting the potential sales of Effie's upcoming yarn.

When, on a return visit to Dubuque, *Variety* accused their audience of demolishing the theater, manager Jake Rosenthal wrote a stern rebuke to the editor:

> I have engaged the sisters for a number of weeks, and in playing them in Dubuque turned patrons away from the theater twelve times during their week's engagement, and there was no disorder of any kind. By letting the public know in advance that good order would be maintained for this act, and that the ladies could give their entire act without molestation, the same as any other act at my house, those who had heard so much about the sisters and who had never had an opportunity to witness the performance, came in droves and brought their friends along four or five times during the engagement. The sisters have received the same good treatment at Des Moines, Ia., and at Springfield, Ill., for the past two weeks, where they also broke records established prior by acts costing four times the money that the sisters receive. The ladies have new wardrobe, but their act is exactly the same in makeup as when they first appeared in their home schoolhouse near Marion, Ia.[28]

The performances may have gone well, but the Sisters' experience was not without its trials and tribulations, and the long arm of the law soon caught up with them yet again. While they were appearing at the Bijou Theater in Des Moines, the women were confronted by Deputy Sheriff Charlie Temple, who demanded their entire wages to settle a debt they had run up in Anita back in June 1899—a debt they had conveniently forgotten all about. In a scene that could have come from the script of a slapstick movie, one evening, after the two women had settled in for the night, "the well-known Cherry Sisters ... had an exciting experience with a folding bed at their hotel. At midnight the hotel clerk heard muffled screams from the direction of their room. Later he heard them again and, hastening to the room found a closed folding bed from which smothered women's voices came," but that's where the comedy ended. The women had been imprisoned for more than an hour; the clerk struggled to release the Sisters from the bed and, once he had, Effie was in such a state that a doctor had to be called.[29]

Effie may have been the most headstrong of the Cherry children, but— as had often been shown in the past—she was not physically the strongest. Shortly after an appearance in Chicago, where the Sisters caused an uproar by preaching about temperance from the stage and demanding that the city take over the ownership of breweries, and that the cost of saloon licenses be raised to an eye-watering $5,000, she was felled by typhoid fever once more. Again Lizzie came out to join them, and to take some of the pressure off Effie, but after a successful fifteen-week tour of the west, the sisters were forced to leave the stage. "We will not work through the summer," Addie announced, "but will spend the most of our time with our sister in the country."[30]

Upon their return to Marion, Addie joined in with the chores on the family farm while Effie convalesced. Luckily she soon recovered and was fit enough for the two of them to return to their house in Cedar Rapids. Although Addie kept true to her promise not to work through the summer, the Sisters did visit Weston and Lexington in Illinois, where they sang a few songs at temperance rallies held by Christian pastor John R. Golden, then standing for office on behalf of the Prohibition Party. Golden was elected to the state legislature shortly afterwards, and Effie for one took great interest in his advancement.

In the New Year, after fulfilling bookings in St. Joseph and Leavenworth, Effie and Addie made yet another attempt at forming their own company. This time around they demonstrated that they were fully aware of where they stood with audiences. "We could put on a legitimate act if necessary," they announced, "but the ridiculous takes much better wherever we have been and we mean to stick to this, as it was in this line that we secured our reputation."[31] After fourteen years on stage, the Sisters finally accepted that they had indeed been aware of who had been conning whom and, having forgotten all about the promise they made a year previously never to tour again, in March 1907 the Cherry Sisters set off once more. "We entered in to this business for about the same reason that all others do—we needed the money. We expect to remain on the road several weeks longer this season."[32] Nonetheless box office returns were poor, and Effie had not fully recovered from her bout of typhoid the previous summer. After completing their advance bookings, with performances in Illinois, Addie and Effie returned once again to the comfort of their Cedar Rapids' home.

10

On the Comeback Trail

At the end of March 1908, after appearing in vaudeville in Chicago, the sisters joined the Merry Maidens, a burlesque company headed by comedian Sam Rice that included buck dancer Lulu Beeson, musical duo Lewis and Thompson, and singer Patti Carney. Rice had seen the Sisters perform in Chicago and thought that they were just the headliners he needed for his ragbag entourage. It is doubtful he would have bothered, had he read the interview Addie gave to one of the Chicago papers: "You see, it's this way. The people don't understand us. We put everything in to our act that is calculated to make it a good one, but it is too good for the average audience." "They don't any of them understand that we write our own words to all the songs," Effie interrupted. "That makes a great difference."[1]

In spite of the Sisters' indifference to their audience, things went well, and ticket sales were healthy. After years of heading their own show, or of playing on variety bills, this was the first time that the Sisters had played to burlesque audiences, but they managed to avoid any impropriety. "We have been with this burlesque company for four weeks now," Addie told reporters when questioned about the morals of their touring partners, "and we haven't seen a single thing but what we consider perfectly proper." But although they may have been enjoying their time on the road, back in Iowa things were not going so well, and while they were playing in Chicago, stories began to circulate in the press that the pair had been forced to sell their home. "First one unscrupulous manager and then another fleeced them unmercifully. They were inveigled in to libel suits for damages, in to this, in to that. They lost money on every hand; soon their elegant home went at a sacrifice sale; their bank deposit dwindled until they were forced again to go on the road as entertainers."[2] The catalog of failure these tales reveled in was simply a rehash of the stories that had been promulgated in the press more than seven years earlier, and they ignored the fact that the Sisters, who spent so much time on tour, had no need to own a house of their own anyway. Property, for the most part, was either in Ella or Lizzie's name; they could stay with either of their sisters or rent accommodation of their own when obliged to stay in Cedar Rapids for more than a few weeks. It must have seemed to the Sisters that every time they stood up, someone wanted to knock them back down again. These personal attacks simply reinforced Addie and Effie's deep distrust of newspapermen.

The troupe played for a week in Duluth, followed by a week in Minneapolis, where the highlight of the show was not the Sisters, but a wedding held on the stage. At other shows the Sisters took a back seat to boxing midgets: one can only imagine their disgust at having stooped so low, yet publicly they continued to talk up their fellow performers, putting pen to paper every time they felt they—or any of their entourage—had been slighted. While on the road with the Merry Maidens, Addie and Effie wrote to *Variety*, taking umbrage with what they saw as unfair criticism of their act.

> In your issue of March 21, you had an article which was one of the most malicious, violent and untruthful writings we have ever read. The person who wrote it is not deserving the name of a man, but is instead a contemptible cur. You said in your paper that we advertised ourselves as 'the worst show on earth,' which makes you a liar, point blank. We have always advertised our act as one of the best, and we would not be far from the truth if we said *the* best. Yes, we played the little theater on State Street, Chicago, for one week. Was that a crime? We would play this little theater one hundred times before we would play The Majestic or any other theater in Chicago when booked by such men as * * * * Although we have the best act in vaudeville and are the best drawing card on the stage, we have no swelled head, as some others have. We have had more knocking since we went into the theatrical business than any act in the history of the world, and we have come to no other conclusion why this is done except we are not of the character of these unprincipled editors and managers who have done the knocking and slandering.[3]

The original article did not claim that the sisters had advertised as the worst act in the world, just that this was the general consensus held by those who had seen them perform. In April they were forced off the stage, not by the critics, but once again by illness. Effie was struck down with appendicitis and, after an appearance in Des Moines, the pair returned to Iowa, and to Ella and Lizzie. Effie had recovered enough for the Sisters to take part in Marion's 4th of July celebrations, and they were paid $100 to appear at a huge outdoor festival at the city racecourse. Although the Sisters had only agreed to perform after receiving an apology from Marion's council for the shocking way in when they had been treated the last time they played there, the *Marion Sentinel* still had its sport, sarcastically stating that "these wonderful girls can prolong life ... the ladies are the most famous and widely known of any sisters either living or dead. They are a joy forever. They write their own songs, compose their own music and design their own costumes. For beauty, talent and originality they surpass anything that will ever come your way again."⁴ Patrons were encouraged to place advance orders for a photograph of the sisters as a souvenir of the occasion, and no doubt many took up the offer. Lizzie was persuaded to join her two sisters so that they could perform three-handers such as "Eulogy on the Cherry Sisters" and "The Gypsy's Warning," and the show was a huge success, with the railroad company having to put on extra trains to bring people to (and take them home from) the site. The good folk of Marion, it seemed, were in a forgiving and reconciliatory mood, and the *Sentinel* reported that "the amphitheater would not hold the people that assembled to witness the program."⁵ The *Marion Register* had the following to say to anyone who dared question if the Cherrys were still a popular drawing card in other cities of the United States: "The New York correspondent of the *Washington Post* gives them a column 'write up' in a recent issue of that paper. The *Banner of Athens*, Georgia, in its issue of the 17th, copies. The *Iowa City Republican* of July 20th gave them a column. In far away Seattle 'Cherry Sundae' is served in the ice cream parlors. From Ocean to Ocean the 'Cherry Sisters' are household words. If the Sisters would listen to the universal call for their entertainment they would forsake their quiet woodland home, go on the stage and 'conquer the vaudeville world' again."⁶

It would not be long before Ella and Lizzie were in trouble again, with a court appearance on 7 October demanded by yet another neighbor, August Pospishil, who owned a couple of small plots next to Indian Creek in Kenwood Park. Lizzie, it seems, had once again taken to driving her livestock across someone else's land without permission, and without paying any notice to Pospishil's gates and fences. But that particular gripe would soon be forgotten, as winter took its toll on the family farm: the weather was harsh and Lizzie and Ella were struggling to keep up with even basic repairs. In a letter to Addie and Effie, Ella wrote "I guess it was 24 degrees below here last week, one inch of snow on the ground. All the hay is gone but a fork full. You don't know how

Ad for the Sisters' appearance in Marion, 4 July 1908.

thankful I am to get the money. I have so many holes to stop that I don't know which to stop first, but I'll take the biggest one." She explained that both women were suffering from colds, and told her sisters to look after themselves. "Be careful this cold weather you don't take cold. I chew Burgundy Pitch for my coff. Lizzie's coff is better … she went out to get herself a bottle of Kemp's Balsam [sic]."[7] Ella's letters were full of concern for their health and welfare; Lizzie's missives were always more concerned with finance, the state of her livestock, or with her daily battles with her stubborn, pinchpenny older sister, but she too showed a touching concern for the welfare of her two youngest sisters. When they were hit by bad weather, Lizzie wrote to admonish them: "Effie, remember your life is worth more than anything on this earth … [if] you must go through this storm always stop at the first place you come to and don't start out again if you have to wait half of the night."[8] Both would occasionally write to say that they had been forced to sell a cow or a colt to pay their bills, and although Ella loved her farm and harbored a deep disdain for life on the stage, in her darker moments she considered throwing in the towel. While Addie and Effie were touring Iowa in early 1911 she wrote to them, asking Addie to send her $50 so that she could pay her bills. Later she wrote to them again, imploring them to help her out. "Say Addie and Effie, do you want me to come and help you out for a dollar a day? If you do I will try it and leave things to go to pieces at home. I simply have *got* to have the money to pay that man in Cedar Rapids. Let me know as it seems I cannot sell my cow and have the chance to buy her back again."[9] But paid appearances were sparse, and even if they had been willing to help Ella out of a hole, they would not have been able to: a booking in Chicago was brought to an abrupt end by yet another court case, and the Sisters were forced to reschedule dates already booked for the Crystal Theater in Waterloo (managed by the rather wonderfully named J. Jolly Jones), while they dealt with this latest crisis.

With little work on the stage, the Sisters were spending more and more time in Cedar Rapids. To keep the wolf from the door Addie went back to raising poultry, and both she and Effie helped to look after some of Lizzie's cows. Effie had her own livestock that Ella took care of, although she seemed set on disposing of them, asking Ella to sell one of her favorite cows to a neighbor for $45. "He said he did not have quite enough money to pay for her," Ella wrote. "I told him to go home and save it. The cow would be here."[10] When money was needed Lizzie was equally pragmatic. "I would sell all of those big fat hens Addie if I was you but see you don't get cheated on the weight when you sell them. Keep the little ones, they will lay the best." She also offered sage advice about lasting out the forthcoming storms, which had been predicted by one of her neighbors. "McDonald said about ... how destructive they are going to be, and that is a bad place where you are for lightning. Don't let your chickens roost in the coop, put roosts across in the trees. If that chicken coop gets blown down it will kill all of your hens, so keep them out of there 'til you get some kind of a summer coop built."[11]

With Lizzie effectively banished from acting on their behalf, Effie took it upon herself to write to the managers of theaters and opera houses in the hope of finding work for the duo. A few scattered dates did come their way, and they could usually rely on help from booking agents in Rock Island, New York and Chicago, cities that had always given them a warm reception, but the number of imitators out there was affecting their earning power. 700 miles away, another duo claiming to be the Cherry Sisters could be seen on the stage of the New Crawford Theater, in Wichita, Kansas, appearing with Sam T. Jack's Gaiety Girls company. Jack had been in the business a long time and had made a fortune running increasingly risqué burlesque shows, but it is unknown if he was aware that the "Cherry Sisters" in his employ were fakes or not. What was fake was the story, in *Billboard*, that "two of the four sisters who caused such a sensation in New York several years ago (Lizzie and Jessie) have since reformed and married," and that "the other two are not only willing to play an engagement at Hammerstein's Victoria, but are endeavoring to prevail upon the two married ones to return to the footlights."[12] The first half of this story was clearly false, if not only because Jessie has been dead six years! However what was true was that Willie Hammerstein had come to their rescue again. Five years after he had taken over the ownership of his father's Victoria Theater, then the only vaudeville house on Broadway, he booked Addie and Effie for a short engagement. Three years later he sent his agent, Jack Curtis, off to Iowa once more to fetch Addie and Effie back with him; the Sisters would appear at the Victoria for a second time in December 1912. Addie and Effie were grateful of the support that their contacts showed them, although Hammerstein's death in 1914 (aged just 38) and the subsequent sale of the Victoria robbed them of another Cherry-friendly venue. They were less happy when a story began to circulate that a woman watching them perform in Fort Dodge was so bored with their entertainment that she yawned extravagantly and dislocated her jaw: apparently her mouth was stuck open for more than half an hour.[13]

The actor and humorist Will Rogers occasionally found himself on the same bill as the Cherry Sisters, now often referred to in the press as the "Vegetable Twins." Rogers is supposed to have remarked that the "Cherry Sisters must have been named before lemons were invented"; some newspapers, knowing of the Sister's litigious nature, went so far as to suggest that they had the actor arrested for the libel, although no such event took place. In Rogers' own scrapbook he referred to the Sisters as "great," and in a letter he wrote to the editor of the *Cedar Rapids Evening Gazette and Republican* he claimed that "they were really the inspiration of me going on the stage."[14] When he visited the city he is reported to have asked "where are the Cherry Sisters? They're more famous than Cedar Rapids itself. I've got to see them."[15]

Rogers may have thought well of them, but the burghers of Des Moines clearly held them in less high esteem. In August 1910 it was announced that portraits of the Ringling Brothers, the five founding siblings of the Ringling Bros. World's Greatest Shows traveling circus, were to go on display in the Iowa Hall of Fame. Four of the brothers were born in McGregor, Iowa, and the family had lived in that town for a dozen years, but Addie and Effie were not happy, and felt that if any entertainers were to be feted then it should have been themselves. "It's just because they are men," Effie declared. "We've brought more fame to Iowa than any ten men, and here the Ringlings are going to be put in the Hall of Fame and we're to be left out in the cold, I suppose. Never mind. Wait until Iowa grants women the suffrage. Then we'll have the pictures of the Ringlings taken from the walls and we'll be pedestaled!" A portrait of the actress Lillian Russell, born in Clinton, Iowa, already hung on the wall of the hallowed Hall but, as Effie added dismissively, "It must have been her complexion that got her there."[16] *Variety* revealed that the Ringling's press agent, Harry Lindley, had strengthened their bid for local immortality by presenting lifetime passes to any and all Ringling Brothers shows to Edgar Harlan, the Hall of Fame's curator.

As if they had not already learned their lesson, in 1913 the Sisters once again tried their hand at running their own company. The duo took over the Haymarket Theater in Chicago, convincing management that their revue would be a huge draw, and that they would be happy for a percentage of the profits rather than a wage. Yet ticket holders arriving for the third night of their residency were met with a closed theater, its windows dark, the only member of staff available a night watchman who announced that there would be no show after all. "The Cherry Sisters have closed," he told the twenty-five or thirty people who arrived at the door. "They jumped out of town last night."[17] The Sisters' grand new company, which "consisted of seven persons, including the sisters, and a moving picture outfit,"[18] was washed up after just two nights; reports vary about the amount taken at the box office, but both *Variety* and the *New York Dramatic Mirror* were in agreement that the total for the two nights came to less than $20. Complaining that the poor turn out was due entirely to a lack of advertising, Addie and Effie skipped town, but not before they "dropped each act on the bill a cute little note stating that salaries would be paid sometime."[19] The members of the company they had left stranded unanimously—and magnanimously—decided not to sue the Sisters for lost earnings. For now.

It was becoming more and more difficult to find theaters that would book an act for a whole week. Many of the houses that the Sisters had once been able to rely on for a decent engagement were turning away from live acts to moving pictures, and many of those theaters that were still booking specialty acts were only willing to give them three nights at most. Things had changed on the home front too. Lizzie was no longer living with Ella, but was looking after the home that she (on paper, at least) owned and that she now shared with Addie and Effie, and occasionally joining the two performing sisters on stage. "We'll go just as long as the people want us," she told a reporter from the *Cedar Rapids Evening Gazette* in a rare telephone interview, responding to reports coming from Chicago about their immanent retirement. "The other girls have been filling a vaudeville engagement and are now on their way home, but I don't believe they ever said they would give up the stage to go farming. I've been staying at home to look after things while the other girls are away but when they return I'm going to take a vacation."[20] As far as the press was concerned, Lizzie accepted that her sisters would never change their ways; however, she confided in her friend Blanche Talbot that she wanted them to give up the stage and return to the bucolic life on the farm. "I am surprised to read that you think [the] sisters will quit [the] business," wrote Blanche. "I presumed on account of the financial conditions of the whole world it affected theirs with all others. It is too bad, for I know they worked hard, they tried, they've done their best—of that I am sure...."[21]

When the Sisters appeared in Burlington the performance was brought to a close after a shower of carrots and onions descended on to the women and a roughly assembled coffin found its way on to the stage. Addie and Effie went off to find a policeman, but when one could not be located in the building, they refused to carry on with the show. After a vitriolic write up in one local paper, the Cherrys wrote to the editor of their chief competitor, the *Burlington Hawk-Eye*, not to complain about being struck by rotting vegetation, nor by the appearance of the black painted "rough box," but once again to contest stories which continued to circulate about their performing behind a protective screen: "The Cherry Sisters wish to state through the columns of the *Hawk-Eye* that the notice which appeared In the Burlington Gazette, written by the manager of the Garrick theater and editor of the Gazette, is false. We never used a 'net' in our act, and no one knows this better than the managers and editors. We could have made this falsehood cost these parties considerable, but we do not care to have our pure name connected with theirs in court. 'Vengeance is mine,' sayeth the Lord. 'I will repay.' Therefore, we will leave them in the hands of a just and righteous God."[22]

In February 1915 they ventured out again, starting with a show in Des Moines. "We like Des Moines," Addie told a reporter from the *Des Moines Tribune*. "We always go well here. This is the first engagement we've taken this spring. We are going to Boone and then we play Omaha. I don't really know the secret of our success on the stage. I think it must be that people see we are just common folk like they are. Then the public likes songs and comedy. People come to see us who don't go to the theater any other time. When we were out in Butte a Methodist minister said to us "I never go to shows, except when you girls come. I always go to see you. You aren't like show people." I think that must be it."[23] Effie, wisely, declined to give her opinion on why their act remained popular with certain audiences, although she did add that "we are considering an offer to go to New York and have a theater of our own. We'll be the headliners and have a bunch of acts with us." Sadly, like so many of their plans, this grand scheme came to naught.

Various reports have claimed that the Cherry Sisters were forced off the stage in 1916 when a flu epidemic caused theaters across the country to close; however the pandemic, which would eventually claim more lives than those lost in World War I, did not begin until March 1918. A polio epidemic gripped New York in 1916, but it is unlikely that this would have kept Addie and Effie from working, and they did play sporadic dates during the year. Quite simply, the reason that the duo gave so few performances between 1915 and 1918 is that fashions were changing and there were few agents who wanted to employ the sisters, or who could see a profit in staging one of their "entertainments." This, no doubt, also explains why they repeatedly attempted to establish their own company; no one wanted to employ them. Notebooks belonging to the sisters are filled with the names and addresses of theatrical agents, bookers, managers and the like, but few of those they solicited for work seemed interested. The pair had hoped that agents in Chicago would have flocked to see them when they played a four-night stint at McVicker's Theater there over Christmas 1915, but no extra bookings followed. The crowd that came to see them (once again augmented by Lizzie) fulfill a three-day booking at the Majestic in Cedar Rapids in May 1916 (after a ballot calling on patrons of the theater to vote for their preferred act was printed in the local papers) must have brought the women some comfort, especially as the previous week they had been forced to share a stage in Des Moines with an act glorifying in the ridiculous name of Gus Elmore's Cannibal Maids (in their very own "picturesquely staged South Sea romance," apparently). The *Cedar Rapids Gazette* reported that their show had changed little in the last two decades: "One dressed in male attire attempts to sing and she succeeds in keeping several bars ahead of the music. The sisters sing a song about a gypsy and try to act it but the effort is painful." Yet they acknowledged that "the audience apparently enjoyed their work because it was unstinted in its applause. Apparently their popularity has not waned,"[24] and so great was the demand to see them that the manager of the Majestic, Mr. Slattery, booked them for two further shows on 3 June, despite boasting that 8,000 people had already been to the theater to see them. For this extra date Effie promised a new song in which she would address the issue of women's suffrage, an increasingly important

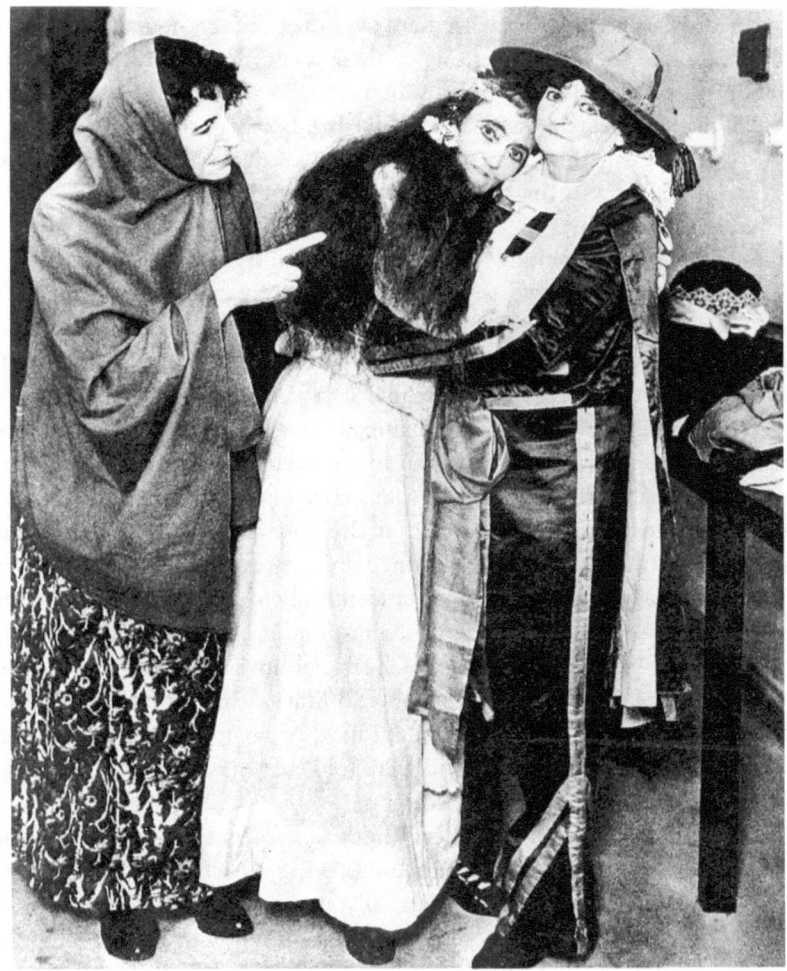

"The Gypsy's Warning," from left: Effie, Lizzie and Addie.

topic for her. After the curtain came down—despite assurances that the Sisters would be off on a tour of the Eastern states–Addie and Effie were unwillingly placed into semi-retirement.

While the more famous half of the siblings were taking what they thought was their final bow, the other pair were up to their old tricks. Ella and Lizzie rented pastureland from Peter Yonkers, whose eighty acres (the same land that had once belonged to the long-suffering John Ross) abutted the western perimeter of the Cherry Family farm, but when it came to settle their bill the women refused to pay up. In retaliation Yonkers—who had a similar experience as a neighbor to the Cherrys as the Cook family had enjoyed, and battled for years with them over the poor maintenance of boundary fences—took possession of one of their cows, but when he went out to check on it one morning he found it had mysteriously vanished. The police were called and a search was made of Ella and Lizzie's property: the missing bovine was found tied up in one of their barns. Charges were brought and a court date was set, but the case was settled when the women paid Yonkers the $45 they owed him.

The two women were fast becoming the scourge of the neighborhood, ending up in court on two separate occasions for criminal damage after smashing down fences erected around the house that Addie and Effie occupied, and causing the landlord, Rebecca Rickard, to ask the court to evict the women from her property. In November 1918 a warrant for their arrest was also sworn out by Ben Roscher, who alleged that Ella and Lizzie had "maliciously and mischievously" smashed down a fence on his land in Marion. Mrs. Roscher had told her husband that Lizzie had informed her that it was she who cut down the fence, and that she and a friend drove across the Roscher's land (their farm was positioned on the western side of the Yonkers" plot) to cut through their barbed wire, seemingly to create a path for her and her sister to use, rather than their having to go around their land to reach the main road. Neither of the elder Cherry siblings intended to be denied access to pasture or to the quickest route to Marion by something as trifling as a neighbor's property, but the court found in favor of the Roschers. Ella and Lizzie were each fined $50, and were told that they faced fifteen days in jail apiece if the fine was not settled.

Like the Cooks and the Yonkers, the Roschers had also suffered several years of abuse from the elder Cherrys. In 1903 Ben Roscher made the mistake of leasing land to Lizzie, and she, naturally, had fallen behind with her rent. Roscher took back his property and leased it, along with the extra grazing rights he had previously given Lizzie, to his neighbor W.B. Randall. Randall erected a new fence around the land that Lizzie had previously called hers, but "Lizzie didn't like the idea of not getting the use of the stalks and let the fence down and allowed her stock, seventeen head of cattle, to run in them. These were driven back and the fence repaired, but it was taken down again. This time Mr. Randall took up one of the cows, to pay for the damage, but this was not paid. An appeal was taken to the township trustees to appraise the damage, which was $2.50, which she still refused to pay. The cow is now for sale, and will be sold tomorrow afternoon if the damages and costs are not paid before then. The costs have grown so that the total will be about $10."[25] A restraining order was issued in the Roscher's favor against the two eldest Cherrys—an injunction the sisters willfully ignored. To their neighbors, living in close proximity to Ella and Lizzie Cherry must have seemed like having the Hatfields and the McCoys on their doorstep.

The upshot of all this was that by mid–1918 the family farm had grown to forty acres and was held entirely in Ella's name; Lizzie was living part-time with Ella and still keeping a few dairy cows in Kenwood Park, where there was a second plot of forty acres. Lizzie, Addie and Effie were renting a house where the two younger girls lived and which Lizzie would occupy alone when Addie and Effie were away; at this address they would supplement their income by taking in the occasional boarder, but with little money coming in the three women decided to take on yet another property in Cedar Rapids where, shortly afterwards, they would set up a small bakery from the front rooms.

11

Can She Bake a Cherry Pie?

Ever since the first commercial screening of a moving picture in a vaudeville theater, in Koster and Bial's Music Hall in New York 1896 (on the corner of Broadway and Thirty-Fourth Street, where the famous department store Macy's now stands), demand for live acts had been on the decline. Addie and Effie may not have been forced off stage by the influenza epidemic, as they would have preferred their public to believe, but across America, theaters were either closing for good or converting in to picture houses, and the vaudeville circuit that had provided the Sisters a living for so long was changing beyond all recognition. "Some of the smaller, storefront theatres could afford a few acts of small time variety in addition to several short films," explains theater historian Cezar Del Valle. "When movie palaces started to develop in the 1910s the main feature was proceed by a stage show. It could be a lavish production relating to the feature or a glorified variety show." Many of the greatest names in vaudeville quickly become established stars in the fledgling movie industry, and when Congress voted to declare war on Germany in April 1917, America's decision to introduce conscription took a huge number of men aged eighteen to forty-five away from their homes, their loved ones, and away from the theaters and opera houses.

Now off the road, but still in need of an income, Addie and Effie decided to concentrate their efforts on the little home bakery they had run from rooms at the front of a rented house on Third Avenue West in Cedar Rapids. Like everything associated with the Cherrys, running this business was not without its complications; the business was listed in Lizzie's name, with Effie officially the store's clerk and Addie a lowly worker. For a time the three of them simply rented the front rooms of the house for the bakery while continuing to live at 500, 23rd Avenue West.

The sisters offered fresh Jersey milk, homemade bread, rolls and—naturally—cherry pies. "It was a great success," Effie wrote. "We worked from eighteen to twenty hours daily; there was such a demand for our bakery goods, and especially for our famous rice bread. We seldom had an hour to call our own, but we wanted to do our little bit through the World War. People came from all over Iowa for our bakery goods, for we did not use any of the cheap substitutes which many of the other bakeries used."[1] Bob Downing, Mae West's stage manager, recalled how he "often stopped to buy sweet rolls at the bakery the Cherry Sisters operated in later years. It was not uncommon to find a sign in their shop window reading: "Fresh bread and bull pups for sale." The girls were extremely taciturn, reluctant to discuss their great success on Broadway, but not unfriendly. They maintained interest in current events."[2]

But Effie yearned to return to the stage; when offers came her way she took them and, as always, the ever-loyal Addie came along too. The bakery was a mere distraction, and anyway, surely Lizzie could manage on her own? The pair joined the Ed Williams Stock Company in June 1918, again playing for three days at the Majestic and, although the dates were explicitly advertised as "the last time they would appear on any stage,"[3] Effie had absolutely

The First Cherry Bakery, 332 Third Avenue, Cedar Rapids, circa 1921 (Orville Rennie and Jane Rennie Collection, 1875-1987. Ms. 178. Special Collections, State Historical Society of Iowa, Iowa City).

no intention of honoring that statement. For the next few months they would happily recycle their material on small stages throughout the Midwest.

As usual, the road traveled by the four sisters was a bumpy one, and they soon found themselves in court once more. This time a judgment that had been awarded against Addie, Effie and Lizzie in favor of Sophronia Grant some years before (and that had caused the two youngest Cherry sisters to leave their rented home) had come back to haunt them. Mrs. Grant was a local merchant who specialized in hair and beauty treatments; she was also the owner of a house that she had rented out to Addie and Effie in November 1906. The original agreement was that the sisters would pay $10.50 a month for the property, and that Mrs. Grant would retain the use of two rooms to store her own furniture in, but the sisters had not paid their rent since November 1911 and Mrs. Grant quite rightly wanted them gone. Addie and Effie refused to move, effectively becoming squatters. Mrs. Grant appealed to the court for $609 in unpaid rent (including interest) plus costs and, after a five-hour hearing, the court ordered that the sisters both pay the amount they owed and that they vacate her property. They agreed to leave the house but apparently forgot all about settling their bill.

Then things started to get messy. When Addie and Effie could not be prevailed upon to pay, the court impounded the furniture they had effectively abandoned at Mrs. Grant's and issued a writ of attachment, which declared that the items could be sold and the money raised be used to pay the debt. Lizzie, never one to shirk her familial responsibilities, waded in to the fray, and insisted that the furniture was hers and not her sisters. In a small notebook, containing a diary for February and March 1916, Lizzie kept her account of the feud:

> Went down to Addie's place to see about getting a man to do the work. Hired Clemins to do the work and told him to go over the next day and tell Jefery he would do it. He went Friday, sure, but Jefery said he had heard from Mrs. Grant's brother (Marick) about two hours before and that he was not going to have any monkeying about and that I had nothing to do with it.

She also branded Mrs. Grant a thief after her agent (Charles A. Jeffries, the "Jefery" Lizzie refers to in her diary) took possession of one of her young horses and "threatened to shoot me in the barn and to have me arrested too if I dared to take the colt out of his barn." Luckily no shotgun was to hand but he "said he was going to get a lawyer. While he was gone the colt got out of the barn, and as the gate was open ran out and down to the girls' place, with his halter dragging after him."[4]

Marick once again took possession of the colt, and refused to give him back to Lizzie unless she could show him papers that proved that she, and neither Addie nor Effie, was indeed the owner, but this Harry Houdini of horses escaped again. A few days later Lizzie

> Went down to the Grant place to get in the house and saw two men coming behind me. I hurried ahead and saw Marick, I said I have come down to do this much and you can turn everything over in to my hands and he said all right. Then up walked two deputy sheriffs and said they had come out to levy on the stock etcetera. I tell them not to put a ticket on the stock as the stock did not belong to the girls, but they went ahead and put the ticket on.... Mrs. Grant's brother unlocked the door and let the sheriffs in the house and took them upstairs to a little room and then they sorted out papers and had Marick swear to it.

After a heated and animated argument over which Cherry owned what, the deputies told Lizzie that "if I said any more they would have me arrested." On 10 March Addie and Effie broke in to their old home and took out several upholstered chairs and other items, which they then secreted about the family farm. The lawyers acting for Mrs. Grant demanded that Addie and Effie return them or face the legal ramifications. Lizzie's interference in the affair understandably upset Mrs. Grant, and after hearing her accusation of theft she took out another writ, this time for $2,000 for slander against Lizzie and did indeed have her arrested. Lizzie countersued for the same amount, insisting that she had been humiliated by Mrs. Grant's action, and that her good name had been besmirched: she "said [the] arrest was open and notorious." Lizzie's plight "had been observed by her neighbors and friends and she as caused deep humiliation, mental anguish and pain thereby."

In September 1919 it was decided by the court that the money owed would be raised by selling the land that Lizzie owned, the twenty acres situated next door to Ella's own twenty acre plot, the very same twenty acres that the family had been brought up on. Lizzie had grand plans to build a new cottage on the land, and her friend Blanche Talbot wrote from Chicago to her to tell her that "when it is finished and you are ready for me to come I will come out for a short visit, nothing would give me more pleasure."[5] However, before the work on the cottage had begun, and before the court could lay claim to the land, Lizzie signed the plot in question over to Ella, in effect doubling the size of the family farm, and claimed that she, like her other sisters, owned no property and so could not be expected to pay their fine. Lizzie signed the land over to her elder sister in April 1920 but, in a poor attempt to hoodwink the court, the documents she submitted to accompany the transfer backdated their transaction to September 1917, before the court decided against her and in favor of Mrs. Grant. No one seemed to concerned when it was discovered that Lizzie had continued to pay the taxes on the land until 1921, and that she had applied for an extension to the mortgage in her own name.

With such an obvious subterfuge having been committed, Mrs. Grant returned to court and a sheriff was appointed to look in to the Sisters' financial affairs. When he could find no evidence of any property belonging to the Lizzie, Addie or Effie, the judge ordered them to appear before him to explain precisely who owned what and how exactly they planned to settle their debt. Mrs. Grant's representative, Henry Rickel, claimed that he could not make head or tail of their complicated financial arrangements, and an exasperated Judge Milo P. Smith suggested, tongue firmly in cheek, that the sisters give a performance in the courtroom, that they charge for entrance and that the door money be used to pay Mrs. Grant. Rickel agreed, but the performance did not take place. A furious Lizzie wrote a damning letter to her younger sisters, blasting both Mrs. Grant and her representative:

> Lawyer Rickel knew I had sold the land to my sister Ella before he went in this deep. Mrs. Grant owes the Cherry Sisters—owes $1000, but the Cherry Sisters do not owe Mrs. Grant one copper cent. Can't this case be thrown out of court so you won't have to go to Des Moines? Rickel had me before Judge Smith so he did not go in to this blind, now he is trying to claim damages. The deed was made out in 1917, some time in September.[6]

Rickel had good reason to want to see the Cherry Sisters embarrassed in court. Many years earlier one of the Sisters had been to see him for advice, and as she was leaving she threw down a battered old twenty-five cent piece, a derisory offering for his time. Since that day the very same quarter had hung by a ribbon in Rickel's office, a reminder to always agree a fee before giving legal counsel ... especially when the Cherrys were involved. This was his chance to make the sister who had slighted him pay.

The case dragged its way through the court for more than five years. In an effort to prevent her from obtaining the deeds to their property, in April 1921 Ella issued her own writ against Sophronia Grant; Mrs. Grant immediately countersued for $175, the amount she figured she was owed for "the wrongful issuing and service of a writ of injunction."[7] The whole sorry affair ended with Mrs. Grant demanding possession of land that Lizzie had signed over to Ella, claiming that Lizzie had done so knowing full well that there was a case pending.

During the long and protracted case, the court learned much about the Sisters' complicated financial arrangements. There was, the siblings revealed, an understanding between them that all four women would share equally in any profits arising from their entertainments. Effie and Addie appeared to have been attempting to keep up with their side of the agreement, contributing some of their earnings to Ella, but—for the period that she was a full-time member of the act–Lizzie had not. With the family farm barely making enough to cover taxes, Ella and Lizzie testified that it was agreed between them that as Lizzie owed her eldest sister around $800 which, according to court records, included $500 as her part of the profits from their entertainments, $200 for Ella's labor on the farm in taking care of Lizzie's live stock, and $100 for money borrowed at various times. To cover this debt she would sign over the twenty-acre plot that adjoined the family farm, and that Ella would assume the mortgage on the land, estimated at a further $800. Despite all that, the land was seized and once again the sisters faced the indignity of seeing their former possessions sold off at public auction on the steps of Marion's courthouse; however Lizzie—as schooled in the ways of the court system as her sisters—appealed the decision. Finally, in January 1925, the Supreme Court accepted that Ella had taken possession of the disputed land in good faith, and that she and Lizzie had not collaborated in an act of fraud, but they still demanded that Lizzie pay Mrs. Grant a total of $300 as full settlement in the outstanding slander case. The two elder sisters must have taken some consolation from the wording of Justice C.W. Vermillion's ruling, which singled out the family's "theatrical talent," and commented on their individual roles in the enterprise: "As to the Cherry Sisters, they achieved fame of a sort upon the vaudeville stage in years gone by. It appears that Lizzie, Effie and Addie were the principal performers, while Ella remained at home and devoted herself to the writing of sketches for the Sisters' performances. There was an agreement that they should share the profits."[8] That last sentence must have pleased Ella no end; she finally had recognition, in print no less, of her position in the family business.

If she ever collected her award or not is unknown, for on 12 April 1934 Sophronia Grant died when a fire engulfed her ten-room house on Zika Avenue, Cedar Rapids. Her death, from asphyxiation as she lay sleeping, came exactly one month after that of her former adversary, Ella Cherry.

As if the court appearances were not enough to keep the Sisters' names in the headlines, another pair of Cherry Sisters surfaced and attempted to take their crowns, touring with the musical farce "Are You A Mason?," although if you checked the small print you might discover that these women were called Mattie and Violet, rather than Addie and Effie. The sisters may have been absent from the footlights, but their name had become a byword for all that was awful. Theda Bara, the great silent movie star, was attempting a stage career at the time, but her appearance in New York in March 1920 was ridiculed, with her acting ability likened to that of Addie and Effie: "Theda Bara's performance in 'The Blue Flame,' a melodrama by George V. Hobart and John Willard, has evoked the most excited criticism from the dramatic writers since the famous Cherry Sisters appeared behind chicken-wire netting on the Bowery."⁹ Before the year was out Ella and Lizzie were in court yet again; this time one J.F. Hornans was suing the pair for the return of a calf they had conveniently forgotten to pay him for.

Perhaps it was constantly seeing others with the same surname in the press that, in 1921, prompted the Sisters to announce their desire to return to the stage. "We have rather enjoyed the bakery business for a change," Effie explained, "but now we are tired of it and are anxious to go back." She told reporters that "the only reason why they hesitated so long was that she had had trouble with her teeth—had many of them removed, in fact, and that had prevented an earlier return to the footlights."¹⁰ In another interview Effie revealed that "we are tired of our bucolic life. We yearn for the applause and the reception we used to get. It is true that the audiences used to throw things at us but that was part of the program. We will sing and act. I don't think we will dance any more, but we will have little sketches—gestures and all. Addie and I wanted to return to the stage a few years ago but the flu epidemic stopped us. It is always something it seems."¹¹ Viewed as either a come back or a farewell to the stage (depending on which sister you talked to), Chicago press agent Cal Harris, who had handled them for a period around the turn of the century, would manage them once again, and Broadway producer Will Morrissey planned to feature the Sisters in a revue featuring excerpts from grand opera. "I expect the Cherry Sisters to repeat their first New York triumphs," Harris boasted. "And why not? Their art, like wine, has improved with age, and they are still in the prime of life."¹²

Postcard showing Greene's Opera House, Cedar Rapids (author's collection).

Addie was nearing sixty-two; Effie was a mere child at

almost 54. Effie was happy to be back in the spotlight, but bristled when Harris fed reporters the lie that "since their retirement they have been out on their big farm milking cows, feeding the chickens, and otherwise keeping themselves busily engaged in healthy operations."[13] For a woman well aware of her position in society, suggesting that she spent her time grubbing around on a dirty farm was an anathema. She let it be known that the duo had not wasted their time in retirement, revealing that "we have a great number of new pieces ready."[14]

The newspapers, as always, followed the latest developments with great interest, but sadly—as had happened after their Chicago showcase in December 1915—the dates that followed were few and far between, and the theaters that would book them were hardly what you might call top rank. When Greene's Opera House, the scene of some of the Sisters' earliest appearances, pulled down the curtain for the final time in February 1922 the writing was on the wall. After serving the public of Cedar Rapids for 42 years, the building, now in a serious state of disrepair, had outlived its original use. Gutted, the building became a parking garage for the nearby Roosevelt Hotel, before being torn down in 1969. On New Year's Eve 1922 the Sisters played Myers Theater in Janesville, Wisconsin, a small town of some 15,000 inhabitants. Originally opened in 1870 as the Myers Opera House, by the early '20s like many other theaters it was struggling to attract an audience, and even in such a small town had to deal with competition from at least three other venues. The Sisters appeared on a bill that included Wild Oscar ("the Only Wild Dutchman in Captivity"), the 4 Wild Cats, and Miss Chocolate Drop. A couple of years later, like so many of its contemporaries, the Myers would switch to showing moving pictures full time.

The world was changing and, for the Cherry Sisters, opportunities were vanishing.

12

Effie for Mayor!

"Vaudeville's Biggest Flop Entering Political Arena," the headline in Variety screamed.[1] Effie Cherry, one half of the infamous "vegetable twins" was to stand for election as mayor of her adopted city, just five years after women in Iowa were given the right to vote in elections.

Women in such positions were rare, but not unheard of, and Iowa was the state that had seen the first ever woman elected to the mayoral office. In 1862 the residents of Oskaloosa selected Nancy Smith for the position, adding her name to the ballot on the day of the election itself as a protest against the only man standing. Mrs. Smith declined the honor, and it would not be until 1887 that Susanna Salter would became the first woman to serve a term as mayor in United States, when she won the election in Argonia, Kansas. Like Mrs. Smith, Mrs. Salter's name had been added to the ballot at the last minute as a joke, a protest against women becoming more politically active. It had been hoped that she would be humiliated by losing, but the prank backfired. News of her success spread across the world, and she paved the way for two more Kansas towns electing women before the decade was through.

Addie, dear, faithful Addie, was there to support her. "You know," Effie told reporters at a press conference given from the serving counter in the front room of their bakery, "Cedar Rapids gets a little quiet now and then, and I thought they needed somebody to kind of liven things up a little. So I say to Addie, 'I'm goin' to run for mayor of this city. What do you think of it?' And Addie says, 'Experience has taught me, Effie, that we can do anything.'"[2]

Ray Swan, manager of the Majestic in Cedar Rapids, approached Effie with a novel idea: he would give her a platform to reach her audience by means of a "guest" spot before each evening's performance at the theater. Tickets for the first three evenings sold out within an hour, and although she was only supposed to speak for five minutes or so before the main program, the appearances were advertised in the *Evening Gazette* as if she were the star of the show.

Introduced as "formerly on of the bright lights of the stage, now one of the bright lights of Cedar Rapids,"[3] Effie strode to the front of the stage dressed entirely in black. Her dress touched the floor, and was matched with long black gloves and a small black hat. Several of those present felt sure had come straight out of the 1890s. One of her big issues, she explained, was the state of the streets. "Decayed garbage is ruinous to the health," she announced to the audience. "It should be removed from the alleys before it gets strong enough to walk away. I have drunk about all the sewer water I can stand. I know, as you all know, that pure drinking water is the most essential thing to good health, far more so than that we should have additions to our parks." The morals of the young were of great concern too. "We should save the boys and girls, for they are the foundation of our great and glorious nation. But when their morals are gone, of what value are they as citizens? The sight of young girls willingly picked up at the curb by automobiles, to go the Lord only known where, has wrung my heart. This is enough to make the angels weep. Oh Daughter of Zion awake from thy slumber and by the grace of God we shall save Cedar Rapids!"[4]

The press, naturally enough, had a field day. Reporters twisted her words or simply made up what they thought their readers wanted. "There are too many old men in shiny automobiles whistling at young girls.... Old men should be at home with their wives and children. When I was a girl I went to bed with the chickens!"[5] Surely anyone who was able to dodge vegetables and eggs as deftly as Effie Cherry would easily be able to dodge the insults that would come her way from her political opponents? Her mailbox was flooded with letters of support, from fans and politicians alike: "I am glad to see that the women of the country are stepping up," wrote one, "and I hope to cast the first vote for a woman President of the U.S."[6]

With newspaper reporters hanging off her every word, Effie was in her element. "There will be no more lovemaking on the streets between the time the movies close and the arrival of the milkman in the morning," she explained. "There will be no more wrestling to jazz music or close-fitting swaying on public dance floors, and the bobbed haired flapper no longer will be allowed to roam the streets unless she is escorted by papa or mamma. This is just the beginning!"[7] She railed against public parks, gymnasiums, bathing beaches and—above all— the sight of a young woman's bare flesh: "We have become worse than the French in exposing flesh," she cried. Lewd literature and immoral entertainment had to go. No one running for mayor of a provincial city ever garnered as many national headlines as Effie Cherry. She seemed unstoppable.

"When I am mayor I'll have the curfew bell ring at 9 pm," she told reporters, offering a 10 pm cutoff during the summer months. "Look at the way the young people carry on! It's awful! I'll have women policemen instead of men. Movies? The only pictures that will get my O.K. are those of national events and crossing the Alps. Taxes? I don't know much about taxes, but I'm for reducing them. First. I'll turn the municipal golf links over to some poor farmer. All it is good for is a pasture, anyway. Bathing beaches? I'll close every one of them until the women agree to wear some clothing while bathing. I'm not a Democrat, Republican or Socialist, but I'm going to run on a 'blue' platform and I'll win." Sadly, she didn't. Despite being taken seriously for the first time in her life the constant grandstanding, coupled with the long hours in the bakery, took its toll. Effie failed to attend a debate between the three candidates just days before the election, and when the results were in it was announced that she had polled 805 votes: her two male opponents—the incumbent mayor C.D. Huston and former mayor J.F. Rall, polled more than 3,000 each, with Rall being reelected. Effie, as usual, blamed the press for her failure. "Since my advent in to politics I have received newspaper clippings from all over the United States, written by one who represents the Associated Press. Now, these newspaper clippings are vile to the extreme and were written for no other thing than to injure me personally. I call this a stab in the dark, and when you consider that I am a woman on whose reputation there is not a stain, it makes it a crime."[8] But whomever—or whatever—she may have blamed, one thing cannot be denied: Effie Cherry broke the mold the day she decided to run for public office, becoming the first woman to ever stand for mayor in Cedar Rapids. "I wanted to be elected by the people who want clean government and water," she told a reporter from the *Cedar Rapids Gazette*. "I wanted to be mayor and make this a good city."[9]

After losing the election, Effie and Addie went back to the stage. Several commentators believed that Effie's attempt to get elected was insincere, a mere publicity ploy to garner interest in the two elderly women and their plans to re-invigorate their career. The extra press she received certainly helped drum up interest in a local talent show the duo were organizing, dubbed "the Show of the Ages," which took place on the stage of the City Auditorium over two nights in September. In an interview given shortly before the mayoral primary Effie openly admitted that, in the event her campaign failed, "it is very probable that we will utilize the publicity the campaign has given us and make a 'once-over' of the old vaudeville circuit."[10]

No sooner had they announced their plans that the pair were contacted by Ray Swan and Merle Trousdale, then owner and treasurer respectively of the Majestic Theater in Cedar Rapids. "Mr. Swan is our own personal business manager," Effie told reporters, adding that "we have signed the contract to appear at the Orpheum in Sioux City on April 17, and Mr. Swan is rapidly booking contracts for us that will probably keep us on the road all summer." Their contract with Swan and Trousdale guaranteed the Sisters $35 a day, plus travel expenses, for up to three performances daily: there would be no money, nor expenses, for the days they did not perform. The men were true to their word, and Trousdale's accounts show that the Sisters were paid up to $245 a week while they worked for them, although the Cherrys were infuriated when Swan called them "the rottenest, rankest, funniest act in vaudeville. The funny part of it is they don't know how awful their stuff is. If they could only realize that the reason for their popularity through their thirty years on the stage was not their ability, but because their act is absolutely punk, perhaps they wouldn't love their 'admiring followers' as much as they do."[11] Trousdale was able to garner them a season's work with his brother's company, the Boyd B. Trousdale Players, on the understanding that they would reprise their old act. The Sisters ended their business arrangement with Swan and Trousdale with their final performance at Chicago's Rialto Theater.[12] The shows were, for the most, politely received, although an appearance in Council Bluffs ended in the Sisters being assaulted:

> A hurry call was sent to Cedar Rapids today for the famous "vegetable screen" of the Cherry sisters, which has lain in a storehouse there for a quarter century, because of a near riot which occurred when the sisters, Effie and Addle, staged their vaudeville comeback here last night. It was just like olden times. Overripe tomatoes, cabbages, stale eggs and even a black cat was hurled at the actresses. Citizens here decided to see to it that the Sisters' act got as loving a reception as it received 25 years ago. When the curtain went up the sisters were greeted with yells, stamping and catcalls. As the act progressed the din became so great that the theater manager sent in a riot call. As the police arrived the vegetable volley was let loose. One spectator hurled a black tom cat on the stage. "It seemed just like olden times," Effie said ruefully as she washed egg stains from her costume. "But we made a big mistake in not bringing our curtain with us. It will be used at every performance hereafter."[13]

It is more than likely that the reporter invented the quote attributed to Effie, but if it is real then it provides the only acknowledgment by any of the sisters that they did, in fact, employ the use of a screen on occasion to protect themselves from the endless shower of detritus hurled at them. Effie also announced that, once the tour was over, she would be taking her own play, "Nobody's Child," to Broadway: "There will be no cherry pies for Cedar Rapids this summer, for Effie Cherry and her sister Addie have closed up their back room bakery shop and are now intensively rehearsing their newest drama, "Nobody's Child" ... and while the famous vaudeville pair do their stuff to the vegetable tune, Cedar Rapids will be without their private supply of doughnuts."[14] Unusually, *Variety* chose to review the Sisters' performance, taking in a show at the Des Moines Orpheum in May:

Effie opens the act, appearing in a blue gown which fits tightly around her neck and sweeps the floor. She sings a song about "Before and After Talking" and immediately disappears. Addie then appears in a rose colored dress and makes a short talk on the modern young man. Poor as it is, it's the best thing the sisters have. Then Effie comes back. She is clad this time in male attire. The pants are dark colored and she wears a light colored sack coat, which looks as though it had just been taken out of a Civil War album. This time Effie sings a song about "She Was My Sister, and Oh I How I Missed Her." By this time Addie has changed to her cherry red dress and they both appear to sing 'Ta-rar-rar-boom-de-ay. For an encore they sing another verse of the same song.

The spectator is going to wonder whether or not the sisters are sincere, or whether they're simply trying to put on a unique act. Your reviewer talked with the sisters in an effort to determine the answer for himself, and he is firmly convinced that they are sincere—and that they have a unique act. Effie talks fluently on everything from prohibition to the Equity strike. She wants particularly to clean up the stage and says she prefers this to closing the shows on Sunday. If it were not for a reputation for being a bad act gained 30 years ago the Cherry sisters could not get a hearing. As it is, they claim they have been offered 40 weeks. The manager who happens to be punished by having them placed on his bill has only one opportunity—that of billing them as a comedy duo. He may be able to get away with it—and again he may not. The Cherry Sisters, when here, were interviewed. Effie explained that they had retired from the stage before, on account of the war. The reporter, a young fellow, took it for granted the recent affair with German was referred to. Stage hands are at odds over the question, however. Some insist that she meant the Civil War, and others say it was the Spanish American.[15]

They struggled to make ends meet, but when Effie fell and broke her hand in late 1924 Addie could not cope on her own, and the bakery was closed. Although the Sisters claimed that their time as bakers was over for good, they would continue with the operation sporadically over the next few years: in 1927 the *Cedar Rapids Evening Gazette* noted that "the Cherry Sisters of vaudeville fame are now operating a bakery here,"[16] and the following year an article in the *Des Moines Register* confirmed that the pair were still plying their trade: "The day the correspondent called, the bakery salesroom of their home at 337 Third Avenue West was a bit spotted with paint. The decorating was interfering with business, but the sisters were continuing to serve old customers and fill special orders. Perhaps they will move soon to a larger store, and operate on a bigger scale."[17] As late as 1932, when *The Chicago Examiner* printed an article about the Sisters precarious financial position, they were still attempting to find the money to pay the rent on the bakery.

While recuperating, Effie turned back to her first love—writing—and authored yet another a novel which, she hoped, would be adapted in to a stage play. Unfortunately "The Blacksmith's Daughter," like "Nobody's Child," "Ellanor," "The Old Hermit's Daughter," and all of her other literary efforts, was destined to remain unpublished. At sixty-two pages long, the work could hardly be called a novel, but she put a lot of faith in the money earning potential of the tale of blacksmith Alfred Deene, his beautiful but chaste daughter Doris, the caddish Jasper Newberry and his quiet, thoughtful brother Don, the man whom Doris eventually marries.

She was still in demand though, and in January 1925, while the Sisters were appearing at the Pantages Theater, she made her radio debut, recording an interview for WCCO in Minneapolis about her experiences playing to houses in Minnesota, and giving a speech on the threat to the nation's youth from vice, from drink, from "wicked and vile" stage shows and from certain magazines and periodicals that "should have had their rights of publication taken away from them long ago, and these writings destroyed and burned. For such literature is more deadly than the sting of the deadly Adder. Do not let the slimey [sic] master of vice creep in to your beautiful city and destroy it."[18] Effie might have been enjoying the opportunity to give one of her blood and thunder speeches, but Addie was less than thrilled at the reaction the Sisters received in the city:

> I think it's perfectly rotten to bill us as "the worst act in vaudeville," as they have billed us here in Minneapolis. Let the public be the judge. If they see that sign they aren't going to come in and see something they don't think is good. Why, when we played through Iowa they used to call us "the two sweethearts of Iowa," and the opera houses always were packed. I guess the only trouble with us is that we never drank beer with the manager. We've lost many a job, but we've always taken care of our reputations. I guess we're the two most exemplary young women in the state of Iowa.[19]

With scant few bookings coming their way, Effie redoubled her political efforts. After all, a mayoral salary would be more than enough to keep them both out of the poor house. Her religious convictions and thoughts on what should be taught to children had been shaken by the trial in Dayton, Tennessee, where a substitute high school teacher, John T. Scopes, had been accused of violating the Butler Act, which made it unlawful to teach human evolution in state-funded schools. Effie sided firmly with William Jennings Bryan, one of the team of prosecutors in the case, whom she saw as protecting America from the heresy of evolution. The publicity surrounding the trial, and her certainty that the morals of the country's young were under threat, helped convince her to enter in to the political arena again. "The city, state and nation is going from bad to worse, physically, financially, mentally and morally,"[20] she exclaimed. "I propose to make the first start to curb the raid downward swing of things. It's the high prices, high taxes, high skirts, high life, one piece bathing suits, high gas, light and water rates and white-collared gasoline hounds that I'm after. Those white-collared hounds who sell us gas are having plenty of fun at our expense. The fumes have caused us no end of trouble and nearly suffocated our next door neighbor recently. Public officials waste too much time playing golf; ankle length skirts will be the style if I have my way. Next, more and bigger policemen."[21]

"I didn't know what it was all about," she explained when discussing her failure first time around, "But I've learned a few things and I'm going to run for mayor and I'm going to be elected. Then I'm going to run for senator. I like politics better than show business. I'll do a few things that'll make 'em sit up and take notice when I'm elected. I was defeated because the story got round that I was going to shut up the dance halls and the theaters. I didn't say anything of the kind."[22] Running for a second time, among her more ludicrous ideas was to have an orchestra play "Home, Sweet Home" every evening at 9 pm to mark the start of the curfew. She also demanded "cleaner motion pictures" years ahead of the Hays Code, and "no swearing in public,"[23] but she kept true to her word by campaigning against taxes, exorbitant prices for utilities such as electricity and gas, and against the fat cats running local politics. "The city hall gang won't listen to anybody unless they are on the inside," she announced. "The man who works with his hands is as valuable to society as he who uses his money. If I am elected mayor I will do all in my power for the betterment of Cedar Rapids. Every dollar taken in and paid out in the city will be accounted for. The citizens will receive full value for every dollar paid out for city expenditures. I want to see Cedar Rapids a clean, moral, and prosperous city. To do this, I have the welfare of the city at heart."[24]

Campaigning began in earnest in September, with newspapers across the country reporting on Effie's platform, and Addie acting as her sister's press agent, sending out photographs and copies of Effie's ten-point platform to any interested parties. Although politics took up most of their time, they did not forsake their audience completely, and in October the Sisters made their radio debut, performing songs and sketches from their stage show to the

Effie Cherry, an official portrait issued to promote her second entry in to the mayoral race, 1926.

audience of Cedar Rapids' WKAA. Harry Parr, manager of the station, told reporters that it was "a pleasure to be able to announce that they will be on the air. The program will be typical, they have promised, featuring some of the numbers they have made famous in their years on the stage."[25] It is strange that Effie would perform for a local radio station, as she blamed another broadcaster, WJAM, for having brought about the end of their bakery: "They got envious of our little bakery, and after the war they bought the property which we had only leased, and the Evening Gazette erected a broadcasting station on the dwelling which was a great failure, and the citizens of Cedar Rapids were glad when they closed it and took down the tower, as we have heard many say."[26] Once again Effie was playing fast and loose with the truth. The offending tower, all 115 feet of it, was actually based at Douglas Perham's electrical shop at 322 Third Avenue West. Perham was an early pioneer of commercial radio, and his station was, as Effie wrote, affiliated to the *Cedar Rapids Gazette*, but although the sisters had initially operated their bakery from the same address, they had already vacated the premises and moved to number 337, on the opposite side of the street, before Perham opened his radio station there.

The Cherrys continued to run their bakery business from the front of 337 for many more years, and the two of them now occupied the ground floor of the same address, with another family living upstairs. On one wall in the hallway of their part of the house, which the sisters shared with their dogs, Foxy (officially "Foxy the Third," and the granddaughter of another terrier that, according to the Sisters, had been poisoned) and Ruby (a stray that had attached itself to Addie), was a large frame, featuring two photographs each of Addie and Effie, one in costume and one seated in their Sunday best, along with the Rawson family coat of arms and a short piece of nonsense that claimed that the badge in question had been awarded to a young man in the English army for exhibiting bravery on behalf of the King. None of the other siblings were represented. It must have seemed to anyone visiting that Addie and Effie had cut Ella and Lizzie out of their life permanently. On the wall opposite hung the four golden horseshoes that the sisters had been presented with in Chicago; next to those hung a portrait of their dear, departed Jessie.

As she had proved by accepting the radio booking, Effie was never one to allow something as insignificant as her principles stand in the way of earning money. Although she frequently railed against the unassailable progress of the automobile, she and Addie gladly accepted a booking from the Iowa Automotive Merchants Association to perform at their annual banquet. Money was money, after all, and the bills still had to be paid. Effie, always good for a quote, blamed the Depression on the automobile, telling reporters that "the government spends tremendous sums on roads and then everyone goes broke paying for their motor cars."²⁷ In an address she wrote, no doubt inspired by her own family's experiences, Effie panned greedy landowners, and insisted that one certain cure for the Depression would be for the State to take back the land.

> There are vast achers, thousands of them, that are owned by wealthy landowners or corporations, throughout the entire country. This should not be allowed. These land owners live in the cities and generally own large manufacturing plants. They never earn their living by farming these lands, they are simply the landlords, like they have in Europe. This ought not to be in America. No one citizen should be allowed, to my mind, to own over one hundred and sixty achers [sic] in his or her own right.²⁸

Effie was a steadfast supporter of Republican senator Smith Wildman Brookhart, who twice represented Iowa in the United States Senate. Brookhart was a God-fearing family man who supported Prohibition, and Effie felt it would be calamitous for the state should he lose his seat. She also made it known that she admired Robert La Follette, the long-serving Republican Senator who, in 1924, ran for President of the United States as the head of his own Progressive Party. Effie's conservative agenda went down well with many, and letters of support, including one from Marion resident John Ives, implored her to "bear down especially hard on the dance, especially these fixed country dance pavilions ... they are simply hell holes of depravity.... I know what I am talking about for I see the effects of it nearly every night during the summer months. Many of these young people dance until they are thoroughly warmed up, then they get in the automobile with a bottle of hooch and cigarettes and drive to kingdom come and God only knows what does and what don't happen."²⁹ She campaigned fiercely, and when the Sisters played six shows over three days at the Majestic at the end of February, Effie once again took advantage of the opportunity to issue her polemic from the stage. The audiences warmly received the Majestic shows, and the Sisters were "greeted by a salvo of applause as each one stepped from the wings of the stage to the glare of the spotlight."³⁰ The Sisters revamped much of their old act for the home crowd, with Effie donning her male drag for "She Was My Sister and Oh How I Miss Her." Even "The Gypsy's Warning" got an outing, this time using an actress from one of the other acts on the bill—Dorothy Byton and her Snappy Steppers—rather than asking Lizzie to help out. "She doesn't have anything to say anyway," Effie explained. "She just stands there, and the Gypsy and the Spanish cavalier do all the talking and singing."³¹ When they performed the same sketch for the American Legion Convention two years later, on a bill that also included hog calling and cow bell ringing, it was the seventy-four-year old Ella and not Lizzie who took the part of the naive young Lady.

The election took place on 16 March, with Effie once again standing against J.F. Rall, the man who had beaten all comers two years" previously. Effie again came third with just 340 votes, almost 3,000 behind Rall. During a long and distinguished career in local politics, the businessman and long-serving Justice of the Peace would be elected mayor of the city four times. Effie did not really stand a chance. Not that the actual result troubled her much. Throughout her life Effie would "adapt" her own story to suit the times, and in her own writings she insisted that "I did win the second time I was candidate for mayor, by an overwhelming majority," and that her ballots had been destroyed by her political opponents. "The man who told me this said he had since been converted and become a Christian, and he told me this with tears in his eyes and his Holy Bible before him, and he asked me to forgive him.... One thing I know. If I had been Mayor Cedar Rapids would have been a better and safe place for our young folks to live in."[32] Two days later she and Addie were back on stage as though nothing had happened, and shortly after they signed a contract with agent Nat Frudenfelt to head a touring revue entitled "Vaudeville Yesterday and Today," on the strict understanding that they would only play "first class, respectable houses."[33] Brookhart, Effie's political idol, lost his own seat in 1932.

Frudenfelt's tour came and went, but few other opportunities arose. They could usually guarantee a couple of local bookings, and the occasional charity benefit, although even these became less frequent. Still, the Sisters' unassailable position as national celebrities continued to bring callers to their door. When screen star Gary Cooper visited Cedar Rapids he was keen to have his photograph taken with the sisters, but although Effie and Addie met the actor and liked him well enough, they refused to pose for an official portrait. A *Gazette* photographer snapped a photograph of the three of them talking together, but the Sisters' backs were turned to the camera. The Sisters agreed that they would both go and see Cooper's latest movie, *The Virginian*, and that they were excited by the prospect of seeing their first "talkie," although as Effie was convinced that the movie industry was corrupting the youth of America it is highly unlikely that they ever did. "The movie shows have been a school to educate our boys and girls in crime down to the finest point," she announced. "There is nothing vicious or vile that they won't throw on the screen; the hold-up, safe crackers, bank robbers, murderers, the immoral vamp ... all given in the most thrilling, blood curdling, vicious, vice-enticing form to lure and tempt the one who goes and sees them."[34]

Almost a decade later, shortly after Hattie Caraway of Arkansas became the first woman to win election to the Senate, Effie revisited her threat to run for office. Always a keen promoter of women's rights, she told reporters that

I would do more than just collect my salary. I believe that woman has been degraded by nudity on the stage today. I'd clean up all the filthy literature and periodicals on news stands and do my best to stop this needless nudity in today's theatrical world. It is woman's place to wage war against sin which has infested us for so long. She has been pulled down terribly. Men will not fight for her any more. It is the women of the nation who should band together to make this world a sane and clean place to live in.[35]

13

On the Comeback Trail (Again)

If times had been hard in the past, things now grew steadily worse. With little income from the bakery, the farm fully signed over to Ella, and the Great Depression tightening its grip on the United States (and across the Western world), Addie and Effie would be obliged to take whatever work came their way, no matter how menial or beneath them. Luckily for them America seemed to be nostalgic for an earlier, simpler age: radio shows and Hollywood movies were exploiting the fascination with all things late-Victorian, choruses of parasol-twirling Floradora girls were a hit once more, and 90s-themed night clubs were doing good business in many major cities.

On 4 February 1930, the Sisters appeared in what, to them, must have seemed the absolute nadir of their performing career. On the stage of the R.K.O. Theater in Cedar Rapids, they took part in a radio broadcast hosted by station WBBM Chicago, but broadcast by local station KWCR. Billed as "The Nutty Club," in October the respected orchestra leader Paul Whiteman would take over as host, but for now the Sisters had to share a platform with famed female impersonator Francis Renault (known as the "slave of fashion"), tramp musician Dixie Bill and others. As if being billed as comic stooge to a man who had made his name impersonating Lillian Russell was not bad enough, KWCR would later amalgamate with WJAM, the broadcaster that Effie blamed for forcing them to call time on their bakery, and become WMT. Effie was sixty-two, Addie a few months past seventy. At a time when most women of their age should have been enjoying a quiet retirement, the Cherry Sisters were still trotting out their moralizing essays and dragging some poor innocent out of the crowd to play stooge during "The Gypsy's Warning."

Although they were not performing as much as they would have liked, or that the mounting bills necessitated, Effie continued to write for the act. In September 1930 she approached Richard J. Madden, an agent and partner in the American Play Company, asking him for his help in staging a play which think will be a great box office winner. I have it all arranged in play form. I think I have it arranged all right. Now, will you please let me know what percent one gets over ten thousand receipts per week, and if they get a cash bonus beside the royalty? I would not say this but with my reputation and the beauty of the play I have written it will be the greatest drama.... I write you because I would not want to trust any producer with my play.[1]

It is more than likely that this was another attempt to get "Nobody's Child" to the stage. Madden declined to take her up on her offer, but in November Effie registered copyright of the play, now titled "Nobody's Child, or the Gypsy's Waif, a Play in Five Acts." More than six years' previously, in March 1924, New York producer Henry Wilson Savage had approached Effie to discuss staging the play, but he was only interested in doing so if she would star in the title role. As Effie's sight was set firmly on the role of mayor of Cedar Rapids at the time she declined his offer, but copyrighting her work now was a sure sign that she expected other theater folk to be interested in the play too. Like all of her unpublished melodramas, "Nobody's Child" was centered around a poor girl lost in the world, only this time the titular waif would eventually discover that she was from aristocratic stock, and her fortune would be restored when she found true love. Each one of Effie's attempts at a novel (or, in this particular case, a play) was little more than a naïve retelling of the Cinderella story, a fairy tale with more than a nod to the Cherrys own dirt-poor upbringing and their aspirations to a life of nobility. They all featured characters clearly based on the five sisters themselves, and all harked back to the tale they had heard their father tell, of the dashing gardener who eloped with the Earl's daughter. And, like all of her other unpublished works, "Nobody's Child" was not very good.

Sporadic offers of work did come their way, but they were few and far between. Every time they appeared before the footlights it was billed as an attempt at a comeback, however the Sisters balked at any suggestion that they had ever retired. "Our careers aren't complete," Effie told a reporter from the *Des Moines Register* when he came to visit them at their home. "The best people will still come to see us, and will pack any house we play in. They know better than to believe the newspapers that say we are ninety, and that we are worn out from dodging vegetables from behind nets!"[2] She also revealed that she was continuing to work on their biography: "Right now I am writing our life histories. We won't say when or how we are going to publish it, but when it comes out you can wager that a bunch of editors will duck for cover. They have slandered us since we were little girls—little orphans making our start on the stage!" Effie, as always, was happy to give her opinion on everything from the current state of the American stage (acts were "twenty thousand times worse today ... worse than burlesque"), to the cause of the Depression ("there are a good many causes, but I believe that the automobile is the worse. All the money the government spends on roads"[3]). Even though they had told a number of reporters from different publications that the bakery had long ceased trading, they were, in fact, still operating: in January she told reporters that "we only do a small business and it hasn't been affected"[4] by the Depression, and a front page story in the *Cedar Rapids Evening Gazette and Republican* of 13 May 1931 told the tale of poor JayVee, a ten year-old boy helping out his desperate family by working for the Sisters. JayVee had been offered the chance to go to camp, but the youngster turned it down. "I deliver bread for the Cherry sisters and I get ten cents a day for it," revealed the boy, whose father had been out of work for over a year, another victim of the Depression. "I don't think we could afford to lose that money at home."[5]

Whenever the Sisters did find work and were taken away from Cedar Rapids, Lizzie would move in to their home on Third Avenue, allowing herself a respite from the increasingly cantankerous Ella, operating the bakery and also looking after the occasional paying boarder. Lizzie was now well in to her seventies, and working in the bakery was becoming too much for her alone. However she continued to keep horses and cows, and—as it ever was—she continually got in to trouble with her neighbors over her inability to recognize boundaries, or to maintain fences and gates. The Reverend F.J. Zavodsky, pastor of the John Huss Methodist Episcopal Church in Chicago, owned the forty acres that joined the eastern boundary of the Cherry Family farm and his tenants were, like the majority of Cherry neighbors before them, constantly battling with Ella and Lizzie over broken fences, gates left open and cows roaming over their land unaccompanied and unwanted. Lizzie bought corn from the good Reverend (through his tenants, the Jepharts), and he in turn allowed her to graze her cattle on the corn stalks left behind, just as the Roschers had done almost three decades earlier. Lizzie regularly complained to the Reverend Zavodsky that she had been conned by the Jephart boys, but in one of his letters to her the good Reverend made it clear that he had the measure of her:

> You write that there were only 24 1/2 bushels of corn according to your measuring, and 35 according to the older boy of my tenant's measuring. In a letter I have just received from Mrs. Jephart she writes that the boy measured *51 bushels*. There is a big discrepancy between your figure and the boy's. You must treat me square! I take the word of the boy. You must pay for 51 bushels! Mrs. Jephart also writes that you let your cows roam all over the fields, that they come even to the house. You must not let your cows to bother my tenants. Mrs. Jephart also writes that you have opened the fence in several places to permit your cows to enter on to my land. You must put up the fence in those places at once. I cannot allow that. I have treated you fair and square and I want you to do the same to me.[6]

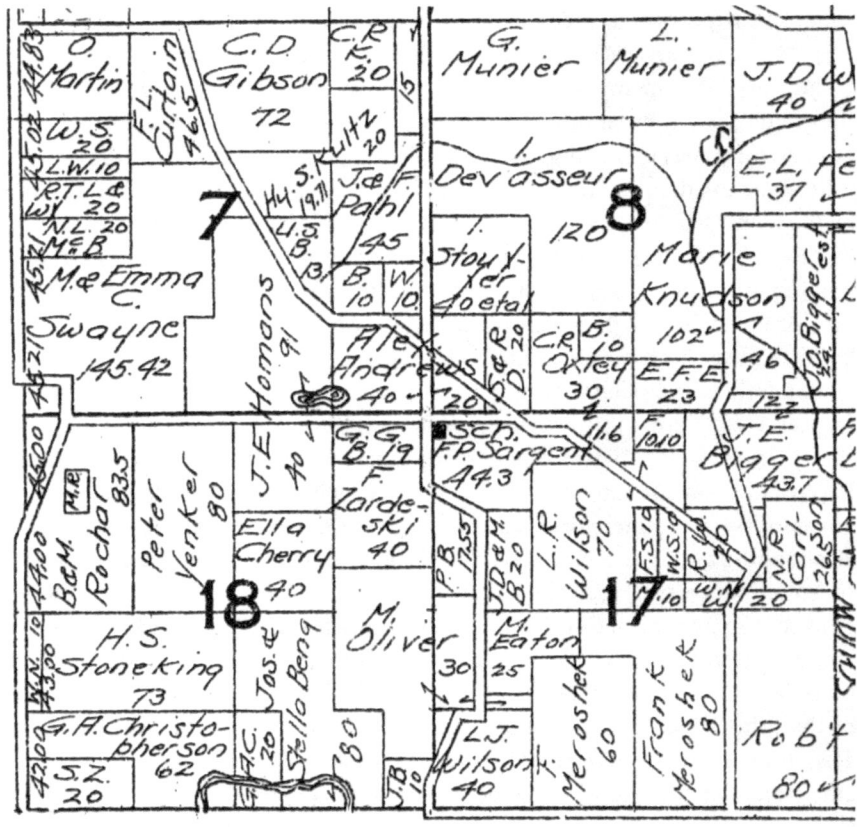

Map showing the Cherry farm, as well as those of their neighbors Peter Yonkers, Ben Roscher and the Reverend Zavodsky.

Effie was adamant that she knew why they were struggling to find work. "Business in the theater is falling off because the managers will not play classical things any more. It isn't so much that the public taste has changed as that the manager's taste has changed. Everything one sees on the stage now is like a Bowery act—sort of rough and crude. Now a good clean Bowery act is all right in its place but managers shouldn't attempt to make whole bills up out of such stuff."[7] Reports appeared in several newspapers stating that the Sisters were running an osteopathic school in Cedar Rapids,[8] but if that were the case they did not stay there long, and dire financial straits, rather than a burning desire to reclaim their crowns as the queens of comedy, necessitated their 1933 tour. "They were so crude," their one-time neighbor M.F. Franchere, a musician whose family owned the biggest retail store in Cedar

13. On the Comeback Trail (Again)

Rapids, revealed. "Their act was a real riot of ridicule. Putting up a screen helped draw the crowds, and the Cherry Sisters' fame spread. They made a lot of money but their managers got practically all of it."[9]

If the changing tastes of the public were not enough, the Depression had hit the Sisters hard too. By the end of 1932 any money that Addie and Effie had managed to salt away had gone, quite possibly lost in the stock market and banking crashes that had recently crippled America's financial institutions. With no money to pay their bills, a lien was put on their household furnishings by their landlord, Walter M. Krebs, for $160 for four months' unpaid rent on the house and bakery. Even if Lizzie had been involved financially with the business, she was unwilling or unable to help out, and this time it fell to the two youngest sisters to clear the debt. Naturally the proud women would deny that they were facing money troubles, but they had indeed been forced to sell pretty much everything they had to pay the bill. The bakery was gone, and Addie and Effie moved to three sparsely furnished rented rooms at 323 Third Avenue South West, no more than a stone's throw away from where they had once operated their successful store. Within a year they would move again, to 620 Seventh Street.

One small bright spark illuminated these dark hours when producer and screenwriter Lou Brock, then head of the short subjects department at R.K.O. Radio Pictures, approached the Sisters to enquire if they would be interested in coming to work for him. Like many other lifelines thrown their way over their career, this tempting offer came to nothing. The company was embarking on a series of musical two-reelers, entitled "Broadway Headliners," and had the Sisters taken up his offer they would have been starring alongside names such as W.C. Fields, Ruth Etting, Betty Grable, and Phil Harris. Yet despite their own experiences in screening moving pictures, and their promise to Gary Cooper that they would go and see him on the big screen, Effie was wary of the medium. "I for one will not go to a show or movie that is not clean, refined and strictly moral if I know it," she wrote in her unpublished autobiography. "For when I leave the theater after a show I want to know that I have heard and seen something praiseworthy, and not feel as though I have been down in the slums and mire and filth to see and hear some debauched, sin stained creature, drunk with vice, reel of a string of profanity and smut, and in the scantiest of clothing do a dance of the underworld." It is doubtful that the pair would have ever worked with Brock, as he was known to be a difficult man to get on with. Although he famously brought Fred Astaire and Ginger Rogers together, and would score several huge hits for R.K.O., he ended up out on his ear after his 1934 movie "Down To Their Last Yacht" flopped. He spent his last days working as the night porter of a hotel in Hollywood.

Reported disparagingly in the press as being "another farewell tour," the Sisters insisted that this was not, in fact, the case, telling anyone who would listen that "we've never really been off the stage." Throughout the 1933 tour Addie and Effie provided the bizarre interlude in the type of saucy burlesque show that the sisters had spent their lives railing against. Hideously out of place, and sandwiched in between acts featuring scantily clad young women and their lecherous comic foils, the Sisters' spot opened with Effie performing her own song "Before and After" as she "marched back and forth across the stage with long strides, clapping her hands. She blithely ignored hoots and catcalls. She held her own competently too, against the orchestra: by neglecting the tune a little she made her voice clearly audible above the accompaniment, and she finished two beats ahead of it."[10] Effie strode off stage and Addie entered, to give their timeworn essay on "The Modern Young Man." Effie (now in full male drag) would return for "She Was My Sister," and for the finale, Addie joined her sister for a rendition of "Eulogy on the Cherry Sisters." Unsurprisingly many of these appearances were accompanied by heckles and Bronx cheers from the audience, although few if any of the paying customers launched produce at the infamous Vegetable Twins. "We knew we were going to play in a burlesque house," Effie explained, "but we didn't know it would be the way it was. Some of the girls go out there on the stage with hardly anything on. And those swear words the comedians say? I hope we never get mixed up in anything like this again."

If life was treating Addie and Effie badly, their lot was nothing compared to that of their two sisters. Ella was nearly eighty years old, and Lizzie just three years younger. Both ladies were frail and Ella was incapable of looking after the farm on her own. The Depression devastated farming in the United States; prices for their crops had fallen so low that many farmers were going bankrupt and losing their homes. Some farming families were burning corn in their stoves because corn was cheaper than coal. Luckily Ella and Lizzie had an endless supply of wood, but even then it had become impossible for them to keep up with the incessant repairs, and the two women had moved in to the basement of the house, the same rooms that they had helped their father dig out beneath their wooden home when they were in their teens. The rooms were poorly ventilated and often smoky. On Christmas Day 1933 Lizzie wrote a barely intelligible letter to Addie and Effie, making light of their plight: "We are well except coughs. Ella says she has got the flu well that is nothing she always says she has got it she is to careless she can't help but catch cold. [sic] Ella does not do much of anything except sit in the old basement. Taxes are not payed.... I have not got many chickens to sell this winter [but] if it doesn't cost too much to send I will send you a chicken."[11]

By February 1934 the conditions that they were living in had attracted the interest of the local authorities, and while Addie and Effie were playing small venues in the East (and Effie was knocking on the doors of publishers in Chicago in a vain attempt to get her novels and play published), both Ella and Lizzie were removed from the dilapidated building and hospitalized. In the last interview Lizzie gave before the sisters were removed, she scolded her two youngest sisters, confiding in *Cedar Rapids Tribune* reporter Ernest Nickel that she had "asked them to quit the stage a hundred times, but that's the only business they know so they always go back ... they just can't stay away from the business."[12] After a short stay in St. Luke's Hospital the two women where transferred to the Linn County Home where, on 12 March 1934, Ella passed away. Her funeral—which, for a woman who seemed to care little about anyone outside of her own family, was surprisingly well attended—was held three days later at the Yocom Chapel, and her remains were interred in Oak Shade cemetery. Keeping up the time-honored tradition of misreporting and misrepresenting them, several newspapers (including the *Mason City Globe* and *The Statesman* in Salem, Oregon) informed its readers that Effie was the Cherry who had fallen from the branch.

Sister Lizzie paid for the funeral, selling three cows to settle the $105 bill for the service and burial. The cost included $5 for the dress Ella was buried in. Addie and Effie made it home from Chicago in time for the internment. Once the funeral was over Lizzie, exhibiting the infamous Cherry streak of stubbornness, demanded that she be allowed to return to the family home. Not that there was much of a home to return to.

In an effort to reclaim a little family dignity, Effie penned a short piece—"A Brief Sketch of the Life and Death of Ella Francis Cherry, Pioneer of Linn County"—that she paid to have published in the *Cedar Rapids Gazette*. The article painted the eldest of the Cherry children as a well-educated landowner, and featured a few lines from a poem that Ella wrote when she was a pupil at the Marion High School:

> *I may travel o'er the mountains*
> *Or cross the burning sands*
> *I can face the raging tempest*
> *I have no fear of man*
> *My eyes are fixed on Jesus*
> *On the granite rock I stand*
> *No foe can ever harm me*
> *With this pebble in my hand.*[13]

The three remaining sisters were barely allowed chance to grieve before they were pulled in to court again. A.W. Gerhardt named the three as defendants in a district court suit, based on promissory notes given to him by Ella in March 1930, for an unpaid debt of $703.71, presumably either the outstanding mortgage on the family farm, or the amount still owed on the land Lizzie had signed over to her to avoid the avaricious Sophronia Grant.[14] To settle the debt the family plot was reduced from forty acres back to its original twenty. Gerhardt, who followed Ella in to the ground less than five months later, had form: in 1930 he had successfully driven the Willson family off their land after they ran up debts in excess of two thousand dollars. The Willson plot was sold from the steps of the same courthouse where, in times past, the Cherry Sisters had seen their own property dispatched, and where many other Depression-hit farmers had watched their livelihoods snatched away.

Addie and Effie found some comfort in rehashing "The Gypsy's Warning" for their home crowd on stage at the Iowa Theater picture house, between screenings of the Irene Dunne comedy *This Man Is Mine*, but within a few weeks they were playing a '90s-themed revival at the Montana Stockgrowers Association Jubilee in Miles City before heading back out on the road. Once again, their 1934 tour was heralded as a "come back," and once again Effie was ready to provide the newspapers with good copy, telling reporters that Sally Rand, the burlesque performer who danced with an ostrich feather fan and occasionally performed a balloon dance with a transparent bubble, "ought to be put in the jail house." Addie was equally dismissive of stage and screen star Mae West, a woman the Sisters felt embodied all that was wrong with the permissiveness of the age. "Why do people flock to see her?" she asked. "She isn't half as good as Sarah Bernhardt, or Lillian Russell."[15] Dressed in floor-length gowns, and looking like an aged drag act, at least they finally got to see the Chicago World's Fair. "We went out several times," Effie admitted, "and enjoyed all the shows and sights,"[16] although they refused to pose for photographs with a group of Oriental dancers. "None of that for us," declared Addie. "We always give a nice, refined act."[17]

This time around, pianist Carl Whyte accompanied the Sisters. Although only in his 30s, Whyte was an experienced performer who had played piano for a number of other acts, and as well as accompanying the sisters he also handled any managerial responsibilities. A huckster who claimed to have approached the organizing committee of London's annual Royal Command Performance in the hope that the Sisters might play there, among the many venue operators he approached, Whyte contacted Bill Hardy, the owner of the a nightclub known as the Gay Nineties in New York. The former speakeasy, now gone legitimate and respectable, seemed like the perfect place for the Sisters to resurrect their act and, according to his own testimony, Whyte's hard work on their behalf saved them from the poor house. "Effie

13. On the Comeback Trail (Again)

and Addie were broke, and evicted from the house they lived in.... I loaned them money on several occasions. I determined to help them and I wrote by hand to every theater, nightclub, burlesque show and county fair in the U.S. to try and book them. Every smart manager said I was crazy.... I never got back any of the loans I made them when I first met them. I kept only enough money from the act to pay my expenses and gave them the rest of it. I got them as high as $150 a week in the heights of the depression."[18]

Even if they had enjoyed the Fair, it was still a miserable time for the three remaining Cherry sisters. Addie and Effie were seeing little financial return for their efforts, and they hated the fact that Whyte was openly promoting them as the World's Worst Vaudeville Act. Their relationship with Whyte was strained (it was widely reported that they refused to speak to him for a week after they heard him cussing), and when one theater put out a sign which trumpeted that the Cherrys were "the Worst Act In the World," a furious Effie made the manager cross out the word "worst" before she would set foot on the stage—not caring one jot that the phrase "the Act In the World" made no sense whatsoever.

In September 1934, in what seemed little more than a pathetic publicity stunt, Whyte announced to the press that he had asked Effie to marry him. "She won't say yes and she won't say no, but I can tell you she doesn't want to let me out of her sight for a second."[19] Hardy brought the sisters to his club in October 1935, but Addie and Effie's show at the Gay Nineties was wretched. Old favorites such as "An Event That Happened in the City of Chicago," and Effie's song "The Railroad Boys" got another outing, and Effie insisted on giving a temperance lecture, despite the club's patrons happily imbibing alcohol, but although the celebrities in their audience—including actress Tallulah Bankhead and zany comedian Gracie Allen—were once again in tears, only this time the tears were borne out of pity and embarrassment rather than laughter. "Please be gentle," the club's M.C. implored. "After all, they are but two little girls trying to get along in the world."

While Addie and Effie were suffering the indignity of recycling their act for indifferent night club patrons and, worse still, appearing in casts that also included former members of the hated Mae West's troupe, poor Lizzie was becoming more and more frail. In a letter they sent her while playing Covington, Kentucky, Addie and Effie wrote about their own money worries: "They don't pay very large salarys so we half to go to quite a few places to get a little. We get more here than any of the other places have paid us, but the railroad fair was quite a bit—twelve dollars apiece but they advanced it but will take it out of our salary. If we get two or three more places I think we can get along all right [sic]."[20] In the same letter, the Sisters told Lizzie

Addie and Effie pictured to promote their appearance at the Gay Nineties (author's collection).

that, once they were more established, they would send her the money to come and join them: "You had better get a place for your cows, for if we get our own show, and I feel sure we will, you will half to be with us [*sic*]." But Lizzie was in no state to join them on stage, and Addie and Effie were either unaware of how desperately ill their only remaining sister was, or they were simply trying to comfort her. Lizzie did not answer the letter. Just before Christmas, while residing at the St. Regis Hotel in Chicago, Effie wrote to a friend in Marion, Gertrude Berry. She told Gertie that they were struggling to make ends meet, writing that "we are not playing, so Addie and I have not got much to do this week, but think we will have work in a few days.... I hope so for we want to be kept at work," and she confided in her how worried she and Addie were for the health of their older sister:

> We wanted to come home and help Lizzie get the paper on her little house, and her heater stove also. I hope she has got someone to do it for her. We worry about Lizzie. We did not want her to stay out there alone this winter. We told her to rent a little room in Marion till we come home, but she is afraid some one will come out and brake [sic] in her house and steal all of her things and do lots of damage to the place. Maybe they would the world is getting pretty wicked not much goodness in it anymore, isn't that so Gertie? Lizzie says she has hard work to get her groceries and things she needs from Marion. I am sure she ought to find a neighbor out there that she could hire to bring out the paper for her house and some groceries.[21]

In January 1936, with the last of her family apparently stranded while touring Missouri and Illinois, Lizzie wrote to Addie and Effie to tell them that "my hands are numb, my feet are numb, I can hardly light the fire." She continued to live in the basement on her own, but at the beginning of February, frail and unable to look after herself, Lizzie was evicted by order of the sheriff's office, and the farm that the Sisters had tried so hard and for so long to cling on to was finally taken away from them. Destitute, she was taken in to care and placed in the Linn County Home, too weak to answer a recent letter from her sisters. The steward of the home, Mrs. I.E. Isham, wrote to Addie and Effie on her behalf. "I read the letter to her and she read the letter also. She was very glad to hear from you, she said she knew now you wouldn't worry about her, that she was where it was warm and [there was] plenty to eat. We are sure having a blizzard this morning.... I am glad Lizzie is with us, for she is in the warm house; it is hard to tell if she would be able to get to town for groceries, and wood could be hard to get. Lizzie seems quite contented. She told us this morning she was glad to be here."[22] Help could not have arrived for Lizzie a moment too soon: on the morning Mrs. Isham wrote to the Sisters the weather in Marion was twelve degrees below zero "and getting colder." Had Lizzie remained on the farm she would surely have fallen victim to hypothermia.

Even if her sisters had had money, there was little they could do to help her. They had traveled to St. Louis on the promise of star billing at the Garrick Theater, but when they arrived there found that the Garrick, a burlesque house, had already planned a two-and-a-half-hour spectacular called "Girls from the Follies." Addie and Effie were shoehorned on to a bill that featured a hodge-podge of comedians, exotic dancers, male and female choruses and other vaudeville acts, but their staid old stories did not fit well, the appalling weather kept the audience away, and they soon left the company. Stuck in St. Louis with no money to get home, Vera Barlow, manageress of the Bowery Music Hall and Bar, took pity on the old timers and signed them for a week, which she later extended. They were to appear, four times nightly, alongside "two singing waitresses, a three-piece negro orchestra and a comedian with a red nose."[23] Their act was short, reprising the same fifteen minute set they had used in the burlesque houses three years previously: if they were called on to perform an encore, an extra verse of "Eulogy on the Cherry Sisters" would usually suffice.

On 24 February the pair composed a letter to Lizzie and told her that "We are going to stay another week where we are which will make three weeks, for it was such bad weather here that we could not get any other place as the theaters were all empty as they said the St. Louis people will not get out when the weather is bad." By the time they wrote to the ailing Lizzie, things were certainly picking up; the small club they were playing in St, Louis was, by their own admission, turning people away at the door, and the owner increased their salary once she realized that they could still draw them in. Thanks to this slight upturn in their fortunes, the Sisters were able to send Lizzie regular care packages and the occasional small amount of money. "We sent you one dollar in a letter and sent you a package with some medicine in for your stomach.... Now Lizzie, don't get lonesome whatever you do, of course that will take away your appetite and make you sick. Now make the best of it and take care of yourself for you have got to take care of your health." In the same letter they held out an olive branch to their sickly sister:

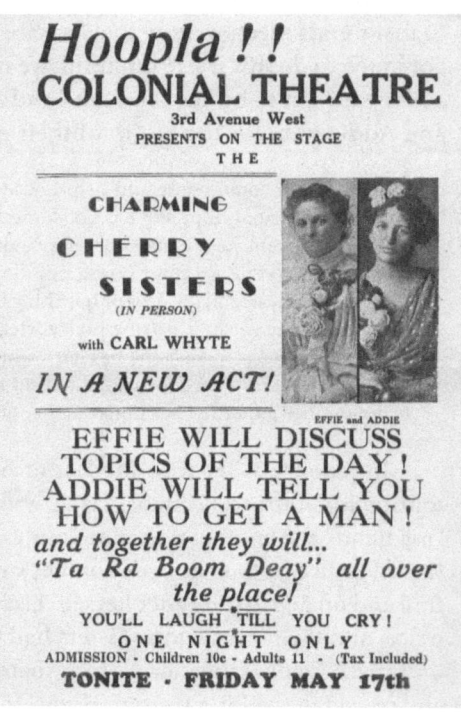

Handbill promoting the Cherry Sisters at the Colonial Theatre, Cedar Rapids, 17 May 1935 (courtesy Marion Historical Society, Iowa).

> An old showman came to see the show and when he saw the crowds he came over to see us, says he will give us $100 per week for the two of us. We are going to ask him if he will give us $150 per week if you are with us, for if we take his offer you have got to go along. Am not going to leave you alone any more, for we see they are bound to kidnap you Lizzie, ha ha! We want you with us and you have got to be with us, and it will be a good thing for you.[24]

Lizzie had just turned seventy-nine: even if she had been in vigorous health it is hard to believe that audiences would have accepted her as the callow young girl in "The Gypsy's Warning." But these letters did much to bolster her spirits, and when they wrote that "a lady who talks on the radio every day," who "always talks to the noted people of the world," had interviewed them and that "her speech was perfectly wonderful and she spoke so high of us,"[25] she must have been fortified by the renewed interest in her Sisters' career. The Sisters were indeed attracting a great deal of attention: "Effie and Addie, the famous Cherry Sisters of Broadway ... are beginning to draw good audiences at the Bowery Music Hall. Many of the neighbors were skeptical when the Cherrys were announced as performers at the Sixth street drum, but the girls' identity seems to have been definitely established. Magazine editors, feature writers and representatives of news services are clamoring for stories about this odd pair, and they're now getting the consideration they believe they deserve."[26] Staying in St. Louis must have been a difficult decision for Addie and Effie to make, but there was money to be made and opinions to be shared. "It was so nice back in the old days," Effie told a reporter from the *St. Louis Star and Times*, "Now it's all burlesque. And the performers are such amateurs!"[27] Effie also told anyone who would listen that she had not given up on her political ambitions, and was again considering running for the Senate.

Even with the difficulties between them in the past, and this sudden burst of interest in their act, it must have been devastating for the Sisters not to be able to be back in Iowa, comforting their last living relative. Addie and Effie wrote almost daily, explaining that they wanted to get home but they had bills to pay and a few more weeks on tour would sort them out. On 28 March Addie wrote a heartbreaking letter to Lizzie, care of the Home: "I know that you will be dispointed that we did not come home from Peoria Ill., but we did not have money enough. I thought he would keep us another week, as we done him the biggest business he ever done." [sic] She added that, "as we had to lay off we can't come home for a week or two. Now Lizzie be good to yourself and maybe we can take you right out on the farm when we come."[28] The following week their farewell tour limped on to Indianapolis. Lizzie Cherry would never see the family farm again.

14

The End

Lizzie died on 11 May 1936. She was seventy-nine, although the *Cedar Rapids Gazette* and many other newspapers erroneously told their readers that she was only sixty-seven. Weak from scratching out a living in the damp, leaking shack she and the rest of her family had once called home, she succumbed to pneumonia and spent her last ten days in hospital in Cedar Rapids. Luckily Addie and Effie managed to make it back to Iowa before their sister passed away, although their return to Cedar Rapids was just as much due to the lack of dates in Illinois as to their desire to be near Lizzie in her final hours.

Lizzie's funeral was held the following day at the Yocom Chapel in Marion: the Reverend Lamont Smith, of the Methodist church at Springfield, officiated. She was buried next to Ella, in Oak Shade Cemetery. Some time after she passed, Effie penned a tribute to her sister:

> *While we are with you in the way,*
> *As on thru' life's short span we go;*
> *It's then I need your loving smile*
> *And gentle words, they cheer me so.*
> *But when I've left this earthly realm*
> *To join the angels on that shore,*
> *Your gentle words and loving smile*
> *I do not need them any more.*
> *Then bring your roses, red and white,*
> *And scatter them above my tomb;*
> *Their blossoms bring sweet blessings bright,*
> *Their fragrance chases out the gloom.*
> *For flowers are emblems of our dead,*
> *Envy them not, these tokens fair.*
> *So bring your flowers, red and white,*
> *And let their fragrance fill the air.*[1]

Reports claimed that Addie and Effie were still living on the family farm in Marion, and the pair told a reporter from the *Gazette* that they were so keen on keeping up the old place and protecting it from vandals that they would be limiting their stage work to the occasional week here and there.² But, like so much of their story, the truth was far more mundane: after Lizzie's death the land that she and Ella had once owned was divided up still further, with sixteen of the twenty acres Lizzie had purchased (and that she had later transferred to Ella) going to Herman Pieper, in lieu of debts. Addie and Effie were now the titleholders of the land, and the tumbledown shack, that their parents had raised them on, as well as four further acres left over from Lizzie's plot. However they had no intention of taking up residence there, and instead continued to live in cheaply rented rooms in Cedar Rapids, venturing in to the city occasionally to pick up their mail or, in late November, to watch the annual Christmas parade.

Addie and Effie on stage at the end of their career (author's collection).

With Lizzie gone, only Addie and Effie remained to carry on the Cherry name. They managed to channel the quarrelsome spirit of their late sister, taking Pieper to court to challenge him over exactly whose acreage was whose, and who—Pieper or the Sisters—had the right to cut down and haul off timber from the land. The case continued for almost two years, but the court finally found in favor of the Cherrys, and they were awarded $136 from Pieper for the wood he had helped himself to. While the pair were preoccupied with logging rights, another act, the "Cherry Sisters, famous hoola dancers,"³ were playing roadhouses in Wisconsin. Addie and Effie would have been mortified had they known bout their vulgar act, but Violet, Pansy and Daisy Cherry soon went the way of all other pretenders to the original Sisters' crown.

Imperious but increasingly weak, the two vowed to carry on. At the

WHO Barn Dance Frolic in Des Moines on 12 December 1936, the Sisters once again performed for the radio. 2,500 people were present to hear the pair go through their routine, and countless thousands more would have heard them over the air. As they waited in the wings of the Shrine Auditorium for their allotted twelve minutes in front of the microphone, Effie was heard to reason that "you're good if they come back. And they've always come back to see us."[4] As they walked to the microphone Effie stuck out her jaw, defiantly, but Addie seemed frail and unsteady. Their voices were thin and the pianist employed to accompany them struggled to do so. At the annual banquet held to honor the work of local Rotarian societies the Sisters received polite applause as they reprised their inter-act turn during a staging of "The Drunkard."

In early April 1938 the two sisters made their final appearance on a stage in their hometown, when they played for four nights at the Strand Theater (which had formerly been known as the Olympic but which now, like so many of the buildings the sisters would have recognized, has been demolished) in Cedar Rapids. This would be the last time that a paying audience would get to see Addie and Effie perform, and capacity crowds greeted the Sisters. In her unpublished biography of the Cherry Sisters, *The Queens of Corn*, author Winifred van Etten wrote that "Addie, old and heavy, had to be helped onto the stage." When they shambled away from the footlights for a final time the Sisters had been performing for more than 45 years. "The Cherry Sisters were a novelty act whose time had past," says theater historian Cezar Del Valle, however in New York, the scene of their biggest success, yet another act was trading on the Cherry Sisters' name, appearing with Gruberg's Carnival as it toured the state for the summer.

Fashion had never troubled the Sisters, and they could often be seen walking near their home, dressed in the same style of clothes they had always worn, with their dresses (accompanied by several underskirts) brushing along the ground as they went

An ad for the Sisters' final performance, at the Strand, Cedar Rapids, 1936.

on their way. Decades earlier local children would have taunted them, and would sing "Cherries ripe and Cherries sweet, you can tell a Cherry by her feet," while being careful not to catch a whack from a riding crop, but now people were much more respectful towards the eccentric-looking pair. Although they had ceased performing, newspapers were still keen to solicit their views on everything from sex to swing. "Why, it ain't even music," Effie told one reporter. "This swing music is the ruination of radio and the movies. It's just crazy stuff. You can have this crazy swing stuff. We'll keep on giving our Gypsy skit, along with our songs and patter."[5] The two sisters had a reputation for being self-contained, and when Addie was knocked down by a truck as the pair of them crossed the road near their home (they were boarding together at 1330, First Avenue North East) she got up, dusted herself down and carried on her way, refusing all offers of help. Times were hard though, and eventually they had to move to smaller, cheaper rooms and both Addie and Effie had to swallow their pride and ask for financial assistance: Effie was issued with a certificate for Old Age Assistance on 1 April 1939, receiving $23 a month from the State. Although no such certificate exists for Addie (Lizzie had also received Old Age Assistance, at a rate of $15 a month, for the last few months of her life), it is safe to assume that both sisters would have been reluctantly accepting help.

On 25 October 1942, at the age of 83, Addie Roselma Cherry died in hospital in Cedar Rapids. She had been ill for just five days. Her funeral took place three days later, and she was buried in the Murdoch-Linwood Cemetery. Effie, who herself had been unwell for some time, was destroyed. The deaths of her other sisters had crushed her, but it was the passing of Addie, her lifelong companion, her partner in crime, her staunchest ally, that was the hardest to bear. Addie's death broke Effie's heart: she went in to a steep decline, and was hospitalized almost immediately after the funeral. Effie remained in her bed at Cedar Rapids' Mercy Hospital (established in 1900 by the Roman Catholic order the Sisters of Mercy) for more than two months.

Frail but inexorable, Effie was still called upon to provide good copy for the newspapers. Interviewed from her hospital bed, she tried once more to lay to rest the old stories about the Sisters performing behind a screen. "It's a lie from beginning to end,"[6] she insisted. "People started that story out of jealously and now people believe it. Why, I never saw a screen in my life— except on a house." Many of the obituaries printed after Addie's death repeated the same scurrilous stories that had followed the Sisters around for their entire career, but the half page she was awarded in *Variety* was particularly acerbic, labeling the Sisters "the lousiest act on the vegetable circuit," and branding them "terrible" and a "mediocrity."[7] Effie was incandescent with rage. "The awful things they said about my darling Addie. Lies! All of them lies! I wouldn't have said such things about a dog!"[8] When a fan wrote to offer her condolences, Effie replied that "I have been very sick. The doctor thought I could never live but I have, though my heart is broken and it seems as though there is nothing to live for anymore. But we have to leave it all with God. His will be done."[9] On leaving hospital she returned to the rooms she had shared with Addie at 508 Fifth Avenue South East. Following the deaths of Ella and Lizzie, Effie had paid for respectful obituaries in the local paper, hoping to counter injurious slurs against the family name. Once Addie was gone she no longer cared what the public thought of the once-famous Cherry Sisters. Her final indignity was to be alone, the orphan she had always claimed to be. Yet although the press reported that she would soon follow her darling Addie, the woman who had appeared to be the most delicate of all the Cherry children continued to cling on to life.

But she could not live forever. Death came for the seemingly indefatigable Effie on 5 August 1944, just a few weeks short of her seventy-seventh birthday. In the spring of 1944 she had a fall that resulted in her receiving hospital treatment for a broken hip, an accident from which she never fully recovered. Frail and gaunt, and with a long history of poor health, she was admitted in to a nursing home just a few days before she took her final bow. Shortly before she suffered her fall, Effie wrote to Carl Whyte, telling him that "I have lost all my sisters. The last one was darling Addie. So far it has been hard for me to bear, but I know she will be with me all the time and that life will not be so lonely."[10]

Newspapers across the country were filled with obituaries, and many devoted full-page articles to the Sisters' story. Almost every one reported her age as sixty-five; even the date of birth on her tombstone was wrong, but then when she snapped "I ain't a-sayin,'" at anyone with the impudence to enquire of her real age what could be expected?

She was buried two days later in Cedar Rapids, the town she had called home for almost half a century. The Reverend Frank H. Ward, whose father had established the town's homeless shelter the Sunshine Mission at around the same time that the Cherry Sisters were starting their career on the stage, conducted a short service. Her funeral was held in the Beatty Chapel, but only a dozen or so elderly women were there to hear the Reverend Ward's words. She was laid to rest next to her adored—and adoring—Addie. Effie's dying wish was that her unpublished biography of her family would finally see print, and that the money raised would pay for suitable grave markers for her and her sisters.[11] Unhappily this would not happen, but with her passing being covered in depth by the local, national and even international press, no doubt she would have been thrilled to have been making headlines one last time. It is doubtful, though, that she would have been happy with the number of articles that, yet again, regurgitated the disputed story of their performing behind a screen ... and that Oscar Hammerstein paid them $1000 a week for the privilege.

Jim Healey, writing in the *Albany Times Union* just 10 days after her death quoted Effie as once having stated that "it is very difficult for one to deliberately act badly. The world is full of people who can act smart. But it takes an awfully smart person to act dumb and naive."[12] Had the joke been on the audience all along? Were Effie and her sisters fully aware of their limitations, and had they hoodwinked the public for almost half a century? "The Cherry Sisters were just good businesswomen," Healey concluded. "They wanted to make money, not careers." The quote is unsubstantiated, but as far back as 1907 the Sisters had suggested that they were conscious of their act being considered ridiculous. The inference is that the sisters were most definitely aware of the reason for their infamy, and that they must have exploited it. Like the similarly untalented Florence Foster Jenkins, the Sisters studiously kept any and all newspaper reports that mentioned them. There can be no doubt that, for the bulk of their career, they knew exactly who was fooling who although, as one editorial put it, "If they were consciously so bad as to become good enough to cash in on it, there is no record of their ever having admitted it."[13] Maybe Effie Cherry had the last laugh after all.

"What I find interesting about the Cherry Sisters is that they entered show business folklore," says Cezar Del Valle. "There were comedians making joke references to the sisters who could never have seen them perform. Mae West never did." Back in 1933 Mae West, an artist who exemplified the permissiveness that the sisters had fought against, poked fun at them in her movie *She Done Him Wrong* (two years later the Sisters would be on the receiving end of another joke in the Rudy Vallee movie *Sweet Music*). Now Bob Downing, stage manager for West's play *Catherine Was Great*, came to their defense:

> I remember them as aging ladies who walked the streets of Cedar Rapids, proudly attired in the fading wardrobe of their heyday. I remember Effie's campaign for the office of Mayor; the biting speeches she delivered in local theaters, condemning the immorality of the younger generation.... However, with Effie passes the final opportunity for stage historians to learn the Sisters' reaction to audiences' reception of their act down the years. Even their neighbors could not learn if the Cherries realized their limitations, and were shrewd enough to capitalize their fame as "the world's worst act," or if they truthfully believed they were variety artists comparable to the great entertainers of their day. Surely no personalities of our stage have endured a more prolonged barrage of catcalls, vegetables and mob derision than the Cherries—with the curious

result that they will be remembered long after many of their more talented contemporaries. All printed reports to the contrary, I wish to deny that the Cherry Sisters ever appeared behind a net. They would have considered such protection as an insult to their agility as dodgers; an affected barrier between themselves and the public they believed they served.[14]

Carl Owen, Ella's friend and one of people responsible for helping to launch the Sisters on to the world's stage, summed up the family quite succinctly: "The Cherry Sisters always felt they were different from everyone else. All their life they thought they knew everything. All that time they were so terribly green."[15]

15

Aftermath

In December 1944, with Effie cold in the ground and no longer able to complain about they way in which she and her sisters were represented in print, *Coronet* magazine published Avery Hale's tongue in cheek article "So Bad They Were Good." "By any standard of criticism, the Cherry Sisters were the worst actresses in the history of the American theater," Hale wrote. "But they made their singular lack of ability pay off handsomely. Old-timers who saw them in their prime are of the opinion that not a single one of the five had a single saving grace. Their voices were twangy and irritating; they were personally ungainly and their choice of apparel was a modiste's nightmare."[1] Quoted from liberally ever since, Hale's account quickly became accepted as an accurate history of the Cherry Sisters.

With no family to claim their meager possessions, Cedar Rapids–like musician, conductor and theater manager Orville Rennie rescued Effie's effects from ending up on a bonfire. Rennie who (according to Carl Whyte) had been employed by Effie in December 1943 to help organize her papers, settled her outstanding bills for the privilege of carting away a trunk containing her unpublished writings—including her three novels, her play, the short biography she had been working on, and several of her mayoral speeches—as well as letters, diaries, scrapbooks, costumes and playbills belonging to the five Cherry Sisters. Mrs. E.V. Fuller, Effie's landlord, was happy to be rid of them, although she made Rennie promise that if he made any money from them then he had to provide Addie and Effie with a memorial befitting their status as queens of the stage.

Rennie was a fast worker. By January 1945 he already had a treatment ready for a film version of the Cherry Sisters story and had lined up meetings with several Hollywood producers—including 20th Century–Fox's Darryl F. Zanuck—who had shown interest in bringing the tale to the big screen.[2] Metro-Goldwyn-Mayer turned him down, as did Lou Levy, then manager of the successful singing act the Andrews Sisters: stage show producer Harry Gourfain approached Levy with an offer but wrote to tell Rennie that "truthfully I think the deal went cold because the Andrews Sisters are, in real life, even homlier than the Cherries."³ Three years later Zanuck was approached once more, this time by actor and producer George Jessel. Hollywood gossip columnist Louella Parsons was convinced that the film would go ahead, writing that "I have often wondered why someone didn't do the life of the Cherry Sisters on the screen.... I have no doubt [Jessel] can get Boss Zanuck to agree, for there are many popular song hits and many famous stage people who were prominent during the Cherry girls' career."⁴

This was not the first time that someone had attempted to bring the story of the Cherry Sisters to the big screen. Although the Sisters missed their chance to make a series of shorts for R.K.O., as early as 1938 actor and producer Louis Sobel had sold an original play, entitled "The Gay Nineties," to Jack L. Warner that, according to Ms. Parsons "covers a span of years and takes in the Lillian Russell period, the Spanish-American War, the Cherry Sisters, Eva Tanguay, 'Ziegfeld Follies,'" and more. The head of the mighty Warner Brothers Studios announced that he had Dick Powell, Humphrey Bogart and Olivia de Havilland lined up to appear in the film, and that Lloyd Bacon had been employed to direct, but sadly the film failed to get off the ground.⁵

When Orville Rennie's movie fell through Dixie Willson (author of *God Gave Me 20 Cents*, and whose brother Meredith Willson had composed the hit Broadway musical *The Music Man*) was commissioned to write a stage musical based on the Cherry Sisters' career. The musical would be produced by Murray Anderson in New York, and was to star singer Beatrice Kay, who had recently appeared in the movie *Billy Rose's Diamond Horseshoe*. Rennie and Willson's plans were thwarted somewhat by the Sisters' piano player Carl Whyte, who claimed that he—as the Cherrys' last manager—was "the only known heir" to the Sisters' legacy and that the biography, and any other material left by Effie, rightly belonged to him.⁶ Whyte, who had spent the years since the Cherrys' final performances working as a pianist in cocktail lounges, wrote an angry letter to Mrs. Fuller, Effie's former landlord, stating that the material belonged to him.

> You had the unmitigated gall to turn these things over to Orville Rennie and cut yourself in on the profits from them for stage and picture rights. Then you attempt to cover up your crime by saying you extracted a promise from Rennie to provide three headstones for the graves of the Cherry Sisters. In one of your letters to me last month you stated that you would never think of taking a penny of the money which came from the sale of Effie Cherry's biography etc. Three head stones' cost would have been a drop in the bucket compared to what the biography etc. would be worth, yet you knew it, as I wrote and told you the value of them. I saved the Cherry Sisters from having to resort to charity in their last years by my unending efforts for them—*and you knew*

it—and Effie Cherry realized it—that's why she arranged with her attorney to give me the first right to them. I would have erected monuments on their graves, instead of headstones.... *Who do you think you are anyway?* What you have done is a criminal offense, and if you don't straighten this out quick with Rennie I'm going to bring you in to court, and lady, it will be a pleasure to show you up for what a *hypocrite you are*.[7]

Whyte took his claims to the press. He asserted that not only had he been working on a movie script of his own based on the lives of the Sisters, but that he and Effie had been lovers, and they had planned to marry. Although she had easily been old enough to have been his mother, Whyte claimed to "have found something almost hypnotic about her." Their affair, he stated, began in 1938 and that he "might have married her, but Addie would have disowned her and that would have broken up their act. But I can tell you I was completely hypnotized by her charms, and her kisses took me completely out of this world."[8] If Whyte's story was true, then their affair was already under way at least four years earlier than he recalled. It had first been revealed in the press in 1934, however Effie made no mention of the romance in any of the documents she left behind, although she did open up about other romances she had enjoyed. "As far as admirers were concerned," she wrote, "I had plenty of them. One dry goods merchant of Cedar Rapids and also one dentist, one was a doctor and also two grocery merchants from a nearby town and a few actors, one farmer and one dairyman who was helping his father. I think this young man was the handsomest of all my young men friends, but they were all fine looking chaps.... Some of these young men have never married. They told me they would never marry when I refused them."[9]

Like much of Effie's writing, some of this smacks of fairytale: the spurned beau denying himself happiness because his first love refused him. An apocryphal story has a young man who came a-calling on the sisters being chased off the farm by the indignant women, his clothes in tatters, and early in their career Jessie candidly admitted that "We are man-haters."[10] Effie vehemently denied that was the case, telling reporters that "the idea probably originated from the fact that they did not go about making 'goo-goo' eyes at the men,"[11] although the sisters Cherry wanted it understood that "the reason none of them is married is that the more they have studied men and dogs the more they have liked dogs,"[12] and that "the man who loves horses, dogs and home is my idea of a real gentleman."[13] As five women who forever saw themselves in the roles of orphans or outcasts, the Cherrys were wary of men, as well they should have been when you consider how they were manipulated by an endless stream of male managers and agents. Whyte insisted that Effie had left him $25 cash in her will, along with copies of her unpublished novel "The

Blacksmith's Daughter," and her unfinished biography of the Cherry Sisters. He also asserted that Effie wrote to him and told him that "When Addie gives her consent we will marry and I sell the novels I have written and build us a castle, with a great big pond in front, filled with golden fish."[14] Was Whyte simply a chancer who thought he might be able to make a quick buck, or had he indeed been Effie's lover, and had Orville Rennie edited him out of their story by destroying any mention of him in the papers he now possessed? As Effie was still alive when romance between the two was first suggested, there is some potential credence to his claim, although the Cherrys were continually manipulating the press, and their own history. Whyte's assertion that he was the intended beneficiary of Effie's estate was made within days of her passing, first appearing in *Billboard* in August 1944, and were made long before he would have heard of any potential plans to earn money from her papers via the big screen.

Whyte was an unreliable chronicler of the Cherrys' story. One of his more outlandish assertions concerned the mystery surrounding their missing brother, Nathan Cherry. Whyte stated that he had been with his sisters when they had played their infamous concert in Dubuque, and that when the sisters fled the town in disgrace, Nathan "hopped on board a load of hogs bound for Chicago and has never been heard from since, although the sisters spent hundreds of dollars on private detectives, seeking him."[15] This was simply not true. None of the contemporary reports of the Dubuque incident mention Nathan being present, and the first mention that he may have gone to Chicago predates the show by five years. But Whyte may have been fed that story by Effie herself, a woman who spent her life reappraising and rewriting her past.

Shortly after these stories appeared, and even though he claimed to have written confirmation from Effie's attorney, James E. Patterson, that "If anyone has the first right to use the Biography in any way, it would be yourself: Effie talked to me about you many times,"[16] Whyte went back to work as accompanist for another act, the Del Rio Midgets. He did not disappear altogether though. Rennie and Willson revisited the idea of a Cherry Sisters stage play several times over the next two decades, and each time they did Carl Whyte resurfaced. Willson complained to Rennie, telling him not to forward any more mail to her from Whyte, whose missives were becoming more and more outrageous, and more and more graphic: I now know what poor Effie Cherrie went thru!" she told Rennie. "He has been flooding me with 20-page letters about all sorts of saddist [sic] subjects ... stories of his meetings with sexual perverts etc."[17] Unable to wear Willson down, Whyte made a pest of himself to her neighbors. Willson instructed anyone receiving letters or postcards from Whyte to throw them straight in to the bin. Carl Whyte eventually gave up playing piano, and went to work for an optical company in St. Louis. He penned a novel based on his experiences but, like all of Effie's work, "At the End of the Rainbow" remains unpublished.

Rennie never gave up. Unable to interest anyone in a film or Broadway musical he investigated the possibility of having their story told in book form. In September 1946 Darrell Garwood, the author of *Artist in Iowa: A Life of Grant Wood*, showed interest but backed away when other commitments took precedent. Orville Rennie then turned to local writer Winifred van Etten and had her prepare a biography of the Sisters. Van Etten, an award-winning novelist and academic who hailed from the Cherry's old stomping ground of Mount Vernon, seemed like an obvious choice, but sadly her comprehensive book, *The Queens of Corn*, would remain unpublished.

By the mid–1950s Rennie had landed a position with radio station KHOW in Denver. Using his contacts in the media he found a company, the Interstate Television Corporation, that was willing to take a chance on the Cherrys. A script for a pilot was prepared and some footage was shot, but again his hard work was overlooked. In early 1960 actress Virginia Sale approached Rennie: she was working with the writer Rosalind Shaffer on a book project which she felt may be dramatized and wished to feature the Cherrys in it. "Our project is not sold yet," she admitted, "but we have high hopes and of course if it ever should be done dramatically I would be playing Effie, I hope ... and we have some fine actresses who would love the other parts."[18] Miss Sale had been discussing the project with Zasu Pitts, who was keen to develop a TV series from the Cherrys story, with herself as Addie ... but despite everyone pushing for the project by August 1961 things once again ground to a halt. After much of the Cherry archive was destroyed in a flood, Orville Rennie and his wife Jane decided to bequeath the remaining material—plus their own papers—to the State Historical Society of Iowa.

Although Orville Rennie may have failed in his quest to make the story of the Cherry Sisters known to the generations who never had the chance to witness the spectacle firsthand, others have been more successful. In 1976, to mark the bicentennial of the American revolution, the Cherrys hometown of Marion held a festival, the chief attraction of which was an original production presented by community theater group the Old Barn Players based on the Sisters' story. A few years later "Cherrysh," a two-act play based on the Sisters and written by former students of Cedar Rapids' Kennedy High School, made its debut. In 1993, to celebrate the 100th anniversary of the Sisters' first performance in Cedar Rapids, "The Blacksmith's Daughter" finally got an outing, almost half a century after its author's death. More recently "The Cherry Sisters Revisited," by playwright Dan O'Brien and with music by Michael Friedman, brought the five women back to American stages. "I've been fascinated by them—their history and their fable—for almost twenty years now," O'Brien explains.

> I was writing a group-generated play about vaudeville for the Trinity Repertory Company in Providence, Rhode Island, and actors in the company were bringing in stories they'd found in their research. As a group of theatre-folk we all took their story quite personally. We found it deeply funny and full of pathos. And mysterious; and this is particularly why I wanted to write about them. The fact that there was little real history about them was intriguing to me. So the question of what they knew about their exploitation, and by extension to what degree their careers was self-exploitation, would be left up to me to explore. But I also didn't want to write your average 'backstage story' about them. I wanted the play itself to be a kind of vaudeville, a darkly comic fable that might call to mind our country's repressed history, yes, but also its present in the form of so-called reality TV and internet fame. This play was the high-water mark of a decade-long fascination with the vaudeville in general. I have always found that world quite haunting; I felt that it was something eerily forgotten, yet uncannily present in our contemporary entertainment. The Cherries felt like a way for the ghosts of our cultural unconscious to have voice again.

Back on home ground three sisters from Marion–Patsi Gann, Wendy Martinson and Sharon Chiaramonte—have been entertaining locals at various events (including the annual Swamp Fox festival) as Addie, Effie and Jessie. "We wrote our own short play, and had to sing off key," says Patsi. "We get the audience involved by booing and throwing fruit. The Cherry Sisters are

Ella and Lizzie's new grave markers (courtesy Jay Kacena, Friends of Oak Shade Cemetery).

an important part of our history, and we're trying to keep their legacy alive." European audiences, never offered the opportunity to gawk at the sisters could finally do so after actress Louise Rakers, founder of the theatrical company Rebella Productions, brought her show "The Cherry Sisters: the Worst Act Ever" to Dutch theaters in 2016, the same year that the Cherry Sisters were featured in an episode of the TV comedy series "Drunk History."

Today little remains of the Cedar Rapids the five sisters once knew. The bakery is no more, and Greene's Opera House, the scene of many a Cherry disaster and once recognized as one of the finest theaters in the mid–West, was torn down in 1969. The once-imposing theater met an inglorious end, having spent its last decades gutted and used as a parking garage. Thanks to the efforts of the Friends of Oak Shade Cemetery, in June 2017 Ella and Lizzie's unmarked graves were finally given headstones, which were donated by Novak and Brannon Monuments of Marion. "Around 100 people attended the service," says Jay Kacena of the Friends of Oak Shade Cemetery. "We love the Cherry Sisters. We are very aware of our heritage and they, after all, played a significant role in our history. In spite of all the fun people have at the expense of those girls we are proud of them, and many of us feel that they got a bad rap. Imagine; on a cold January night in Iowa 125 years ago, the Cherry Sisters laced up their boots, gritted their teeth, marched into town and put on a show that we're still talking about today! They deserve to have their names engraved in granite." Local trio the Deep Dish Divas–Deb Hunemuller, Carrie Kriz and Karen Pierce—performed "Rock of Ages" and "Ta-ra-ra Boom-de-ay," and an eulogy was given by Sonya Darrow and Kelly Shriver Kolln, two Cedar Rapids residents who, three years' previously, had written and performed their own one-act play, "The Cherry Sisters' First Trial." Each of the markers featured an illustration of two cherries. Lynette Brenzel, Executive Director of the Marion Heritage Center and Museum, who was closely involved with the rededication ceremony, agrees with Kacena: "The Cherry Sisters are loved in Marion. We're really proud of them."

In 1955, a retrospective article on the Sisters' career featured a comment from one of their Cedar Rapids' neighbors. "They lived at the right time," the sage offered. "In these days of television they would never have been noticed."[19] Far from it. In the three-quarters of a century since Effie breathed her last, the world has been treated to Tiny Tim and Mrs. Miller, to William Hung and Wing, each of them celebrated by their fans for their oddness, feted for their brilliance and yet vilified by critics for deviating from what the majority accept as being acceptable. In these days of multi-channel, 24-television, where it seems almost anybody is allotted their fifteen minutes of fame, the Cherry Sisters would have been superstars. As Ella's old school friend Mary Dunham put it:

> I have nothing but respect for the Cherry Sisters. It is a hard way to earn a living, or would be for the most of us. But if they wish to do it, they have a right to choose their own way. That they have had the pluck to persevere and to make money at it, proves them to be smart and shrewd, and that they have merit of the kind that is strong enough to succeed in ways not of the ordinary. May they go on their way retaining the honesty which makes them worthy of respect, and the courage which has pre-empted for them a place and a work in a world that owes them an honest living.[20]

And what did happen to all of that money? James Thompson, former proprietor of the Delphis, Cedar Rapids' first picture house, confirmed what the Sisters themselves always suspected: "The Cherry Sisters drew thousands of spectators and they gave the patrons their money's worth, but the sad thing about it was the girls were never paid anywhere near in proportion to what they drew. The booking agents became rich at their expense [but] the Cherry Sisters should have become wealthy."[21]

Cherry Sisters button badge, circa 1896 (courtesy Marion Historical Society, Iowa).

Appendix 1

The Cherry Sisters in Concert

Although their career on the stage lasted for more than forty years, the Cherry Sisters' act did not alter much. The program was longer in the earlier years, when they would provide an entire evening's amusement, and when they were able to give a complete "entertainment" a show could last for ninety minutes or more. For the majority of their career they performed twice a day (matinees and evenings), although in later years they were often given as little as twelve minutes to fill, and would perform the same short routine up to four times a day.

For a short period their cousin, Isabell Rawson, joined the sisters on stage. The following program was compiled by Lizzie, and was scribbled by her on the back of a concert handbill from 1894. As she noted, "all is original."

"Song"—performed by Jessie Cherry.
"The Drummer"—performed by Isabell Rawson.
The Seasons in Four Acts: "Spring"- Jessie Cherry; "Summer—Daughters of Liberty"—Effie Cherry; "Autumn"—Addie Cherry; "Winter"—Isabell Rawson.
"The American Flag"—performed by Jessie Cherry [presumably "Fair Columbia"]
"Ballard" [sic]—performed by Effie Cherry and Isabell Rawson [presumably "Irish Ballad"]
"Prohibition Essay"—performed by Addie Cherry.
"Naomi the Indian Maiden"—performed by Lizzie Cherry, cavalier Effie Cherry.
"Song, Music and Dancing"—performed by Jessie Cherry and Miss Isabell Rawson.
"Colored Ballard" [sic]—composed and performed by Ella Cherry.
"Rifle Shooting"—performed by Lizzie and Addie Cherry.
"Chanting Song"—performed by Effie Cherry.
"Barefooted Iona, the Orphan Flower Girl"—composed and performed by Jessie Cherry.

Appendix 1

"January Scene in Four Acts"—performed by Lizzie Cherry.
"Eulogy on the Cherry Sisters"—composed and performed by the Sisters.
"This program worth a dollar for only 25 and 40 cents. 25 for children under 10 years old. Come early and avoid the rush strict cash at the door no tickets. Doors open 7, performance begins half past."

On 29 May 1897, at one of Lizzie's final performances with Addie, Effie and Jessie, the sisters performed the following:

"Eulogy on the Cherry Sisters"—composed and performed by the sisters.
"Corn Juice"—composed and sung by Jessie.
"Irish Ballad"—composed by Lizzie and sung by Addie and Lizzie.
"The Traveling Man"—composed and sung by Effie.
"Bicycle Ride to the Fair"—composed and sung by Jessie.
"The Mystery of the Nineteenth Century"—an essay composed and performed by Addie.
"When I Asked Her if I Might"—composed and sung by Effie.
"Trilby"—based on the novel by George du Maurier, performed by Addie and Jessie.
"The Gypsy's Warning"—with Addie as the Cavalier, Effie as the Gypsy, and Lizzie as the lady.
"Fair Columbia"—composed and sung by Jessie.
"The Editor"—composed and sung by Addie.
"Railroad Boys"—composed and sung by Effie.
"College Boys"—composed and performed by Jessie.
"McKinley's Cold Cure"—composed and sung by Effie.
"The Orphan Flower Girl"—composed and sung by "barefooted Jessie."
Tableaux: "Rock of Ages" and "Goddess of Liberty"—performed by the company.

In one of their final performances as a trio, in Little Rock in 1902, Addie, Effie and Jessie presented the following:

"Eulogy on the Cherry Sisters"—composed and performed by the sisters.
"Fair Columbia"—composed and sung by Jessie.
"Irish Ballad (The True Biddy Just from the Emerald Isle)"—composed by Lizzie and sung by Addie and Effie.
"My Bicycle Ride"—composed and sung by Jessie.
"The Traveling Man (a personation true to life)" [sic]—composed and sung by Effie.
"Essay: a Tragedy Seen on The Streets of Chicago"—performed by Addie.
"My First Cigar"—written and performed by Jessie.
"Before and After"—composed and sung by Effie.
"The Gypsy's Warning"—with Addie as the Cavalier, Effie as the Gypsy, and Lizzie as the lady.
"Corn Juice"—composed and sung by Jessie.

"The Hero of Manila"—written and performed by Effie.

"The Hypnotizing of Trilby" ("after being put under the powers of hypnotism, Miss Jessie will sing 'Ben Bolt'")—based on the novel by George du Maurier, performed by Addie and Jessie.

"The Orphan Flower Girl"—composed and sung by Jessie.

Tableaux: "America Crowning Cuba," "Rock of Ages" and "Good Night"—performed by the company.

Appendix 2

A Cherry Sisters Timeline

1821: Thomas Cherry is born in Rhode Island. (1870 census)

1831: Laura Rawson is born in Vermont. (1860 census)

1854: September 7—Ellen Frances (Ella) Cherry is born in Marlborough, Massachusetts. (1870 census)

1856: Thomas and Laura Cherry, along with their infant daughter, move to Iowa.

1857: February 10—Elizabeth Viola (Lizzie) Cherry is born. (1860 census)

1859: October 27—Ada (Addie) Roselma Cherry is born in Mount Vernon, Iowa. (1860 census)

1862: Nathan Cherry is born in Linn Grove, Iowa. (1870 census)

1865: Inez (Ina) Cherry is born in Linn Grove. (1870 census)

1867: August 26—Effie Isabell Cherry is born in Wheaton, Illinois. (1870 census)

1869: Anna Cherry is born; death date unknown. (1870 census)

1871: November 27—Jessie Cora Cherry and her twin brother, Alfred Thomas, are born.

1872: The Cherry family moves to Marion.

September—Alfred Thomas Cherry dies, on the family farm in Marion.

1876: Laura Cherry, The mother of the family, dies in Marion.

1884: Nathan leaves the farm. His sisters will never see him again.

December 24—Inez Cherry dies, in Marion.

1888: June 15—Thomas Cherry, the father of the family, dies in Marion.

December 20—Ella wins a new bonnet in a competition at the Mentzer Hose Company Christmas fair in Marion. (*Cedar Rapids Evening Gazette*, 21 December 1888)

1892: January 29—Lizzie is the defendant in a court case brought by Charles Cook, to be heard at the Superior Court in Cedar Rapids at the beginning of February. Cook was the Cherrys' neighbor. (*Cedar Rapids Evening Gazette*, 29 January 1892)

Fall—Lizzie and Effie leave the farm to set up a small dairy business in Marion.

1893: January 12—The first advertisement appears in the press for the Cherry Sisters' debut (*Marion Sentinel*, 12 January 1893)

January 20—The Cherry Sisters' debut at Daniels Opera House, in Marion, Iowa. (*Marion Sentinel*, 12 January 1893)

February 17—Greene's Opera House,

Cedar Rapids: first recorded incident of objects being thrown. (*Marion Sentinel*, 16 February 1893)

February 21—According to a report, the Sisters "propose to erect a screen that will cover the entire front of the stage to the ceiling." (*Cedar Rapids Evening Gazette*, 21 February 1893)

February 23—Fred P. Davis, city editor for the *Cedar Rapids Evening Gazette*, is arrested and charged with libel. (*Cedar Rapids Evening Gazette*, 24 February 1893)

March 3—The first mention of the idea of a "trial" being held at Greene's Opera House. ("Genius Nipped in the Bud," *Cedar Rapids Evening Gazette*, 3 March 1893)

March 8—The original, court appointed, date for the preliminary hearing in Fred Davis's libel trial. (*The Algona Upper Des Moines*, 1 March 1893)

March 9—Report that the sisters have been invited to perform in Quincy, Ill., and Des Moines. ("The Cherry Sisters," *Cedar Rapids Evening Gazette*, 9 March 1893)

March 14—The Sisters are back at Greene's for a performance followed by a mock trial. The night was a sell-out. (*Cedar Rapids Evening Gazette*, 11 March 1893)

March 18—Watson's Opera House, Vinton, Iowa. (*Vinton Semi-Weekly Eagle*, 17 March 1893)

March/April—A performance at Clinton, Iowa. (*Davenport Democrat and Leader*, 14 May 1893)

April 13—Marshalltown, Iowa. (*Marion Sentinel*, 13 April 1893)

April 14—Cedar Falls, Iowa. (*Marion Sentinel*, 13 April 1893)

April 24—Cedar Falls, Iowa. The box office took $150. (*Marion Sentinel*, 27 April 1893)

April 25—East Side Opera House, Waterloo (postponed). (*Waterloo Daily Courier*, 24 April 1893)

April 28—East Side Opera House, Waterloo: Ella's final appearance (for now) with the original incarnation of the troupe. (*Cedar Rapids Evening Gazette*, 1 May 1893)

May 5—Toledo, Iowa. (*Marion Sentinel*, 18 May 1893)

May 10—Only Effie and Jessie appear at the Burtis Opera House, Davenport after Lizzie and Addie missed their train. (*Rock Island Argus*, 11 May 1893)

May 17—Riot in Dubuque. (*Rock Island Argus*, 22 May 1893)

May 18—Bellevue, Iowa, to an audience numbering just two. (*Cedar Rapids Evening Gazette*, 24 May 1893)

May 19—Lyons (Clinton), Iowa.

May 20—Grand Opera House, Burlington, Iowa. (*Cedar Rapids Evening Gazette*, 11 May 1893)

May—Muscatine, Turner Opera House: audience 25. (*Cedar Rapids Evening Gazette*, 24 May 1893)

May 25—Academy of Music, Fort Madison, Iowa. (From handbill)

May 26—Clinton, Iowa. ("Iowa News," *Minneapolis Tribune*, 27 May 1893)

June—A caricature of the Cherry sisters appears in scandal sheet the National Police Gazette.

June 22—First reports of the sisters court case against their tenant, Houts.

September 11—The quartet play Greene's Opera House in Cedar

[1893] Rapids again. (*Marion Sentinel*, 13 September 1893)

October 10—A performance in Central City, Linn County: "The house was a financial success and the sisters covered themselves all over with glory, winning oceans of applause. They speak highly of their reception and treatment by Central City, and of the efforts of Mayor Davis and his corps of police to maintain order and give them a fair show to display their attractions." (*Jackson Sentinel*, 12 October 1893)

October 23—After failing to pay for their lodgings in Savannah, the Sisters travel to Lyons without their baggage. (*Waterloo Daily Courier*, 25 October 1893)

October 25–26—The sisters play Fulton, Iowa. (*Waterloo Daily Courier*, 25 October 1893)

October 27—The "famous Cherry Sisters" go to Clinton, Iowa to sue the *Daily Herald* for libel. (*Chicago Inter Ocean*, 28 October 1893)

November 20—The Sisters sue the Clinton Herald for libel for $1,000.

1894: March 31—Daniels Opera House, Marion. (From flyer/letter in Collection)

May 23—The Sisters travel to Philadelphia. (*Dixon Evening Telegraph*, 31 May 1894)

May 29—Central City, Iowa. (*Dixon Evening Telegraph*, 5 June 1894)

May 30—Heynan's Hall, Miles, Iowa. (*Dixon Evening Telegraph*, 8 June 1894)

June 8—Opera House, Dixon, Illinois. (*Dixon Evening Telegraph*, 9 June 1894)

August 4—The sisters, at home in Marion, take out an advert in the *New York Dramatic Mirror*: "wanted, an expert manager at once" for the Cherry Sisters Opera Company. (*New York Dramatic Mirror*, 4 August 1894)

September 1—The sisters, currently in Aurora, Illinois, take out a second advert in the *New York Dramatic Mirror* for a manager. (*New York Dramatic Mirror*, 1 September 1894)

1895: March 16—Daniels Opera House, Marion. Flyers proclaim the troupe as "the Celebrated Northern Stars, Queens of Comedy and Song, the renowned Cherry Sisters." (From handbill in Rennie Collection)

May—A show scheduled for Tipton, Iowa is abandoned due to poor audience numbers. (*Marion Register*, 5 June 1895)

June 24—The sisters attack Charlie Floyd, the editor of the *Center Point Tribune* with riding crops, and are each fined $12 plus costs (*The Scranton Tribune*, 26 June 1895). At their show that night, just $9 is taken at the box office. (*Marion Sentinel*, 27 June 1895)

July—Lyons (Clinton), Iowa. (*Marion Sentinel*, 18 July 1895)

July 18—Opera House, Lisbon, Iowa. (*Marion Register*, 17 July 1895)

July—Shellsburg, Iowa. (*Vinton Eagle*, 30 July 1895)

August 15—Mechanicsville, Iowa. (*Marion Sentinel*, 15 August 1895)

August 23—Riot in La Porte, Iowa. (*Cedar Rapids Evening Gazette*, 26 August 1895)

September 1—Ella is arrested after threatening J.A. Rose with a shotgun. ("The Cherry Sisters," *Cedar*

Rapids Evening Gazette, 4 September 1895)

November 8–9—Daniels Opera House, Marion, Iowa. The Sisters are now advertising themselves under a new name: The Jubilee Concert Company. (*Cedar Rapids Evening Gazette*, 9 November 1895)

November 16—Daniels Opera House, Marion, Iowa. The show descends in to a riot. (*Marion Pilot*, 21 November 1895)

November 18–19—Marengo, Iowa.

November 20–21—Brooklyn, Iowa.

November 28—The Sisters play for the benevolent Protective Order of Elks in Cedar Rapids. (*Cedar Rapids Evening Gazette*, 29 November 1895)

December—Davis Opera House, Clinton, Iowa. (*Sterling Standard*, 21 November 1895)

December 5—The Sisters entertain at a fundraising party hosted by Mrs. John B. Bever of Cedar Rapids, before meeting with Civil war veteran and politician Colonel Robert Ingersoll at the Grand Hotel. (*Marion Register*, 1 December 1895)

December 23—Opera House, Coggon, Iowa. (*Cedar Rapids Evening Gazette*, 20 December 1895)

December—Grinnell, Iowa. (*Vinton Eagle*, 27 December 1895)

1896: January 18—Greene's Opera House, Cedar Rapids. (*New York Dramatic Mirror*, 25 January 1896)

February 8—Opera House, Gladbrook, Iowa. (*Des Moines Register*, 11 February 1896)

February 15—Cedar Rapids, a performance for the Ladies' Auxiliary of the Order of Railway Conductors. (*Marion Sentinel*, 13 February 1896)

March 4—Decorah. On arrival at the station the Sisters "were met with carriages and a brass band, and their entertainment was a howling success." (*Marion Sentinel*, 12 March 1896). "The audience did howl themselves hoarse. The best part of the entertainment, however, was not the howling of the audience; it was in watching the Cherries endeavor to proceed along the lines of the program and at the same time avoid being struck by the aged hen fruit which occasionally exploded upon the stage. It is said that the Cherry Sisters cleared $50 out of the performance here, and we really cannot tell on whom the joke of the whole thing was—the audience or the sisters of euphonious surname. The girls may play a return date here later on, when the thrifty hen is attending better to business." (*Decorah Journal*, reprinted in the *Cedar Falls Gazette*, 26 March 1896)

March—The Sisters perform at the Auditorium Music Hall, Maryland.

March 7—Osage, Iowa. (*Waterloo Daily Courier*, 7 March 1896)

March 16—Clarksville, Iowa: the show is abandoned after one song. (*Marion Pilot*, 19 March 1896)

March 18—Opera House, Greene, Iowa: "Ho! The famous Cherry sisters are coming to Greene with their fun show, March 18. Turnips, cabbages, old shoes, most anything to throw at the actors is what makes the fun." (*Iowa Recorder*, March 1896)

May 8—The four Sisters are playing for a week at Whitehall's Bijou Family Theater, Washington, Iowa.

[1896] June 10–11—Opera House, Maquoketa, Iowa. (*Marion Sentinel*, 11 June 1896)

July 20—Williamsburg, Iowa. (*Marion Register*, 22 July 1896)

August 6—Palisades, Iowa: a show for the National Union Society. (*Marion Sentinel*, 6 August 1896)

September 1—Phipp's Opera House, Boone, Iowa. (*New York Dramatic Mirror*, 5 September 1896)

September 18—Van Horn, Iowa. (*Vinton Eagle*, 18 September 1896)

September 21—Grand Opera House, Peoria, Illinois. (*New York Dramatic Mirror*, 26 September 1896)

September 22—Empire Theater, Quincy, Illinois. (*New York Dramatic Mirror*, 10 October 1896)

September 23—The Grand, Burlington, Iowa.

October 9—Iowa Falls. (*Ackley World*, 16 October 1896)

October 21—Grand Opera House, Peoria, Illinois. (*New York Dramatic Mirror*, 31 October 1896)

October 22—Empire Theater, Quincy, Illinois. (*New York Dramatic Mirror*, 31 October 1896)

October 24—Mason City, Illinois. (*Iowa Recorder*, 27 October 1896)

November 9—The Sisters travel to New York. (*New York Dramatic Mirror*, 11 November 1896)

November 11—The Sisters play to an invited audience at the Olympia.

November 16—The Cherry Sisters open at Oscar Hammerstein's Olympia Theater in New York.

December 15—The quartet make their debut at the Imperial, Chicago. (*New York Dramatic Mirror*, 19 December 1896)

1897: January 3—The Star Theater, Cincinnati, Ohio. (*Iowa Recorder*, 19 January 1897)

January 10—The Hagan, St. Louis. (*New York Dramatic Mirror*, 16 January 1897)

January 19—Tivoli Theater, Chicago.

January 23—The Sisters' contract for the Tivoli Theater, Chicago is extended by a further week. (*New York Dramatic Mirror*, 6 February 1897)

February 1–6—Tivoli Theater, Chicago. (*New York Dramatic Mirror*, 6 February 1897)

February 7—It is announced that the sisters are to embark on a tour of the Western states, appearing in a production of Uncle Tom's Cabin. (*Rochester Democrat and Chronicle*, 7 February 1897)

February 8–13—Waldmann's Opera House, Newark, New Jersey, as part of Reilly and Wood's Big Show.

February 15–20—The Columbia Theater, Providence, Rhode Island (as part of Reilly and Wood's Big Show). (*New York Dramatic Mirror*, 27 February 1897)

February 22—The Sisters are booked for a return visit to Proctor's, for the Washington's Birthday celebrations. (*New York Dramatic Mirror*, 20 February 1897)

March 6–12—Hyde and Behman's Theater, Brooklyn. (*New York Dramatic Mirror*, 13 March 1897)

March 13—The Sisters, staying at the Clarendon Hotel, Brooklyn NY, write a letter to the editor of the *New York Dramatic Mirror* to complain about Mr. Price, the business manager of Proctor's Pleasure Palace. ("A

Letter from the Cherries," *New York Dramatic Mirror*, 20 March 1897)

March 15—The Auditorium Music Hall, Baltimore with Reilly and Wood's show.

March 22-27—The Sisters play for a week at the Court Theater, Buffalo, as the closing act of Reilly and Wood's vaudeville company. (*New York Dramatic Mirror*, 20 March 1897)

March 28—The Sisters, along with Reilly and Wood's vaudeville company, appear at Harry Williams' Academy of Music, Pittsburgh.

April—The Sisters are left stranded after Pat Reilly abandons them and refuses to pay their last week's wages. (*New York Dramatic Mirror*, 17 April 1897)

May 3—The Sisters begin a week at the Bijou Theater, Washington in a bill with Dan McCarthy and James W. Reagan. (*New York Dramatic Mirror*, 8 May 1897) The stay is later extended to two weeks.

May 10—The Sisters pay the deposit on ten acres of land in North Marion, but the asking price ($10,000) proves too much and the purchase is not completed.

May 17-18—Burtis Opera House, Davenport, Iowa. (*New York Dramatic Mirror*, 22 May 1897)

May 18—Dan McCarthy breaks with his management, complaining about acts such as the Cherry sisters being included on the same bill. (*New York Dramatic Mirror*, 29 May 1897)

May 19-20—Two nights at Foster's, Des Moines.

May 20—It is reported that the Sisters have purchased ten acres, known as Paddington Farm, for $10,000 (probably the same plot as mentioned on 10 May): "The Cherry sisters purchased ten acres of land known as the Paddington farm on the electric car line, adjoining Bower's nursery on the North, for an estimated $10,000, The purchase followed their successful eastern tour." (*Marion Sentinel*, 20 May 1897)

May 21—Grand Opera House, Ottumwa, Iowa, where the "the audience was so disorderly the sisters refused to proceed and the performance was brought to a close." (*New York Dramatic Mirror*, 5 June 1897)

May 24—Grand Opera House, Fairfield, Iowa "to a packed house." (*New York Dramatic Mirror*, 5 June 1897)

May 28—Greene's Opera House, Cedar Rapids. (*Cedar Rapids Gazette*, 30 May 1937)

May—Nashua, Iowa. (*Iowa Recorder*, 8 June 1897)

May 31—Grand Opera House, Ottumwa, Iowa "Cherry Sisters appeared May 31. But the audience was so disorderly the sisters refused to proceed and the performance was brought to a close." (*New York Dramatic Mirror*, 5 June 1897)

June 1—A performance by the Cherry Sisters at Brown's Opera House, Waterloo is reported as remarkable because "not an egg was thrown, not a cabbage fell." (*The Carroll Herald*, 8 June 1897)

June 2—Des Moines, for a weeklong engagement at Croker Park. (*New York Clipper*, 3 July 1897)

June 5—A performance by the sisters at Croker Park, Des Moines is interrupted by a barge load of bottle-throwing hoodlums.

[**1897**] June 5—Lizzie leaves the Cherry Sisters. ("Lizzie Leaves her Sisters," *Leavenworth Times*, 9 June 1897)

June 9—Knoxville, as a four piece (probably with Ella).

June 17—Two performances at Stewart Park in Dubuque, at the Elks' Summer Picnic. (*New York Dramatic Mirror*, 3 July 1897)

June 21—The trio begin a weeklong engagement in Sioux City. Due to the Grand Opera House being closed, the shows take place under canvas. (*New York Dramatic Mirror*, 3 July 1897)

June 25—Pavilion, Sioux City, Iowa. (*New York Dramatic Mirror*, 10 July 1897)

June 28–July 3—The Cherry Sisters are at the Dohany Theater, Council Bluffs, Iowa. (*New York Dramatic Mirror*, 17 July 1897)

July 4–5—The Trio were due to appear at the Keokuk Opera House, Iowa, but such was the demand for tickets that the shows were transferred to the Casino Summer Theater, Hubinger Park. The Sisters give two performances, to a total of 15,000 people. (*New York Dramatic Mirror*, 17 July 1897)

July 7—Lizzie buys a plot of land from G.A. Johnson for $300. (*Marion Register*, 7 July 1897)

July 21—Warren Opera House, Greenfield, Iowa, "to large business." (*New York Dramatic Mirror*, 14 August 1897)

July 23—Opera House, Indianola. (*The Des Moines Register*, 24 July 1897)

July 25—On the same day that the Sisters sign a contract with the Puget Sound Theatrical Agency of Butte, Montana, the sisters play their first night of a four day booking at the Hotel Orleans, Spirit Lake, Iowa. (*Cedar Rapids Evening Gazette*, 21 July 1897)

August 7—Fort Dodge, a show for military personnel.

August 12—Germania Opera House, Carroll, Iowa. (*The Carroll Herald*, 10 August 1897)

August 13—Call's Opera House, Algona, Iowa.

August 14—Opera House, Estherville, Iowa.

August 18—Wisner Opera House, Eldora, Iowa. (*Ackley World*, 13 August 1897)

August 20–22—The Watch Tower Theater, Rock Island, Illinois. Two performances a day (three on Sunday), with tickets given away free by the Tri-City Railway Company.

August 28—At a show in Clarion, Iowa, several arrests were made, including a young boy who threw eggs at the Sisters. (*Iowa Recorder*, 31 August 1897)

August 30—The Auditorium, Galesburg. (*New York Dramatic Mirror*, 4 September 1897)

September 2–4—The Auditorium, Peoria, Illinois. (*New York Dramatic Mirror*, 18 September 1897)

September 6–7—Chatterton Opera House, Springfield, Illinois.

September 8–12—Harlem Park Theater, Rockford, Illinois: "Seating capacity will be increased by 500 seats." (*New York Dramatic Mirror*, 11 September 1897)

September 22—Phipp's Opera House, Boone, Iowa. (*New York Dramatic Mirror*, 2 October 1897)

September 23—Watson's Opera House,

Vinton, Iowa: advance notices claim that four Sisters, including Lizzie, will be appearing. (*Vinton Eagle*, 21 September 1897)

September 24—Dubuque, and another hail of "dead rats, eggs and tomatoes." (*The Des Moines Register*, 26 September 1897)

September 26–October 2—Gilliss Theater, Kansas City, Missouri for a week: "The fearful and wonderful performances of the Cherry Sisters were the feature of the vaudeville at the Gillis.... They objected to the fusillade of missiles, and rang down the curtain." (*New York Dramatic Mirror*, 9 October 1897) Adverts announced that four sisters would be performing, but only Addie, Effie and Jessie appeared.

September—"An audience at Independence assailed the Cherry sisters with dead rats, eggs and tomatoes, and the curtain was rung down." (*Iowa Reporter*, 5 October 1897)

October 8–9—Crawford Grand, Leavenworth.

October 15–16—Crawford's Opera House, Topeka, Kansas. (*New York Dramatic Mirror*, 23 October 1897)

October 19–21—Columbia Hall, St Joseph, Missouri.

October 21—In St Joseph, the sisters are accused of absconding without paying their hotel bill.

October 29–30—Grand Opera House, Fort Smith, Arkansas. (*New York Dramatic Mirror*, 30 October 1897)

October 31—Fayette, Iowa.

November 11—Elgin, Illinois.

November 9—Hildreth Opera House, Charles City, Iowa. (*New York Dramatic Mirror*, 20 November 1897)

November 11—Opera House, Elgin, Iowa. (*New York Dramatic Mirror*, 27 November 1897)

November 14—Davidson Theater, Milwaukee, Wisconsin. "The Cherry Sisters, who were billed as the chief feature, were hooted off the stage, and the performance proved of such poor quality that the management wisely canceled the engagement, and the house will be dark the remainder of the week." (*New York Dramatic Mirror*, 27 November 1897)

November 15—Fort Scott, Kansas.

November 17—Opera House, Parsons, Kansas. Cancelled. (*New York Dramatic Mirror*, 27 November 1897)

November 19–20—Whitley Opera House, Emporia.

November 23–24—Grand Opera House, Kalamazoo. (*New York Dramatic Mirror*, 4 December 1897)

November 29–30—Arkansas City. (*Arkansas City Daily Traveler*, 5 October 1897)

December 12—Clifford's Gaiety Theater, Chicago for a week, with their burlesque company. "The Cherry Sisters ... proved to be as big a card as ever, filling the Gaiety." (*New York Clipper*, 18 December 1897)

December 22—Opera House, Dixon, Illinois to a "large house that failed to appreciate them." (*New York Dramatic Mirror*, 15 January 1898)

December 23—Academy of Music, Sterling, Illinois. (*New York Dramatic Mirror*, 8 January 1898)

December 26—Clifford's Savoy, Chicago, for a week with their burlesque company.

1898: January 3—Aurora Opera House,

[1898] Aurora, Illinois. (*New York Dramatic Mirror*, 22 January 1898)

January 5–6—Zimmermann Opera House, La Salle, Illinois "to a small audience." (*New York Dramatic Mirror*, 22 January 1898)

January 10—The Sisters played Washington Hall, Clinton, Iowa, "and were enthusiastically received." (*New York Dramatic Mirror*, 22 January 1898)

January 12—The Auditorium, Moline, Illinois. (*New York Dramatic Mirror*, 29 January 1898)

January 14—Harper's Theater, Rock Island, Illinois: "Small audience, performance execrable." (*New York Dramatic Mirror*, 29 January 1898)

January 17—Riot in Iowa City. ("Whispers at the Wings," *Sportsman* (Melbourne), 8 March 1898)

January 21—Evan's Theater, Red Oak Iowa, "to a large house, best performance of the kind ever given in the house." (*New York Dramatic Mirror*, 5 February 1898)

January 24—Corning Opera House, Iowa.

January 26—Evidence in the case of the Cherry Sisters v. Miller is heard in the central courthouse, Des Moines. ("The Court Record," *The Des Moines Register*, 27 January 1898)

January—A performance in Prescott is cancelled due to poor ticket sales.

January 29—Patt's Opera House, Creston, Iowa. (*New York Dramatic Mirror*, 5 February 1898)

February 1—Opera House, Glenwood, Iowa.

February 3—Atlantic, Iowa; the audience walked out during the show ("Iowa Notes," *The Des Moines Register*, 6 February 1898), and the Sisters have to return to their hotel under escort. (*The Des Moines Register*, 4 February 1898)

February 10—Sac City (*The Odebolt Chronicle*, 10 February 1898). This was the performance that Billy Hamilton reviewed.

February 11—The Sisters are booked to play the Opera House, Correctionville.

February 15—Grand Opera House, Sioux City, Iowa. (*New York Dramatic Mirror*, 5 March 1898)

February 16—New Theater, Missouri Valley, Iowa. (*New York Dramatic Mirror*, 5 March 1898)

February 18–19—Phipp's Opera House, Boone, Iowa. (*New York Dramatic Mirror*, 5 March 1898)

February 20—"A damage suit has been commenced by Opera House manager Laub against the Cherry Sisters because they deemed Correctionville too small for their attention and cancelled their date without his consent. Their baggage was attached to satisfy his claim." ("Cherry Sisters in Court," *Kansas City Journal*, 21 February 1898)

February 21—the Sisters are due to appear at the Fifth Avenue Opera House, Arkansas but fail to appear. (*Arkansas City Daily Traveler*, 22 February 1898)

February 24–25—The Sisters are in Washington, where they "gave a parlor entertainment at the Morgan to a select few of the assemblymen which was highly enjoyed by those present. The sisters are very desirous of having a law enacted making it a misdemeanor for editors of newspapers to publish derogatory articles or defame one by caricature. The sisters say it is shameful the way the press treats them and they propose to put a stop to it or go out of the show business into the law business. They won a suit in Des Moines last week, receiving some gate receipts. They have begun a suit against the State Leader for $15,000, and there are others." ("Not Observing Lent," *Cedar Rapids Evening Gazette*, 28 February 1898)

February 26—The Sisters lose a court case against C. D. Miller, and are fined $32.53 including costs. (*The Des Moines Register*, 26 February 1898)

March 8–9—McCasland's Opera House, East St. Louis. The show scheduled for the 10th is cancelled. (*New York Dramatic Mirror*, 26 March 1898)

March 12—Lyceum Theater, Bloomington. Illinois (matinee). (*New York Dramatic Mirror*, 26 March 1898)

March 12—Grand Opera House, Mount Vernon, Illinois. (*New York Dramatic Mirror*, 12 March 1898)

March 16—Lyceum Theater, Bloomington. Illinois (matinee). (*New York Dramatic Mirror*, 2 April 1898)

March 16—Shoaff's New Opera House, Paris, Illinois. (*New York Dramatic Mirror*, 2 April 1898)

March 22—Grand Opera House, Terre Haute. (*New York Dramatic Mirror*, 2 April 1898)

March 25—Sixth Avenue Theater, Beaver Falls. (*New York Dramatic Mirror*, 16 April 1898)

March 31—Globe Opera House, Hamilton, Ohio. (*New York Dramatic Mirror*, 16 April 1898)

April 1—Grand Opera House, Greenville, Ohio (*New York Dramatic Mirror*, 2 April 1898)

April 4—Market Square Theater, Urbana, Ohio. (*New York Dramatic Mirror*, 16 April 1898)

April 7—Masonic Opera House, Ironton, Ohio.

April 8—Listed by the *New York Dramatic Mirror* as playing The Bradley, Richmond, Indiana. (*New York Dramatic Mirror*, 9 April 1898)

April 8—Grand Opera House, Portsmouth, Ohio.

April 10—Grand Opera House, Greenville, Ohio. (*New York Dramatic Mirror*, 30 April 1898)

April 11—Chestnut Street Opera House, Lancaster. (*New York Dramatic Mirror*, 30 April 1898)

April 16—Nielsen Opera House, Sandusky. (*New York Dramatic Mirror*, 16 April 1898)

April 20—The Sisters sue the publishers of the *Des Moines Leader*.

April 25—Sixth Avenue Theater, Beaver Falls. (*New York Dramatic Mirror*, 23 April 1898)

May 10—Grand Opera House, Greenville.

May 21—Crescent Opera House, Fond du Lac. (*New York Dramatic Mirror*, 4 June 1898)

May 23–24—Waterloo, Iowa (Memorandum book, Rennie Collection)

May 26—Grande, Baraboo, Wisconsin. (*New York Dramatic Mirror*, 11 June 1898)

May 28—Opera House, Winona, Minnesota. (*New York Dramatic Mirror*, 11 June 1898)

June 22—Sieg Theater, Marshalltown, Iowa. (*New York Dramatic Mirror*, 9 July 1898)

[1898] July 22–24—The three Sisters play the Watch Tower Theater, based in an amusement park in Rock Island. Tickets for the concerts were given away free, and newspapers report that even though they gave a third performance on their last day, hundreds had to be turned away. (*New York Dramatic Mirror*, 30 July 1898)

August—Opera House, Jefferson, Michigan.

August 15–20—Peoria, Illinois. (*New York Dramatic Mirror*, 20 August 1898)

August—At a performance in New Sharon, Iowa several members of the audience are hurt by cantaloupe melons launched from the gallery. (*The Des Moines Register*, 3 September 1898)

August 30–31—the Sisters are due to play the Opera House in Anita, but no tickets are sold and the Sisters leave town without performing.

October 18—Funke Opera House, Lincoln, Nebraska. ("The Cherry Sisters," *Nebraska State Journal*, 19 October 1898)

October 20—Malvern, Iowa.

October 31—Martin's Opera House, Ackley, Iowa. (*Ackley World*, 2 November 1898)

November 12—Derthick Opera House, Belvedere, Illinois. (*Belvedere Standard*, 10 November 1898)

November—K. P. Lodge, Freeport, Illinois.

November (Thanksgiving Eve)—Beloit, Wisconsin.

December 4—The Cherry Sisters Vaudeville Company begins a weeklong residence at Howard's Theater, Chicago. Over 5,000 tickets had been sold in advance. (*New York Dramatic Mirror*, 10 December 1898)

1899: January 6—First mention in the press of the Sisters' impending visit to Havana.

January 8—They begin a weeklong engagement at the Drexel Theater, 39th Street, Chicago, playing twice a day (Chicago Daily Tribune, 8 January 1899). Their booking is later extended by a further week. (*New York Dramatic Mirror*, 28 January 1899)

January 23–February 6—the Sisters play a two-week engagement at the Empire Theater, Buffalo, two houses daily. Originally booked for one week, demand for ticket was so great that the theater's management kept them on for a second week. They missed the first show, a matinee on Monday as their train arrived late, but the audience was given free tickets for a later date. ("Among All the Play Houses," *Buffalo Courier*, 24 January 1899)

February 6–11—The Sisters perform at the Bijou Theater in Toronto.

February—"The Cherry Sisters, after being left In the lurch by manager W. S. Robinson of Toronto [manager of the Bijou], applied to the relief officer for tickets to enable them to reach Philadelphia, but as the cost would be $35 the request was refused. The United States Consul also refused the desired aid. Judgment for the full amount claimed, $37 in each case, was given against Robinson, whom the Cherry Sisters charged with refusing to pay wages due. The case will be appealed." (*New York Dramatic Mirror*, 4 March 1899)

March 6—The Sisters begin a weeklong engagement at the Wonderland Theater in Rochester, N.Y., with extra matinees on Wednesday and Saturday. Support is from a pantomime troupe led by George H. Adams. (*Rochester Democrat and Chronicle*, 5 March 1899)

April 1—Beck's Wonder World, Cincinnati, Ohio. (*New York Dramatic Mirror*, 8 April 1899)

April 7—McGregor Opera House, Brazil, Indiana. (*New York Dramatic Mirror*, 22 April 1899)

April 10—Grand Opera House, Terre Haute, Indiana. (*New York Dramatic Mirror*, 22 April 1899)

April 15—The Cherry Sisters appear on stage at the Grand Opera House, Terre Haute—located, rather aptly, on the corner of Seventh and Cherry Streets. (Sunday Star, April 17)

April 17—Broadway Theater, Lincoln, Illinois. (*New York Dramatic Mirror*, 29 April 1899)

April 20—The Sisters' case against the owners of the *Des Moines Leader* begins in court.

May 10—Parker's Opera House, Mason City, Iowa. (*New York Dramatic Mirror*, 27 May 1899)

May 17—Iowa Falls. (*Ackley World*, 24 May 1899)

June 2—Masonic Opera House, Oskaloosa, Iowa. (*The Des Moines Register*, 7 June 1899)

June 3–5—Grand Opera House, Ashland, Wisconsin.

June 16—New Grand Opera House, Watertown, South Dakota. (*New York Dramatic Mirror*, 24 June 1899)

June 25–30—The Sisters make their debut at the Hilltop Casino at the Pavilion, Duluth. (*Duluth Evening Herald*, 26 June 1899)

July 22—Pabst Theater, Wausau, Wisconsin. (*New York Dramatic Mirror*, 29 July 1899)

August 2—The Bergman, McGregor, Iowa. (*New York Dramatic Mirror*, 12 August 1899)

August 6–12—Watch Tower theater, Rock Island. (*Rock Island Argus*, 29 July 1899)

August 13—Oriental Theater, Prospect Park, Moline. "Cherry Sisters at Prospect Park Sunday. The Cherry Sisters will give an inimitable performance at the oriental theater at Prospect Park Sunday, assisted by Prof. Harry Parker, aeronaut and acrobat. Also Edison's polyphone. A big show for 10 cents. Don't miss it. Afternoon and evening. Also trapeze performance and band concert." (*Rock Island Argus*, 12 August 1899)

August 17–19—Schuetzen Park, Davenport, Iowa. (*New York Dramatic Mirror*, 26 August 1899)

August 28—September 5—Oriental Theater, Prospect Park, Moline "by the Cherry Sisters with their vaudeville company." (*Rock Island Argus*, 2 September 1899)

September—Addie, Effie and Jessie sue "their sister Lizzie in the Linn county district court. The amount in controversy is $630, and represents a quarrel over money and property." (*Vinton Review*, 28 September 1899)

October 1–7—The Sisters play the Des Moines Carnival. (*Marion Sentinel*, 28 September 1899)

October 3—In Des Moines, the Sisters

[1899] write to the manager of Hyde and Behman's, in Brooklyn, in the hope of securing a two-week engagement: "We have one of the best companies money can secure; we have the Peerless Cherry Sisters surrounded with a company of the best artists in the profession and know we can do you the best business of the season." ("Those Cherry Sisters," Chicot, *New York Morning Telegraph*, 10 October 1899)

October—Alden. (*Ackley World*, 25 October 1899)

November 8—Auditorium, Owatonna, Minnesota. (*New York Dramatic Mirror*, 25 November 1899)

November 18—The Armory, Austin, Minnesota. (*Mower County Transcript*, 22 November 1899)

November 23—The Sisters play an Actors Fund benefit in the afternoon, at the Metropolitan Opera House, Minneapolis. (*Minneapolis Tribune*, 22 November 1899)

November 23–25—Raudenbush Hall, St. Paul Minnesota, with Hazel Jackson and Little Ruby. (*St. Paul Globe*, 23 November 1899)

December 25–early January—Palace Museum, Minneapolis, with Joseph Doyle and Mollie Granger. On the third night the Sisters abandon the show after being showered with vegetables: they returned the following evening, but they did not see their contract out. (*New York Clipper*, 6 January 1900)

1900: January 30–February 4—Coeur d'Alene, Spokane.

January 31—Beckwith Memorial Theater, Dowagiac, Michigan. (*New York Dramatic Mirror*, 10 February 1900)

February 18–24—Sutton's Theater, Butte, Montana. (*New York Dramatic Mirror*, 6 March 1900)

March 5—Funke opera house, Nebraska. (*The Nebraska State Journal*, 4 March 1900)

March—In Butte, Montana, a mini riot breaks out, when "a few men became so wildly excited that they attempted to throw chairs." (*Marion Sentinel*, 22 March 1900)

March—Anaconda, California, where they "attracted to the stage large quantities of eggs and potatoes." (*The Portsmouth Herald*, 23 March 1900)

March 26–April 7—Chutes Amusement Park, San Francisco for two weeks; two shows a day. (*The San Francisco Call*, 26 March 1900)

May 1—Street carnival, Sacramento, California.

June 12—"The delightfully unconventional Cherry Sisters, who joined in singing the requiem over Oscar Hammerstein's Olympian hopes here several years ago, are out in California. They still act as their own press agents, as the following from the San Francisco Music and Drama will indicate: 'The Cherry Sisters invaded the office of Music and Drama a few days ago with their war paint on and stated that if an apology was not immediately forthcoming for the very fair and just criticisms which had appeared in the paper concerning their freak act they would lock the office doors and sing. The fighting editor promptly capitulated' and the Cherrys departed, wreathed in Cedar Rapid smiles." ("Gossip," *New York Morning Telegraph*, 12 June 1900)

July 20–September 1—Salt Lake City, Utah "in their own pavilion," near to the Salt Palace Saucer velodrome.
September—Nebraska, street fair. (*The North Platte Semi-Weekly Tribune*, 21 August 1900)
September 23–30—New Lyceum Theater, Denver, Colorado, on a bill that also included the Davis Children (Horace, Joe and Madeline), the Quinn Trio and Virginia Schaefer, whistler. (*New York Clipper*, 6 October 1900)
October 29–November 3—Heck's Wonder World, Cincinnati, Ohio. (*New York Clipper*, 10 November 1900)
November 19—The Grand, Danville, Illinois. (*Danville Democrat*, 20 November 1900)
1901: January 6—Morrison, Illinois. (Jessie's Diary for 1901)
January 7—Savannah, Carroll County, Illinois. (*Dixon Evening Telegraph*, 9 January 1901; Jessie's diary lists this as taking place on 13 January)
January 10—Fulton, Illinois. (*Dixon Evening Telegraph*, 11 January 1901)
January 11—Milne's Opera House, Morrison, Illinois. (Jessie's Diary)
January 19—Grand Opera House, Fairfield, Illinois. (*New York Dramatic Mirror*, 13 February 1901)
January 21—Mount Carroll, Illinois. (*Dixon Evening Telegraph*, 23 January 1901)
January 22—Stockton, Illinois. (Jessie's Diary)
January 24—Warren, Illinois. (Jessie's Diary)
January 25—Shannon, Illinois. (Jessie's Diary)
January 26—Lanark, Illinois. (Jessie's Diary)
January 28—Pearl City, Illinois. (Jessie's Diary)
February 7—Gutenberg, Iowa. (Jessie's Diary)
February 8—At an Elk's Club charity fair in Omaha, dolls made to look like the Cherry Sisters are auctioned.
February 10—Oxford Junction, Iowa. (Jessie's Diary)
February 20—Cedar Falls, Iowa. (*Marble Rock Journal*, 28 February 1901)
March 3—Lake City, Iowa. (Jessie's Diary)
March 18—Rockford, Iowa. (Jessie's Diary)
March 26—Opera House, Minneapolis. (*The Minneapolis Journal*, 27 March 1901)
April 6—Seamore, Iowa. (Jessie's Diary)
May 2—It is reported that the Sisters are to perform at the upcoming Iowa Republican Convention. (Marion Pilot, 2 May 1901)
May—Warsaw, Iowa. (*The Quill* [La Harpe, Illinois], 23 April 1901)
May 8—Oxford, Iowa.
May 28—The Supreme Court delivers its verdict in the case of Cherry vs. the *Des Moines Leader*.
June 11—Colimes, Iowa. (Jessie's Diary)
June 15—Lisbon. (*Marion Sentinel*, 27 June 1901)
July 2—La Porte.
July 17–18—Opera House, Bowen, Illinois. (*The Bowen Chronicle*, 18 July 1901)
July 18—It is reported that the Sisters are going to launch their own newspaper, *The Theatrical and Society Compendium*. (*The Pantagraph* [Bloomington, Illinois], 18 July 1901)
August 1–7—Harlem Park, Rockford:

[1901] the Sisters are reported to have been paid $300 for the week. (*The Daily Chronicle*, 13 August 1901)

August 23—The show in Theiler's Park, Joliet (later renamed Rivals Park) is cancelled due to poor ticket sales. The Cherrys, unable to pay their hotel bill, have their luggage impounded by the police. (*Rock Island Argus*, 23 August 1901)

September 4—The sisters win a rare court case, and are awarded $120 against the Knights of the Globe, a fraternal organization based in Illinois, for lost earnings as the result of the cancelled performance at Theiler's Park, Joliet. (*Rock Island Argus*, 5 September 1901)

September 23—The Sisters perform at the Economic in Clinton, Iowa for an entirely female audience, and announce that they will only play in front of women in the future. ("Cherry Sisters Won't Appear Before Men," *The Topeka Daily Capital*, 25 September 1901)

September 30–October 5—The sisters are one of the attractions at Wichita's Big Carnival. (*Wichita Daily Beacon*, 24 August 1901)

October 5—"CHERRY SISTERS STILL ALIVE. From the hopeful State of Iowa comes fresh verification of the Biblical axiom about a prophet being without honor in his own country. They had a carnival out at Marshalltown the other day, and the Cherry Sisters, probably as representative products of the State, were engaged to appear as one of the chiefest attractions. They were pleased to so appear, but their kindly feelings in the matter disintegrated, it is said, when they arrived upon the scene and saw the way in which they were billed. They threaten, according to report, to sue the Marshalltown Carnival Company for damages, objecting to such billing as 'Iowa's Famous Song Birds! Bad Eggs, Black Powder, and Ten-gauge Guns Barred!' Furthermore comes a rumor that the Cherries have determined upon a new rule and hereafter will ex elude men from their audiences, posting the sign 'For Women Only' at the box-office during each engagement. Now, will the men be good?" (*New York Dramatic Mirror*, 5 October 1901)

October 7–12—According to Ella, the Sisters are scheduled to play the Cedar Rapids Carnival. (*Marion Pilot*, 3 October 1901)

October 31—Oakland, Iowa. (Jessie's Diary)

November 20—The Overland, Nebraska City: "Poor house and performance." (*New York Dramatic Mirror*, 7 December 1901)

November 28—Dohany Opera House, Council Bluffs. (*Omaha Daily Bee*, 29 November 1901)

December 8—Miaco's Trocadero, Omaha, Nebraska for a week: "Drew fairly good houses." (*New York Clipper*, 21 December 1901) According to Jessie's diary the sisters took $823.65 at the box office, with their share being $247.25

December 19—Addie Cherry is "taken sick with a fever" (Jessie's Diary). She had measles. (Van Etten, p141)

1902: February 4—Toler Auditorium, Wichita. (*The Wichita Daily Eagle*, 29 January 1902)

February 8—New Ragsdale Opera House, Newton, Kansas. (*The Evening Kansan-Republican*, 6 February 1902)

February 14—Shaw Theater, Hutchinson. (*The Hutchinson News*, 11 February 1902)

February 18—Woods' Opera House, Wellington, Kansas. (*New York Dramatic Mirror*, 8 March 1902)

February 21—Pittsburg, Opera House, cancelled due to bad weather. (*The Pittsburg Daily Headlight*, 21 February 1902)

February 25—Topeka, Kansas (cancelled). (*Topeka Daily Capital Sun*, 23 February 1902)

February 26-March 9—Two weeks at the Standard Theater, Fort Worth, Texas. (*New York Clipper*, 15 March 1902)

March 10-11—The Sisters play the Grand, Waco, Texas. (*New York Dramatic Mirror*, 29 March 1902)

March 13—The Sisters' appearance at the Opera House, Denison, Texas is postponed after they miss their train and fail to appear. (*New York Dramatic Mirror*, 29 March 1902)

March 17—The Sisters play the Opera House, Denison. (*New York Dramatic Mirror*, 29 March 1902)

May 24-July 4—Summer Season at Delmar Garden, St. Louis in their own theater (probably a tent), after which the trio "retire" to Marion. ("Youngest of the Cherry Sisters is off the Stage Forever," *St. Louis Post Dispatch*, 18 October 1903)

October 4-5—Midway Carnival, Omaha. (*Omaha Daily Bee*, 5 October 1902)

October 18—After appearing for a week in Fort Smith (under their own tent), the Sisters attempt to skip town but are prevented from leaving until they settle their bills.

November 17—West End Park, Little Rock for a week (possibly cancelled or closed early?) (*Arkansas Democrat*, 13 November 1902)

November 21—The Sisters play a benefit at Houck's Music Hall, Little Rock, Arkansas—with a promise that one half of the proceeds will be donated to a local children's home. (*Daily Arkansas Gazette*, 18 November 1902)

1903: January 3—The Sisters are reported to have left Hot Springs, Arkansas under a cloud: "The Cherry Sisters packed their grips yesterday and silently stole away. Before leaving they said they had had enough of the Springs, and would not play there again if they were each presented with a private residence and bathhouse…." Whatever their gripe was it would soon be overlooked. ("Cherry Sisters Steal Away," *New York Sunday Telegraph*, 4 January 1903)

February 22-23—Headlining appearance at Chute's Park Theater, Los Angeles, for a special Washington's Birthday celebration.

April 18—it is reported that the Cherry Sisters are the "owners and managers of a hotel down at Hot Springs, Ark." ("Caught in the Crowd," *Chicago Tribune*, 18 April 1903)

September 3—Reports appear that Jessie has been ill with a fever, but is recovering well.

September 30—Jessie Cherry dies at 535, Quapaw Avenue, Hot Springs,

[1903] Arkansas, of typhoid. (*Daily Arkansas Gazette*, 2 October 1903)

October 6—Jessie is buried in Cedar Rapids. (*New York Clipper*, 17 October 1903)

October 9—It is reported that D.N. Hitchcock, of the Reservation Inn, has been assaulted by two men in a dispute over unpaid wages; both were employed by the Cherry Sisters, who had been running the Inn's dining room. (*Arkansas Democrat*, 9 October 1903)

1904: July 31—August 3 Addie and Effie play for a week at the Wenona Beach Park Casino, Bay City as part of a touring package that also includes Orville and Frank, and Manning and Du Crow. (*New York Clipper*, 30 July 1904)

August 4–7—The Sisters appear at the Riverside Park Casino, Saginaw. (*New York Clipper*, 30 July 1904)

1905: January 8—People's Theater, Cedar Rapids for a week, with George and Sophie Allyn, Jack Bentham and Blanche Freeman, J.L. Samuels, Ray W. Fay and the polyscope (*New York Clipper*, 20 January 1905) The Selig Polyscope Company was a motion picture business, founded in Chicago in 1896 by William Selig.

February 20–25—The Unique Theater, Indianapolis for a week. (*The Indianapolis Star*, 19 February 1905)

April 22—The Anchor, Saybrook. According to the newspaper, four sisters appear. (*The Weekly Pantagraph*, 28 April 1905)

May 8—People's Theater, Cedar Rapids for a week. (*New York Clipper*, 20 May 1905)

July 3–8—The Midland, Fort Dodge, Iowa. (*New York Clipper*, 8 July 1905)

1906: February 12–17—Bijou Theater, Dubuque. (*The Galena Tribune*, 15 February 1906)

February 19—Bijou Theater, Des Moines for a week. (*The Des Moines Register*, 18 February 1906)

March 5–10—Bijou Theater, Decatur. (*The Decatur Herald*, 27 February 1906)

March—The sisters play the Bijou Theater, Dubuque.

March 10—"The Cherry Sisters, Addie and Effie, are enjoying their last farewell tour, by actual count, says a Des Moines paper, the fourth. The round of blood-curdling stories of folding bed accidents and the like which always accompany their journeys have come forth like old acquaintances. These performers are at their old sketch, which means that they are trying to impersonate somebody or something though with much less success than can be well imagined. However, they appear to be a success in the way of drawing big crowds." (*Billboard*, 10 March 1906)

March 19–25—Bijou Theater, Atlanta, Georgia.

March 27–28—Calumet Theater, South Chicago (*The Topeka Daily Capital*, 29 March 1906)

April 2–7—Euson's Theater, Chicago.

April—Bijou Family Theater, Kenosha, Wisconsin. (*New York Dramatic Mirror*, 21 April 1906)

April 16—Idea Vaudeville Theater, Fond du Lac, Wisconsin.

April—Bijou Family Theater, Racine,

Wisconsin: "the rush so great [that] people were turned away at nearly all performances." (*New York Dramatic Mirror*, 28 April 1906)

April 23-28—Fond du Lac, Wisconsin. (*New York Dramatic Mirror*, 28 April 1906)

April 30-May 5—Bijou, Oshkosh, Wisconsin. (*New York Dramatic Mirror*, 5 May 1906)

June 9—"We have just closed a fifteen weeks' engagement over the Western and International circuit. Owing to Effie Cherry not having been very strong since she had the typhoid fever we will not work through the summer, bat will spend the most of our time with our sister in the country." (*New York Clipper*, 9 June 1906)

July 16—All four Sisters appear at a temperance meeting held in Lexington, Illinois. (*Weekly Pantagraph*, 20 July 1906)

July 19—Ella, Lizzie, Addie and Effie take part in a temperance rally held in the streets of Weston, Illinois. (*Weekly Pantagraph*, 27 July 1906)

December 31-January 5—People's Theater, St Joseph, Missouri. (*New York Clipper*, 5 January 1907)

1907: January 7-12—People's Theater, Leavenworth, Kansas. (*New York Clipper*, 12 January 1907)

January—Lyric Theater, Sioux City. (*The Nashua Reporter*, 10 January 1907)

January 13-19—Orpheum, Omaha, Nebraska. (*New York Dramatic Mirror*, 19 January 1907)

January 20-26—Parlor, Omaha, Nebraska. (*New York Clipper*, 26 January 1907)

January 27-February 2—Yale, Theater, Kansas City. (*New York Clipper*, 2 February 1907)

February 4-9—Family Theater, Davenport, Indiana. (*New York Clipper*, 9 February 1907)

February 11-16—Bijou, Quincy, Illinois. (*New York Clipper*, 16 February 1907)

February 18-23—Industrial Theater, Moline. (*New York Dramatic Mirror*, 23 February 1907)

March 4-10—Star Theater, Chicago. (*New York Clipper*, 9 March 1907)

March 9—"CHERRY SISTERS TO REST. The Cherry Sisters, whose memorable performance at Hammerstein's Olympia several years ago created a sensation, inform THE MIRROR that the season of their concert company will close at Moline. Ill., owing to the Illness of Miss Effie. They will rest at their country home, near Cedar Rapids until next season." (*New York Dramatic Mirror*, 9 March 1907)

March 11-16—Empire vaudeville house, Freeport. Illinois. (*Freeport Journal-Standard*, 11 March 1907)

March 18-21—Bijou, Galesburg, Illinois. (*Variety*, 23 March 1907)

March—Industrial Theater, Moline, Illinois. (*New York Clipper*, 9 March 1907)

1908: January 12-18—Teddy Theater, Chicago, with Bell's Animals, Mae Mason, and the Spanish Bullfighters. (*New York Clipper*, 25 January 1908)

January 27-February 1—Lyric Theater, Chicago Heights with Magical Marvin and the Three Harrisons. (*New York Clipper*, 1 February 1908)

February 3-8—Iola Theater, Chicago. (*New York Clipper*, 8 February 1908)

[1908] February 17-29—Empire Theater, Chicago. (*Saturday Blade*, 22 February 1908)

March 15—Star Theater, St. Paul, for a week with the Merry Maidens. (*New York Dramatic Mirror*, 4 April 1908)

March 23—Addie and Effie begin a weeklong engagement at the Metropolitan, Duluth, supporting the Merry Maidens. (*The Labor World*, 21 March 1908)

March 30-April 4—The Dewey Theater, in Minneapolis with the Merry Maidens. (*Star Tribune*, 2 April 1908)

April 5-8—New Empire Theater, Des Moines with the Merry Maidens. (*The Des Moines Register*, 6 April 1908)

July 4—The Sisters play in Marion. Ahead of their performance, the local council issues an official apology for the way the sisters were treated at their performances in 1895.

July 26-August 1—The Sisters are booked to play Peoria, Illinois. (date later changed) (*New York Dramatic Mirror*, 8 August 1908)

August 2-9—At the Al Fresco Park in Peoria, Illinois the Sisters play to an estimated 30,000 people. (*New York Dramatic Mirror*, 29 August 1908)

September 24-26—Two performances a day at the Delphis Theater, Cedar Rapids. (*Cedar Rapids Evening Gazette*, 24 September 1908)

December 17-20—Family Theater, Rock Island. (*The Rock Island Argus*, 16 December 1908)

December 28-January 2—Columbia Theater, Chicago. (*New York Clipper*, 2 January 1909)

1909: January—Pekin Theater, Chicago. (*New York Clipper*, 16 January 1909)

February 1-6—Crystal Theater, Chicago. (*New York Clipper*, 30 January 1909)

February 22-27—Palais Royal, Chicago. (*New York Clipper*, 27 February 1909)

March 1-6—Vaudette Vaudeville Theater, Englewood, Chicago twice a day for a week. (Advert in *The Englewood Economist*, 2 March 1909)

March 13—The *New York Dramatic Mirror*, announces that Willie Hammerstein has signed the Cherry Sisters "for an indefinite engagement at the Victoria Theater, beginning in April." (*New York Dramatic Mirror*, 13 March 1909)

March 20—*Billboard* erroneously reports that "two of the four sisters who caused such a sensation in New York several years ago (Lizzie and Jessie) have since reformed and married" and that "the other two are not only willing to play an engagement at Hammerstein's Victoria, but are endeavoring to prevail upon the two married ones to return to the footlights." (*The Billboard*, 20 March 1909)

1910: June 22—The Cherry Sisters appear with Duncan the Hypnotist at the Air Dome theater, Monmouth, Illinois. (*Republican-Atlas*, 23 June 1910)

August 3—Al Fresco Park, Peoria, Illinois (for two weeks).

September 8—Variety reports that Addie and Effie are protesting the inclusion of portraits of the Ringling Brothers in Iowa's Hall of fame. ("Kings for Hall of Fame," *Variety*, 10 September 1910)

1911: January 24—Alcazar, Madison St, Chicago (three nights). (*New York Clipper*, 4 February 1911)

February 6–11—Clark Theater, Chicago. (*Variety*, 11 February 1911)

February 13—Sittners Theater, Chicago for one week. (*Variety*, 18 February 1911)

March 6–8—Crystal Theater, Waterloo, Iowa; rescheduled from the previous week after the Sisters were detained in Chicago. (*Evening Times–Republican*, 9 March 1911)

March 13–18—Fort Dodge (*Evening Times–Republican*, 17 March 1911)

June 4–9—Portola Theater, San Francisco, with the Three Armentos, Frank Bell and his dogs, Maud Still, Hazel Bedette, and others plus moving pictures. (*New York Clipper* 17 June 1911)

1912: December 6—Addie and Effie appear at the Lake View Workers' Bazaar, held at Edgewood No. 3 School, Ellis Park, Cedar Rapids. (*Cedar Rapids Evening Gazette*, 5 December 1912)

December 9—The Sisters are once again booked to perform at Willie Hammerstein's Victoria Theater, on the corner of 42nd Street and Broadway. (*Variety*, 22 November 1912)

1913: February 24–26—Arcade Theater, Minot, North Dakota. (*The Ward County Independent*, 20 February 1913)

March 6–8—Brinkman Theater, Bemidji, Minnesota, with specialty act Pratt's High School Terriers and a movie show. (*The Pioneer*, 6 March 1913)

March 31–April 2—Garrick, Burlington. (*Cedar Rapids Evening Gazette*, 31 March 1913)

April 3—Burlington, Iowa: "A regular old time Cherry sisters demonstration, with trimmings of fruit and vegetables, marked the close of a vaudeville engagement by the sisters at a Burlington theater recently. When the women had about finished their act, a shower of carrots and onions greeted them. They were struck with the missiles and left the stage in search of a policeman to arrest the audience, but did not return." (*Marion Sentinel*, 10 April 1913)

April 17–20—Idea Theater, Fond du Lac. (*Fond du Lac Commonwealth Reporter*, 17 April 1913)

May 14—Haymarket Theater, Chicago. The first night of a variety show put on by the Cherry Sisters Vaudeville Company, another attempt by Addie and Effie to manage their own affairs. Opening night revenue was $11.15

May 15—Haymarket Theater, Chicago. $8.60 taken at the box office.

May 16—After just two dates, the Cherry Sisters Vaudeville Company—which includes seven acts and a motion picture—shuts up shop. A show scheduled for this night is cancelled, and the sisters skip town without leaving a forwarding address. ("Back to Farm For Cherry Sisters," *Billboard*, May 23, 1913)

May 17—The Sisters were due to join Norman Friedwald and his Jolly Minstrel maids at the Broadway Theater, Muskogee, Oklahoma. (*New York Clipper*, 30 May 1914)

[1913] May 18—The Sisters play two shows in the evening at the Empire, Rock Island, supporting Sophie Tucker (*Rock Island Argus,* 17 May 1913)

May 19-20—The Family Theater, Rock Island, Illinois. (*Rock Island Argus,* 19 May 1913)

1914: May 17-21—The Sisters appear at the Broadway theater, Muskogee, Oklahoma as part of Norman Friedewald's Jolly Minstrel Maids company. (*New York Clipper,* 30 May 1914)

1915: January 17-20—Empress Theater, Des Moines, Iowa. (*The Des Moines Register,* 17 January 1915)

January 30—Waterloo, Iowa. (From handbill in Rennie Collection)

May 3-8—Gayety Theater, Omaha, Nebraska for a week. (*Omaha Daily Bee,* 4 May 1915)

December 23-26—The Sisters are playing at McVicker's Theater, Chicago. (*Variety,* 29 December 1915)

1916: May 17-22—Empress Theater, Des Moines, with Gus Elmore's Cannibal Maids. (*The Des Moines Register,* 7 May 1916)

May 25-27—Three shows a day for three days at the Majestic Theater, Cedar Rapids. (*Marion Sentinel,* 25 May 1916)

June 3—The Sisters give three performances (one matinee and two evening shows) at the Majestic Theater, Cedar Rapids. ("Cherry Sisters to Play Return Date," *Cedar Rapids Daily Republican,* 31 May 1916)

1918: June—"After an absence of several years the Cherry Sisters have been persuaded by Ed. Williams to return to the footlights for his performances of 'Mam'zelle.' The girls have shaken out their wardrobe, collected their greasepaints and rehearsed their numbers and are prepared to repeat their success of earlier years. Following 'Mam'zelle' will be 'The House of Glass,' featuring Tiny Leone. Mr. Williams states that in spite of adverse conditions his companies at Quincy, Ill., Kokomo, Ind., and Cedar Rapids, Ia., are playing to record business." (*New York Dramatic Mirror,* June 1918)

June 22—Addie and Effie, joined by Lizzie, appear for a weeklong engagement at a theater in Cedar Rapids. ("Cherry Sisters End Their Stage Career," *The Sioux County Index,* 28 June 1918)

June 28—First mention in press of Sisters running a bakery: "Poor investments have caused them to lose the farm and in recent years they are said to have been in straitened financial circumstances. They now run a little bakery on the west side of the river." ("Cherry Sisters End Their Stage Career," *The Sioux County Index,* 28 June 1918)

1919: June 25-26—Tackett's Theater, Coffeyville. (*The Coffeyville Daily Journal,* 24 June 1919)

October 8—Performance at the Winter Garden, Wichita, Kansas. ("Amusements," *The Wichita Daily Eagle,* 8 October 1919)

1921: March—"Will Morrissey announces a review that will bring back the famous Cherry Sisters to Broadway next month. A feature of the piece will be excerpts from grand opera in which both he and the sisters will appear." (*New York Dramatic Mirror,* March 1921) Morrissey is a composer, performer and producer, and author of a number of Broadway shows.

July—Addie and Effie announce that they will begin their "First Farewell Tour" (actually their third series of farewell dates) in New York in the Fall, promoted by their former press agent and manager Cal Harris. ("Cherrys to Come Back," *Brooklyn Daily Eagle*, 31 July 1921)

July 18—Williamsburg, Iowa. (*Marion Weekly Sentinel*, 14 July 1921)

August 16–21—The Sisters play the Twenty-First Annual Marion Interstate Fair; one of seven vaudeville acts, playing several times a day. (*Cedar Rapids Evening Gazette*, 21 July 1921)

1922: December 31—Myers Theater, Janesville, Wisconsin. The Sisters play a special New Year's Eve show. (*Janesville Daily Gazette*, 30 December 1922)

1924: February 29—Effie Cherry announces her intention to run for mayor of Cedar Rapids.

March 4—Effie appears on the stage of the Majestic Theater, Cedar Rapids to give a talk during her mayoral campaign. (*Southeast Missourian*, 5 March 1924)

March 18—Effie comes third in the race for mayor.

March 19—Addie and Effie announce that they have signed a contract for a "comeback" tour with the Orpheum Circuit.

March 22—Addie and Effie sign a contract to take part in a tour promoted by the Boyd B. Trousdale Players. (Contract in University of Iowa collection).

April 13—Addie and Effie begin a "comeback tour" with an appearance at the Crystal Theater, Waterloo, Iowa. (*Waterloo Evening Courier and Reporter*, 12 April 1924)

April 17—Orpheum, Sioux City, Iowa.

April 24—Their appearance on stage in Council Bluffs ends in a near riot, with "overripe tomatoes, cabbages, stale eggs and even a black cat" hurled at stage. ("Cherry Sisters Find Comeback 'As Was,'" *Syracuse Journal*, 25 April 1924)

May 29—Fundraising society the Cheese Club of Brooklyn announce that they hope to engage the Sisters to appear in their upcoming charity revue "One Hulluva Night." (*Brooklyn Daily Eagle*, 29 May 1924)

August 27—*Variety* reports that Addie and Effie are to produce a talent show in Cedar Rapids. "O shades of the Roman Stadium, the dying gladiators and the rest of the Midnight Scandals! The Cherry Sisters will produce and present at the City Auditorium Sept. 11–12 a production that will give home town Thespians a field as wide as the Russian steppes. Opportunities for local aspirants to strut their stuff will be unlimited. Following the fling at producing, the sisters will swing into a good old-time political campaign in support of La Follette. Effie will immediately take the stump and tour the country, making speeches on behalf of 'Fighting Bob.' Addie will remain at home and when not too busy with directing the activities of the local La Follette Club she will get together the old trousseau preparatory to the time the Cherry Sisters

[1924] will again swoop down on the mirthful way along Broadway." ("2 Cherrys Producing Local Talent Show," *Variety*, 27 August 1924)

September 18-19—City Auditorium, Cedar Rapids, with their "Show of the Ages" local talent show. (*Cedar Rapids Evening Gazette*, 16 September 1924)

1925: January 5-10—Pantages Theater, Minneapolis. (*Cedar Rapids Evening Gazette*, 7 January 1925)

August 8—Effie announces her plans to stand for mayor a second time. (*Lewiston Daily Sun*, 10 August 1925)

September 8—Wapsie Valley Fair, with full vaudeville program. Week-long festival; the Cherrys only play one night. Billed as "their only appearance in eastern Iowa." ("Wapsie Valley Fair All of Next Week," *Marion Sentinel*, 3 September 1925)

October 12—Addie and Effie make their radio debut, performing on Cedar Rapids' WKAA. (*Cedar Rapids Republican*, 11 October 1925)

1926: February 15—Addie and Effie appear on radio station KWCR in Cedar Rapids. (*Cedar Rapids Republican*, 7 February 1926)

February 19—Addie writes to the editor of *Variety*, asking him to print Effie's picture alongside details of her political platform.

February 25-27—Addie and Effie to appear at the Majestic, Cedar Rapids, performing both matinee and evening shows.

March 16—Effie fails in her attempt to become mayor of Cedar Rapids, having polled just 347 votes.

March 18—Greene, Iowa. (*The Greene Recorder*, 31 March 1926)

December 27—Sioux City for a week. (*The Argus-Leader*, 22 December 1926)

1927: May 17—The Sisters provide entertainment for the closing night banquet of a three-day baker's convention at the Hotel Montrose, Cedar Rapids. The *Gazette* notes that the sisters are still "operating a bakery here." (*Cedar Rapids Sunday Gazette and Republican*, 18 May 1927)

1928: September 10—The Sisters, as part of a cast of 100, play a midnight show for the American Legion convention at the Memorial Building, Cedar Rapids. They perform "The Gypsy's Warning," with Ella. The show is advertised as their "farewell appearance." (*Cedar Rapids Sunday Gazette and Republican*, 9 September 1928)

September 19—Addie and Effie begin a three-day engagement at the Majestic, Cedar Rapids. (*Cedar Rapids Gazette*, 20 September 1928)

October 3—Fall Festival, Iowa Falls. (*Waterloo Daily Courier*, 29 September 1928)

October 26—The Sisters perform at the annual banquet held by the Iowa Automobile Merchants Association, held in Cedar Rapids. (*Cedar Rapids Sunday Gazette and Republican*, 9 September 1928)

1929: January 17—The Sisters are one of the acts providing entertainment at the Cedar Rapids Federation of Labor dinner. (*Cedar Rapids Evening Gazette and Republican*, 15 January 1929)

March 23—The Cherry Sisters are booked to appear in The Shrine

Jollies of 1929, a charity event at the Shrine Temple, Des Moines. (*The Des Moines Register*, 24 March 1929)

1930: November 13—Effie registers copyright in her play "Nobody's Child, or the Gypsy's Waif, a Play in Five Acts." (*Catalog of Copyright Entries*, 1930)

1931: July 2—The Sisters are in Davenport, Iowa, to appear on a local radio station and give a performance at the Kiwanis Club. (*Cedar Rapids Evening Gazette and Republican*, 2 July 1931)

July 31–August 2—Sylvan Theater, Greenwood Park, Des Moines. (*The Des Moines Register*, 29 July 1931) The Saturday evening show was cancelled due to bad weather, and the Sisters were held over for an extra night (Monday 3 August). They played to almost 1,000 people a night, in a 15 minute set that included "A Good Time Is Coming," "The Modern Woman," "She Was My Sister" and "Eulogy on the Cherry Sisters." ("Cherry Sisters revert to 90s," *The Des Moines Register*, 1 August 1931)

August 4–9—Addie and Effie play the dance pavilion at Cedar Park, performing a 15 minute set as part of the "Show of Yesterday and Songs of Today," with Bob Zila. (*Cedar Rapids Evening Gazette and Republican*, 2 August 1931)

August 23—Lake Comar, Story City (matinee and evening) with their "Show of Yesterday." ("Cherry Sisters at Comar Sunday," *Ames Daily Tribune*, 22 August 1931)

1932: January 8—"The famous Cherry Sisters are hostesses at an osteopathic school in Iowa." (*Smithtown Messenger*, 8 January 1932)

January 25—The Sisters appear at the Majestic, Cedar Rapids. (*Variety*, 26 January 1932)

August 27—The Sisters perform at the annual Bean Day community celebration in Newhall, Iowa. (*Waterloo Daily Courier*, 19 August 1932)

December 4—A report appears in the press stating that Addie and Effie are planning a return to the stage. (*Spokesman-Review*)

1933: January 5—The Sisters are appearing at the Garrick Burlesque House in St. Louis, alongside Wally Vernon and Ann Corio.

January 7–8—Addie and Effie play in Des Moines "on farewell tour." (*Milwaukee Sentinel*, 9 January 1933)

July 31—Addie and Effie finally achieve a lifetime ambition, and visit the Chicago World's Fair. ("Cherry Sisters at World's Fair," *Daily Register*, 31 July 1933)

September 14—Australian newspaper the *Adelaide Sport* reports that three of the "elderly spinsters, who still cling to ankle length skirts and high waists are planning to put on their old act just as they did more than 30 years ago." (*Adelaide Sport*, 14 September 1933)

September 16–22—The Sisters are engaged for a week to appear at the Gayety Theater, Milwaukee through Milt Schuster of the Schuster Booking Agency, Chicago. ("Where Cherry Sisters Star Is In Burlesque," *Milwaukee Journal*, 17 September 1933)

September—Addie and Effie appear at

[1933] the New Lookout House, Covington, Kentucky, "two shows nightly, 10:30 and 12:30."

1934: February 27—Ella and Lizzie are evicted from the family farm and taken to St. Luke's Hospital, Cedar Rapids. ("2 Cherrys In County Home," *The Des Moines Register*, 7 March 1934)

March 5—Ella and Lizzie are committed to the Linn County Home. ("2 Cherrys In County Home," *The Des Moines Register*, 7 March 1934)

March 12—Ella Cherry dies in Marion.

March 15—Ella's funeral takes place at the Yocum Funeral Home chapel in Marion. (*The Des Moines Register*, 14 March 1934)

March 23–24—The Sisters appear at the Iowa Theater, Cedar Rapids, three shows a day. Their spot—they perform "The Gypsy's Warning" (presumably with someone other than Lizzie) as an added live attraction to a screening of an Irene Dunne film. ("Cherry Sisters to Revive Days of Gay Nineties," *Cedar Rapids Tribune*, 23 March 1934) Their show was held over for a third day. (*Cedar Rapids Gazette*, 25 March 1934)

March 23—Addie and Effie entertain at a party held by Mrs. George Douglas at her home in Cedar Rapids. (*Cedar Rapids Gazette*, 25 March 1934)

May 25–26—The Sisters perform at the Montana Stockgrowers' Association Jubilee. ("Old West Lives Again In Fete," *Des Moines Register*, 26 May 1934)

June—President Theater, Des Moines, Iowa. (*Cedar Rapids Tribune*, 8 June 1934)

September 3—The Sisters, with Carl Whyte, appear at the Mississippi Fairgrounds, Davenport, Iowa. ("Cherry Sisters to Appear at Iowa Farmers' Show," *Chicago Daily Tribune*, 6 August 1934)

September 4—Addie, Effie and Carl Whyte play the West Hotel, Minneapolis. The Sisters take parts in the temperance drama "The Drunkard." ("Cherry Sisters To Revive Worst Vaudeville Act," *The Minneapolis Star*, 4 September 1934)

September 26—Addie and Effie begin a month long residency at a nightclub (the Nut House) in Chicago, and announce their plans to play the following spring at a command performance in front of the British royal family. (*Milwaukee Journal*, October 4, 1934)

October 26—The Sisters and Whyte are at the New Lookout House, Cincinnati, for a week, with a chorus known as "the Beef Trust." (*The Cincinnati Enquirer*, 28 October 1934)

November 10—Garrick Theater, St. Louis for a week with their show "Legs and Laughter." (*The St. Louis Star and Times*, 7 November 1934)

1935: February—Omaha, Nebraska. (*Lansing State Journal*, 26 February 1935)

March 31–April 2—Fitchburg Theater, Fitchburg, Massachusetts, in the "Bowery Follies." (*Fitchburg Sentinel*, 27 March 1935)

April 6—Iowa Theater, Cedar Rapids. (*Cedar Rapids Gazette*, 6 April 1935)

May 12—Embassy Night Club, Cedar Rapids. (*Cedar Rapids Gazette*, 12 May 1935)

May 15—Olympic Theater, Cedar

Rapids, with Carl Whyte. (*Cedar Rapids Gazette*, 15 May 1935)

May 17—Colonial Theatre, 3rd Avenue West, Cedar Rapids, "in a new act," with Carl Whyte. (From handbill)

May 18—Old Timer Club, Cedar Rapids. (*Cedar Rapids Gazette*, 18 May 1935)

June 6—Olympic Theater, Cedar Rapids. This is announced as "the last time they will appear at the Olympic." (*Cedar Rapids Gazette*, 5 June 1935)

September 14—Two performances at the Annual Celebration, Swisher, Iowa. (*Cedar Rapids Gazette*, 13 September 1935)

October 1—Addie and Effie arrive in New York, and greet the press ahead of their appearance at Billy's Gay Nineties.

October 3—The Sisters open at Billy's Gay Nineties. (*Daily News*, 9 October 1935)

October 5—Addie and Effie are interviewed by Charles Estcourt, Jr., of the Buffalo Evening News, backstage at New York night club Billy's Gay Nineties.

October 19—Adie and Effie begin a week's booking at the New Saverin Café, Buffalo. (*Buffalo Evening News*, 17 October 1935)

1936: February 1—The Sisters open at the Garrick, St. Louis, as part of a burlesque bill entitles "Girls From the Follies." (*The St. Louis Star and Times*, 29 January 1936)

February 4—Lizzie is evicted from the family farm and is placed, by the sheriff's office, in the Linn County Home. ("4th Cherry Sister," *Variety*, 5 February 1936)

February 10–29—Addie and Effie are playing the Bowery Music Hall and Bar, in St. Louis. (*The St. Louis Star and Times*, 11 February 1936)

April 4—Colonial, Indianapolis. ("In New Show," *The Indianapolis Star*, 3 April 1936)

May 11—Elizabeth Viola Cherry dies, in hospital in Cedar Rapids. ("Elizabeth Cherry Dies," *Cedar Rapids Gazette*, 12 May 1936)

December 12—The Sisters appear at the WHO Barn Dance Frolic in Des Moines, broadcast on radio. ("Cherry Sisters Brag of Drawing Bigger Crowds than Ina Clair," *Cedar Rapids Gazette*, 27 December 1936)

1937: April 27—The Sisters appear as the headline act at a Gay 90s-themed banquet held at the Pla-Mor Ballroom by Cedar Rapids' Rotarians. More than 900 Rotarians from more than 65 clubs all over Iowa attend. (*Cedar Rapids Gazette*, 27 April 1957)

August 26—Cass Opera House, Sumner, Iowa. (*The Fredericksburg News*, 26 August 1937)

1938: April 3–6—The Cherry Sisters make their final appearances, at the Strand Theater, Cedar Rapids. (*Cedar Rapids Gazette*, 31 March 1938)

June 21–June 26—"The Cherry Sisters" appear with Gruberg's Carnival in Rochester, N.Y. This was probably Wilhelmina and Lottie May Pannsy, a pair of chorus girls who were playing at around the same time. (*Billboard*, 2 July 1938)

June 27–July 2—"The Cherry Sisters" appear with Gruberg's Carnival in Jamestown, N.Y. (*Billboard*, 16 July 1938)

1942: October 25—Addie Cherry dies, aged 83, in Cedar Rapids. (*St Petersburg Times*, 28 October 1942)

1944: August 5—Effie Cherry, the last of the sisters, dies in a nursing home in Cedar Rapids, aged 76. August 7—Effie is buried in Cedar Rapids. "Only a dozen elderly women attended the funeral." (*Buffalo Evening News*, 8 August 1944)

Chapter Notes

Introduction

1. "Eulogy on the Cherry Sisters," lyrics by the Cherry Sisters.
2. "Mobbed by Hoodlums," *The Alton Evening Telegraph*, 19 November 1895.
3. "The Cherry Sisters Coming," *The New York Dramatic Mirror*, 14 November 1896.
4. "Cherry Sisters," *Dixon Evening Telegraph*, 8 June 1894.
5. "Shows for This Week," *The Illustrated Buffalo Express*, 22 January 1899.
6. "Aimed at the Actors," *The Evening Star* (Washington, D.C.), 21 October 1906.
7. T. Allston Brown, *History of the New York Stage*, Vol. 2 (New York: Dodd, Mead, 1902), p. 474.
8. Effie Cherry, *Reminiscences*, unpublished. Orville Rennie and Jane Rennie Collection, 1875–1987. Ms. 178. Special Collections, State Historical Society of Iowa, Iowa City.
9. Ibid.

Chapter 1

1. Effie Cherry, "The Autobiography of the Cherry Sisters," unpublished. Orville Rennie and Jane Rennie Collection, 1875–1987. Ms. 178. Special Collections, State Historical Society of Iowa, Iowa City.
2. Ibid.
3. *Cedar Rapids Gazette*, 21 January 1893.
4. *Marion Sentinel*, 12 January 1893.
5. "Effie Cherry Tells Minneapolis Reporter What She Is Going to Do When She's Mayor of Our City," *The Cedar Rapids Gazette*, 7 January 1925.
6. "What the Theaters Are Offering this Week," *Los Angeles Herald*, 6 August 1905.
7. "Amusements," *The Daily Gate City*, 24 December 1914.
8. "The Event of the Season," *Marion Sentinel*, 26 January 1893.
9. "An Interview with Effie and Addie Cherry," *The Republican*, 15 February 1925.
10. "The Event of the Season," *Marion Sentinel*, 26 January 1893.
11. *Cedar Rapids Gazette*, 21 January 1893.
12. Quoted in Winifred Van Etten, *The Queens of Corn*, p. 47. Box 4, Folder 1, Orville Rennie and Jane Rennie Collection, 1875–1987. Ms. 178. Special Collections, State Historical Society of Iowa, Iowa City.
13. "A Show by Prairie Girls," *The Sun* (New York), 29 March 1896.
14. *Cedar Rapids Evening Gazette*, 11 May 1893.
15. "The Autobiography of the Cherry Sisters," Effie Cherry, unpublished.
16. "Genius Nipped in the Bud," *Cedar Rapids Evening Gazette*, 3 March 1893.
17. *Cedar Rapids Gazette*, 18 February 1893.
18. Ibid.
19. "The Autobiography of the Cherry Sisters," Effie Cherry, unpublished.
20. Ibid.
21. *The Wichita Daily Eagle*, 14 February 1894.
22. *Cedar Rapids Evening Gazette*, 21 February 1893.
23. "Libel Charged," *Cedar Rapids Evening Gazette*, 24 February 1893.
24. *Boston Evening Transcript*, 17 March 1893.
25. "Genius Nipped in the Bud," *Cedar Rapids Evening Gazette*, 3 March 1893.
26. Quoted in "They're After Fred," *The Rock Island Argus*, 6 March 1893.
27. *Marion Sentinel*, 9 March 1893.
28. "A Cedar Rapids Attraction," *The Davenport Weekly Leader*, 2 March 1893.
29. "Can He be Forgiven?," *Cedar Rapids Evening Gazette*, 14 March 1893.

30. Letter from the Cherry Sisters to the editor and reporters of the *Waterloo Reporter*, 1908. Orville Rennie and Jane Rennie Collection, 1875-1987. Ms. 178. Special Collections, State Historical Society of Iowa, Iowa City.
31. "Green Gally Gawks," *Cedar Rapids Evening Gazette*, 15 March 1893.
32. *The Upper Des Moines*, 22 March 1893.
33. "Green Gally Gawks," *Cedar Rapids Evening Gazette*, 15 March 1893.
34. *Ibid*.
35. "The Cherry Sisters Chestnut," *Cedar Rapids Evening Gazette*, 15 March 1893.
36. "Green Gally Gawks," *Cedar Rapids Evening Gazette*, 15 March 1893.
37. "The Autobiography of the Cherry Sisters," Effie Cherry, unpublished.
38. "The Cherry Sisters Chestnut," *Cedar Rapids Evening Gazette*, 15 March 1893.

Chapter 2

1. Effie Cherry, "The Autobiography of the Cherry Sisters," unpublished.
2. *Ibid*.
3. Luther A. Brewer and Barthinius L. Wick, *History of Linn County Iowa* (Cedar Rapids: Torch, 1911), p. 469.
4. "Marion, the Milwaukee of Iowa," *The Marion Sentinel*, 19 August 1965.
5. Effie Cherry, "The Autobiography of the Cherry Sisters," unpublished.
6. "Our Washington Letter," *Marion Register*, 19 May 1897.
7. John Godfrey Saxe, "The Turkey and the Crow," in *Fables and Fairytales* (Boston: James R. Osgood & Co., 1875).
8. "Postscript on the Fabulous Cherry Girls," *Cedar Rapids Gazette*, 17 September 1944.
9. "Around the Town," *Cedar Rapids Gazette*, 20 March 1958.
10. Effie Cherry, "The Autobiography of the Cherry Sisters," unpublished.
11. Letter from Lizzie to Addie and Effie Cherry. Original letter lost, quoted in Van Etten, p. 36.
12. Quoted in Van Etten, p. 37.
13. Effie Cherry, "The Autobiography of the Cherry Sisters," unpublished.
14. "Marion Locals," *Cedar Rapids Evening Gazette*, 21 December 1888.
15. *Ibid*.
16. James L. Ford, "The Guileless Cherry Sisters Saw the Town," *New York Journal*, 13 December 1896.

Chapter 3

1. "The Event of the Season," *The Davenport Democrat and Leader*, 3 May 1893.
2. E.W. Osborn, "Cherry Sisters Jarred Gotham," *Springfield Republican*, 12 September 1925.
3. *The Davenport Democrat and Leader*, 14 May 1893.
4. *Cedar Rapids Evening Gazette*, 1 May 1893.
5. "Oh! What a Night!," *The Davenport Democrat and Leader*, 11 May 1893.
6. *Davenport Daily Republican*, 10 May 1983.
7. *Davenport Weekly Leader*, 10 May 1983.
8. "Oh! What a Night!," *The Davenport Democrat and Leader*, 11 May 1893.
9. *Dubuque Telegraph*, 5 May 1893.
10. *The Sun* (New York), 12 November 1896.
11. Effie Cherry, "The Autobiography of the Cherry Sisters," unpublished.
12. "A Show by Prairie Girls," *The Sun* (New York), 29 March 1896.
13. "Is It True What They Say About the Cherry Sisters?," *The Des Moines Register*, 7 August 1955.
14. "Actors Mobbed in Dubuque," *The Inter-Ocean*, 18 May 1893.
15. "Worse and Worse," *Davenport Democrat and Leader*, 21 May 1893.
16. "Actors Mobbed in Dubuque," *The Inter-Ocean*, 18 May 1893.
17. "It Was Brutal," *Dubuque Daily Herald*, 18 May 1893.
18. Effie Cherry, "The Autobiography of the Cherry Sisters," unpublished.
19. "Fame and Rotten Eggs," *The Upper Des Moines*, 24 May 1893.
20. *Ibid*.
21. "Looking in to It," *Dubuque Sunday Herald*, 21 May 1893.
22. "The Abuse of the Cherry Sisters," *Dubuque Daily Herald*, 19 May 1893.
23. "It Was Brutal," *Dubuque Daily Herald*, 18 May 1893.
24. "Thinking It All Over," *Dubuque Daily Herald*, 20 May 1893.
25. "Fame and Rotten Eggs," *The Upper Des Moines*, 24 May 1893.
26. "Worse and Worse," *Davenport Democrat and Leader*, 21 May 1893.
27. "Looking in to It," *Dubuque Sunday Herald*, 21 May 1893.
28. "Fame and Rotten Eggs," *The Upper Des Moines*, 24 May 1893.
29. "It Was Brutal," *Dubuque Daily Herald*, 18 May 1893.

30. Effie Cherry, "The Autobiography of the Cherry Sisters," unpublished.
31. *Davenport Democrat and Leader*, 23 May 1893.
32. *Cedar Rapids Gazette*, 24 May 1893.
33. "A Card From Manger Roehl," *Dubuque Daily Herald*, 20 May 1893.
34. "Looking in to It," *Dubuque Sunday Herald*, 21 May 1893.
35. "Refused to be Sworn," *Dubuque Daily Herald*, 23 May 1893.
36. "Looking in to It," *Dubuque Sunday Herald*, 21 May 1893.
37. *Ibid.*
38. "The Cherry Sisters at Dubuque," *Marion Sentinel*, 25 May 1893.
39. "Worse and Worse," *Davenport Democrat and Leader*, 21 May 1893.
40. *Cedar Rapids Gazette*, 8 June 1893.
41. *Cedar Rapids Gazette*, 26 May 1893.
42. "Plenty of Cherry Pie," *Dubuque Daily Herald*, 25 May 1893.
43. *Cedar Rapids Gazette*, 10 June 1893.
44. "Quit the Stage," *The Rock Island Argus*, 14 June 1893.
45. Effie Cherry, "The Autobiography of the Cherry Sisters," unpublished.
46. *Cedar Rapids Gazette*, 14 August 1893.
47. Undated letter, written by Lizzie Cherry on the reverse of a handbill for a Cherry Sisters concert in Fort Madison, Iowa. Orville Rennie and Jane Rennie Collection, 1875–1987. Ms. 178. Special Collections, State Historical Society of Iowa, Iowa City.
48. "The Wild Cherries," *The Rock Island Argus*, 11 September 1893.
49. *Cedar Rapids Weekly Gazette*, 17 August 1893.
50. *Chicago Inter Ocean*, 28 October 1893.
51. Letter to Lizzie Cherry from Jessie Cherry, undated, quoted in Van Etten, p. 71.
52. *Cedar Rapids Gazette*, 30 October 1893.
53. Original letter lost; quoted in Van Etten.
54. Letter to Lizzie Cherry from Helen Andrews, undated. Orville Rennie and Jane Rennie Collection, 1875–1987. Ms. 178. Special Collections, State Historical Society of Iowa, Iowa City.
55. *The Marion Sentinel*, 22 August 1895.

Chapter 4

1. "Cherry Sisters Again," *Marion Sentinel*, 27 June 1895.
2. "Oldest Booking Agent, Now in S.C., Tells Anecdotes," *Santa Cruz News*, 13 July 1937.
3. "More About the Cherries," *The Sun* (New York), 25 October 1896.
4. "The Cherry Sisters," *The Marion Pilot*, 29 August 1895.
5. *Ibid.*
6. *Ibid.*
7. "The Cherry Sisters," *Cedar Rapids Evening Gazette*, 4 September 1895.
8. Handwritten note on the reverse of handbill. Orville Rennie and Jane Rennie Collection, 1875–1987. Ms. 178. Special Collections, State Historical Society of Iowa, Iowa City.
9. "Mobbed by Hoodlums," *Alton Evening Telegraph*, 19 November 1895.
10. "Comedy Ends in Suits," *The Boston Post*, 25 November 1895.
11. "Mobbed by Hoodlums," *Alton Evening Telegraph*, 19 November 1895.
12. "The Cherry Sisters," *Marion Register*, 20 November 1895.
13. *Ibid.*
14. *New York Sun*, July 5, 1908.
15. *Cedar Rapids Evening Gazette*, 21 February 1893.
16. *Cedar Falls Gazette*, 17 March 1896.
17. Fred Allen, *Much Ado About Me* (Boston: Little, Brown, 1956), p. 307.
18. "Broadway After Dark," Ward Morehouse, *New York Sun*, 11 August 1944.
19. Effie Cherry, "The Autobiography of the Cherry Sisters," unpublished.
20. *Ibid.*
21. *Ibid.*
22. *Dubuque Times* reprinted in *Cedar Rapids Republican*, 13 March 1896.
23. *Cedar Falls Gazette*, 17 March 1896.
24. "News of the North West," *The Algona Upper Des Moines*, 18 March 1896.
25. Van Etten, p. 118.
26. Quoted in the *Marion Sentinel*, 30 July 1896.
27. "Our Washington Letter," *Marion Register*, 19 May 1897.

Chapter 5

1. "Olympia Opened," *New York Dramatic Mirror*, 30 November 1895.
2. *Ibid.*
3. *New York Dramatic Mirror*, 21 November 1896.
4. "A Show by Prairie Girls," *The Sun* (New York), 29 March 1896.
5. "More About the Cherries," *The Sun* (New York), 25 October 1896.
6. "The Cherry Sisters," *Marion Sentinel*, 29 October 1896.

7. "Notes from Stageland," *The Sun (New York)*, 26 November 1896.
8. "The Cherry Sisters Talk," *The Sun (New York)*, 6 December 1896.
9. *New York Dramatic Mirror*, 21 November 1896.
10. *The Sun* (New York), 12 November 1896.
11. *New York Dramatic Mirror*, 14 November 1896.
12. Joseph Kaye, "Around the Memoir Table," *Syracuse Journal*, 21 June 1927.
13. *The Sun* (New York), 12 November 1896.
14. James T. Powers, "To Ella Cherry of the Cherry Sisters," *New York World*, December 1896.
15. Effie Cherry, "The Autobiography of the Cherry Sisters," unpublished.
16. *The New York Journal*, 15 November 1896.
17. *The Sun* (New York), 19 November 1896.
18. "First Times in New York," *The Sun* (New York), 17 November 1896.
19. *New York World*, 17 November 1896.
20. "Supplement," *The New York Times*, 15 November 1896.
21. "Four Freaks from Iowa," *The New York Times*, November 17, 1896.
22. Charles Pike Sawyer, "Mirror of the Week," *New York Evening Post*, 1 April 1922.
23. "The Queer Cherry Sisters," *The Pittsburgh Press*, 22 November 1896.
24. James L. Ford, "Jay Performers and Jay Audience," *The New York Journal*, 17 November 1896.
25. "Notes from Stageland," *The Sun* (New York), 26 November 1896.
26. *Chicago Daily Tribune*, 17 November 1896.
27. "Heard at the Theaters," *New York Journal*, November 18, 1896.
28. "A Show by Prairie Girls," *The Sun* (New York), 29 March 1896.
29. Buster Keaton with Charles Samuels, *My Wonderful World of Slapstick* (New York: Doubleday, 1956), p. 68.
30. "Cherry Sisters," *The Davenport Democrat and Leader*, 16 November 1896.
31. "To Protect the Cherries," *New York Herald*, 21 November 1896.
32. *The Sun* (New York), 19 November 1896.
33. "Cherry Sisters Try Wan Comeback, But Pity Supplants Vegetables," *The Tennessean*, 2 January 1937.
34. "Queer Costumes on the Boulevard," *New York Tribune*, 27 November 1896.
35. *The Times-Picayune*, 7 December 1896.
36. *Democrat and Chronicle* (Rochester, New York), 21 November 1896.
37. "Chroniclings," *Rochester Democrat and Chronicle*, 16 November 1896.
38. "Songs and Singers, Plays and Players," *Rochester Democrat and Chronicle*, 29 November 1896.
39. "Piteous Farce of the Cherry Sisters," *New York Press*, 22 November 1896.
40. Ibid.
41. "Notes from Stageland," *The Sun* (New York), 26 November 1896.
42. "Piteous Farce of the Cherry Sisters," *New York Press*, 22 November 1896.
43. "A Hilarious Aftermath," *The World* (New York), 23 November 1896.
44. Ibid.
45. Ibid.
46. *New York Dramatic Mirror*, 5 December 1896.
47. "The Cherry Sisters Talk," *The Sun* (New York), 6 December 1896.
48. Ibid.
49. *The Salt Lake Herald*, 6 December 1897.
50. James L. Ford, "The Guileless Cherry Sisters Saw the Town," *New York Journal*, 13 December 1896.

Chapter 6

1. "Hawkeye Hummers," *Rock Island Argus and Daily Union*, 21 August 1897.
2. "The Cherry Sisters at Chicago," *Rock Island Argus*, 16 December 1896.
3. "The Players for This Week," *The New York Journal*, 7 March 1897.
4. "Possessors of All Gall," *Cedar Rapids Evening Gazette*, 28 July 1897.
5. "A Show by Prairie Girls," *The Sun* (New York), 29 March 1896.
6. "The Cherries Are Overripe," *St. Louis Post Dispatch*, 11 January 1897.
7. Ibid.
8. Jessie Cora Cherry, "Alone in the Street." Orville Rennie and Jane Rennie Collection, 1875–1987. Ms. 178. Special Collections, State Historical Society of Iowa, Iowa City.
9. Quoted in the *Marion Pilot*, 21 January 1897.
10. *New York Dramatic Mirror*, 13 March 1897.
11. "The Cherries and Miss Dressler," *New York Dramatic Mirror*, 13 March 1897.
12. *New York Dramatic Mirror*, 13 March 1897.
13. "A Letter from the Cherries," *Variety*, 20 March 1897.
14. *New York Clipper*, March 20 & 27, 1897.

15. *New York Dramatic Mirror*, 20 March 1897.
16. "At the Royal," *Sportsman* (Melbourne), 17 August 1897.
17. *Daily Standard Union* (Brooklyn), 6 March 1897.
18. *Daily Standard Union* (Brooklyn), 9 March 1897.
19. *Oskaloosa Daily Times*, 29 September 1896.
20. *The Baltimore Sun*, 16 March 1897.
21. "The Cherry Sisters," *The Buffalo Courier*, 23 March 1897.
22. *The Baltimore Sun*, 15 March 1897.
23. *Marion Pilot*, 15 April 1897.
24. "Cherry Sisters Flitted," *Pittsburgh Daily Post*, 5 April 1897.
25. *The Waterloo Courier*, 19 May 1897.
26. "McCarthy's Difficulties," *Buffalo Courier-Record*, May 20 1897.
27. *Evening Star* (Washington, D. C.), 4 May 1897.
28. *Evening Times*, 4 May 1897.
29. "Our Washington Letter," *Marion Register*, 19 May 1897.
30. "The Stage," *San Francisco Call*, 20 June 1897.
31. "Managed Famous Cherry Sisters," *Cedar Rapids Evening Gazette*, 9 January 1915.
32. "Cherry Sisters Part," *The Decatur Herald*, 6 June 1897.
33. "Lizzie Leaves Her Sisters," *Leavenworth Times*, 9 June 1897.
34. Charles E. Lauterbach, *Jolly Della Pringle: Star of the Western Stage* (Jefferson, NC: McFarland, 2015), p. 26.
35. "A Note from the Cherry Sisters," *New York Dramatic Mirror*, 24 July 1897.
36. "Hawkeye Hummers," *Rock Island Argus and Daily Union*, 21 August 1897.
37. *Steamboat Rock Echo*, 19 August 1897.
38. "A Bunch of Cherries," *Esterville Daily News*, 19 August 1897.
39. "Sherman Brown Describes Cherry Sisters' Visit to Milwaukee," *Milwaukee Sentinel*, 14 June 1931.
40. *New York Dramatic Mirror*, 27 November 1897.
41. "The Cherry Sisters," *Glenwood Opinion-Tribune*, 8 July 1897.
42. "The Cherry Sisters," *Mason City Globe—Gazette*, 25 October 1962.
43. Stan Gores, "Cherry Sisters Sang at Crescent Opera House," *Fond Du Lac Commonwealth Reporter*, 10 January 1969.
44. "They Are Rotten," *The Wellington Daily News*, 13 February 1902.
45. "More Woe For the Cherries," *Kansas City Journal*, 3 October 1897.
46. "Poor Havana!," *The Sunday Leader*, 8 January 1899.
47. *The Nashua Reporter*, 2 February 1899.
48. *The Des Moines Register*, 4 August 1898.
49. "The Cherry Sisters," *The Marion Sentinel*, 29 November 1900.

Chapter 7

1. *Marion Pilot*, 24 February 1898.
2. "Cherry Sisters Again," *Tri-States Union*, 20 January 1898.
3. *Marion Register*, 19 January 1898.
4. Referenced in Van Etten, p. 134.
5. "Youngest of the Cherry Sisters Is Off the Stage Forever," *St. Louis Post Dispatch*, 18.
6. "From Iowa City," *Cedar Rapids Evening Gazette*, 18 January 1898.
7. *New York Dramatic Mirror*, 5 February 1898.
8. "A Harvest of Fools," *Glenwood Tribune*, 3 February 1898.
9. *The Odebolt Chronicle*, 17 February 1898.
10. "The Cherries Were Here," *The Odebolt Chronicle*, 17 February 1898.
11. *Rock Island Argus*, 14 July 1898.
12. "Hawkeye Hummers," *The Rock Island Argus*, 21 August 1897.
13. "The Cherry Sisters," *Nebraska State Journal*, 19 October 1898.
14. *Ibid.*
15. *The Courier* (Lincoln, Nebraska), 15 October 1898.
16. "Single Bed Was Enough," *Sterling Standard*, 1 December 1898.
17. *The Belvidere Standard*, 24 November 1898.
18. *The Belvidere Standard*, 10 November 1898.
19. Advertisement, *New York Clipper*, 26 November 1898.
20. *New York Dramatic Mirror*, 31 December 1898.
21. *The Inter-Ocean*, 5 December 1898.
22. *The Belvidere Standard*, 24 November 1898.
23. "The Cherry Sisters," *Ackley World*, 2 November 1898.
24. *New York Dramatic Mirror*, 4 March 1899.

Chapter 8

1. "Cherry Sisters May Remove to Rockford," *The Belvidere Standard*, 24 November 1898.

2. "Cherry Sisters in Court," *The Daily Iowa Capitol*, 20 April 1899.
3. "Case of Addie Cherry vs. The Leader Heard," *The Des Moines Register*, 21 April 1899.
4. Burdett A. Rich and Henry P. Farnham, eds., *The Lawyers Reports Annotated*, volume 54 (Rochester, NY: Lawyer's Co-operative, 1902), pp. 855–859.
5. *Marion Pilot*, 5 October 1899.
6. "In Answer to the Marion Register," *Marion Pilot*, 21 September 1899.
7. "Gossip," *New York Morning Telegraph*, 12 June 1900.
8. "Notice," *Salt Lake Herald*, 2 August 1900.
9. Promotional handbill. Orville Rennie and Jane Rennie Collection, 1875–1987. Ms. 178. Special Collections, State Historical Society of Iowa, Iowa City.
10. "Cherry Sisters Are Broke," *Ackley World*, 21 November 1900.
11. "Court Says Cherry Sisters Got Deserts," *Chicago Tribune*, 31 May 1901.
12. "Cherries Lose," *Davenport Democrat and Leader*, 29 May 1901.
13. *El Dorado Daily Republican*, 31 May 1901.
14. Letter from Jessie Cherry to Elizabeth Cherry, undated. Orville Rennie and Jane Rennie Collection, 1875–1987. Ms. 178. Special Collections, State Historical Society of Iowa, Iowa City.
15. Letter from Jessie Cherry to Elizabeth and Ella Cherry, San Francisco, April 1900. Orville Rennie and Jane Rennie Collection, 1875–1987. Ms. 178. Special Collections, State Historical Society of Iowa, Iowa City.
16. "Cherrys Will Continue to Follow Footlights," *Rock Island Argus*, 19 July 1901.
17. *The Pantagraph* (Bloomington, Illinois), 18 July 1901.
18. "Ladies Day with Cherries," *Omaha Daily Bee*, 14 December 1901.
19. Jessie's Diary for 1901. Quoted in Van Etten, p. 167.
20. "Original in Their Roles," *Omaha Daily Bee*, 9 December 1901.
21. *Ibid.*
22. "Cherry Sisters," *Lead Daily Call*, 12 December 1901.

Chapter 9

1. Letter from Jessie to Lizzie Cherry, undated (circa 1902), Orville Rennie and Jane Rennie Collection, 1875–1987. Ms. 178. Special Collections, State Historical Society of Iowa, Iowa City.

2. Reprinted in the *Marion Sentinel*, 27 March 1902.
3. "Cherries Are Almost Ripe," *Omaha Daily Bee*, 16 January 1902.
4. "The Cherry Sisters," *Wellington Daily News*, 13 February 1902.
5. Letter from Lizzie Cherry to Addie, Effie and Jessie, 1902. Quoted in Van Etten, p. 167.
6. "The Morals of St. Louis," The Cherry Sisters, *St. Louis Post-Dispatch*, 8 September 1902.
7. "Cherry Sisters Steal Away," *New York Sunday Telegraph*, 4 January 1903.
8. "Caught in the Crowd," *Chicago Tribune*, 18 April 1903.
9. Letter from Lizzie to Addie, Effie and Jessie Cherry, 1903. Quoted in Van Etten, p. 177.
10. Letter from Ella to Addie, Effie, Jessie and Lizzie Cherry, 12 August 1903. Orville Rennie and Jane Rennie Collection, 1875–1987. Ms. 178. Special Collections, State Historical Society of Iowa, Iowa City.
11. Letter from Ella Cherry (undated), circa 1903. Orville Rennie and Jane Rennie Collection, 1875–1987. Ms. 178. Special Collections, State Historical Society of Iowa, Iowa City.
12. "A Letter from Effie Cherry," *Marion Sentinel*, 10 September 1903.
13. "Effie and Addie Fare Thee Well," *Cedar Rapids Daily Republican*, 20 February 1906.
14. Letter from Ella to Addie, Effie, Jessie and Lizzie Cherry, 1 October 1903. Quoted in Van Etten, p. 187.
15. Effie Cherry, "The Autobiography of the Cherry Sisters," unpublished.
16. Keith Kerman, "The Cherry Sisters on the Stage Again in Burlesque," *St. Louis Post Dispatch*, 22 January 1933.
17. *Arkansas Democrat*, 9 October 1903.
18. "The Cherries Are Vain," *The Decatur Herald*, 8 March 1906.
19. "Value of Three Original Records," *Edison Phonograph Monthly*, November 1904.
20. "Sisters Leave Farm to Give Vaudeville Quite a Shock," *Chicago Tribune*, 30 June 1955.
21. "The Cherry Sisters Are Back," *The Kansas City Star*, 16 January 1916.
22. "Want Voice of Dead," *Freeport Journal-Standard*, 8 April 1905.
23. Jessie Cora Cherry, "Fair Columbia," 1892. Orville Rennie and Jane Rennie Collection, 1875–1987. Ms. 178. Special Collections, State Historical Society of Iowa, Iowa City.
24. Advertisement, *The Phonoscope* 1, no. 2 (December 1896).
25. *Iowa Recorder*, 21 February 1906.
26. "The Cherries Are Vain," *The Decatur Herald*, 8 March 1906.

27. Letter from the Cherry Sisters to G.M. Gelureks, 5 August 1910. Orville Rennie and Jane Rennie Collection, 1875–1987. Ms. 178. Special Collections, State Historical Society of Iowa, Iowa City.
28. "Artist's Forum," *Variety*, 10 March 1906.
29. *Dixon Evening Telegraph*, 6 March 1906. The *San Antonio Gazette* (14 April 1906) claimed that this was a tall tale that newspapers often told about the Cherrys.
30. *New York Clipper*, 9 June 1906.
31. "Cherry Sisters," *Freeport Journal-Standard*, 12 March 1907.
32. Ibid.

Chapter 10

1. "Afternoon on the West Side Rialto, *Chicago Inter-Ocean*, 16 February 1908.
2. "The Cherry Sisters Again," *Des Moines Register*, 22 March 1908.
3. "Artists" Forum," *Variety*, April 1908.
4. "The Fourth at Marion," *Marion Sentinel*, 25 June 1908.
5. *Marion Sentinel*, 16 July 1908.
6. *Marion Register*, 24 July 1908.
7. Letter to Addie and Effie from Ella Cherry, 13 January 1909. Orville Rennie and Jane Rennie Collection, 1875–1987. Ms. 178. Special Collections, State Historical Society of Iowa, Iowa City.
8. Letter from Lizzie to Effie Cherry, 22 May 1911. Orville Rennie and Jane Rennie Collection, 1875–1987. Ms. 178. Special Collections, State Historical Society of Iowa, Iowa City.
9. Letter from Lizzie Cherry to Addie and Effie, with postscript added by Ella, 7 June 1911(?). Orville Rennie and Jane Rennie Collection, 1875–1987. Ms. 178. Special Collections, State Historical Society of Iowa, Iowa City.
10. Letter to Effie from Ella Cherry, 29 January 1911. Orville Rennie and Jane Rennie Collection, 1875–1987. Ms. 178. Special Collections, State Historical Society of Iowa, Iowa City.
11. Letter from Lizzie to Effie Cherry, 22 May 1911. Orville Rennie and Jane Rennie Collection, 1875–1987. Ms. 178. Special Collections, State Historical Society of Iowa, Iowa City.
12. *The Billboard*, 20 March 1909.
13. *Evening Times-Republican*, 17 March 1911.
14. "Will Rogers Says," *Cedar Rapids Evening Gazette and Republican*, 28 April 1928.
15. "A Few Conversational Sentences by Rogers," *Cedar Rapids Evening Gazette and Republican*, 27 April 1928.
16. *Belvidere Daily Republican*, 29 August 1910.
17. "Cherry Sisters Go Back to Farm," *Chicago Daily Tribune*, 16 May 1913.
18. Ibid.
19. "Oh, You Cherry Sisters," *Variety*, 21 May 1913.
20. "Cherry Sisters Not to Give Up Stage For Farm," *Cedar Rapids Evening Gazette*, 16 May 1913.
21. Letter from Blanche Talbot to Lizzie Cherry, 16 January 1919. Orville Rennie and Jane Rennie Collection, 1875–1987. Ms. 178. Special Collections, State Historical Society of Iowa, Iowa City.
22. *Buffalo Evening News*, 30 April 1913.
23. "Cherry Sisters at Des Moines," *Marion Sentinel*, 4 February 1915.
24. Quoted in the *Marion Sentinel*, 8 June 1916.
25. "Marion News," *The Cedar Rapids Evening Gazette*, 20 February 1903.

Chapter 11

1. Effie Cherry, "The Autobiography of the Cherry Sisters," unpublished.
2. "The Cherry Sisters," *The New York Sun*, 8 August 1944.
3. "Cherry Sisters to Make Farewell Bow," *Cedar Rapids Republican*, 18 June 1918.
4. Memorandum book belonging to Lizzie Cherry (unsigned), marked February 1916. Orville Rennie and Jane Rennie Collection, 1875–1987. Ms. 178. Special Collections, State Historical Society of Iowa, Iowa City.
5. Letter from Blanche Talbot to Lizzie Cherry, 16 January 1919. Orville Rennie and Jane Rennie Collection, 1875–1987. Ms. 178. Special Collections, State Historical Society of Iowa, Iowa City.
6. Lizzie Cherry, undated memo concerning the lawsuit brought by Sophronia Grant. Orville Rennie and Jane Rennie Collection, 1875–1987. Ms. 178. Special Collections, State Historical Society of Iowa, Iowa City.
7. "Sues on Account of Writ," *Cedar Rapids Evening Gazette*, 30 April 1921.
8. "Cherry Sisters Win High Court Battle," *Cedar Rapids Evening Gazette*, 14 January 1915.
9. "Theda Bara Roasted by Dramatic Critics," *Daily Palladium*, 18 March 1920.
10. "Cherry Sisters Return to Stage," *Cedar Rapids Evening Gazette*, 4 August 1921.
11. "Cherry Sisters Threatening to Return to Stage," *Freeport Journal-Standard*, 9 August 1921.
12. *Brooklyn Daily Eagle*, 31 July 1921.

13. "Twenty Years After," *The Indianapolis Star*, 31 July 1921.
14. "Cherry Sisters Return to Stage," *Cedar Rapids Evening Gazette*, 4 August 1921.

Chapter 12

1. "Vaudeville's Biggest Flop Entering Political Arena," *Variety*, 5 March 1924.
2. "One of Famed Cherry Sisters Enters Politics," *Star Tribune* (Minneapolis), 29 February 1924.
3. "Curfew for Young C.R. Sinners," *The Cedar Rapids Gazette*, 26 February 1950.
4. Ibid.
5. "Stage," *Muncie Evening Press*, 4 March 1924.
6. Postcard from Fred Bennyhoff to Effie Cherry, 3 March 1924. Orville Rennie and Jane Rennie Collection, 1875–1987. Ms. 178. Special Collections, State Historical Society of Iowa, Iowa City.
7. "Morality Issue in Mayor Race," *The Oshkosh Northwestern*, 29 February 1924.
8. "Effie Cherry Calls Newspaper Stories a Slur on Character," *Cedar Rapids Republican*, 28 March 1924.
9. "Effie Still Waiting on Customers," *The Cedar Rapids Gazette*, 18 March 1924.
10. "Cherries Ripe, Cherries Red; Cherry Sisters Eastward Head," *Billboard*, 29 March 1924.
11. "Theater Manager Says Cherry Sisters' Act 'Rankest Ever,'" *Omaha Daily News*, 22 April 1924.
12. "Managed Noted Cherry Sisters," *The Mason City Globe-Gazette*, 9 August 1944.
13. "Cherry Sisters Find Comeback 'As Was,'" *Syracuse Journal*, 25 April 1924.
14. "Cherry Sisters Plan to Rehearse Parts," *Lincoln Evening Journal*, 26 March 1924.
15. *Variety*, 14 May 1924.
16. "Bakers Chief in Praise of City," *Cedar Rapids Sunday Gazette and Republican*, 18 May 1927.
17. "The Cherry Sisters Nice, Clean Act Is on the Stage Again," *The Des Moines Register*, 2 September 1928.
18. From a copy of the original speech, in Effie's handwriting, sent to Mrs. Gertrude Berry of Marion, Iowa. Part of the collection of the Marion Heritage Center and Museum, Iowa.
19. "Effie Cherry Tells Minneapolis Reporter What She Is Going to Do When She's Mayor of Our City," *The Cedar Rapids Gazette*, 7 January 1925.
20. "Effie, of Cherry Sisters, Is Candidate for Mayor," *The Indianapolis Star*, 31 January 1926.
21. "Last of Cherry Sisters Fading," *Chicago Daily Tribune*, 13 December 1942.
22. "Effie Cherry Tells Minneapolis Reporter What She Is Going to Do When She's Mayor of Our City," *The Cedar Rapids Gazette*, 7 January 1925.
23. *Motion Picture News*, 20 February 1926.
24. "Effie Cherry Hurls Another Broadside in Her Mayoralty Fight," *Cedar Rapids Republican*, 31 January 1926.
25. "Cherry Sisters on WKAA Program," *Cedar Rapids Republican*, 11 October 1925.
26. Effie Cherry, "The Autobiography of the Cherry Sisters," unpublished.
27. "Cherry Sisters, Fear Worst for Theater, Threaten Comeback," *Brooklyn Daily Star*, 30 January 1932.
28. From a copy of the original speech, in Effie's handwriting, sent to Mrs. Gertrude Berry of Marion, Iowa. Part of the collection of the Marion Heritage Center and Museum, Iowa.
29. Letter from John Ives to "Effie Cherrie," 3 March 1926. Orville Rennie and Jane Rennie Collection, 1875–1987. Ms. 178. Special Collections, State Historical Society of Iowa, Iowa City.
30. "Majestic Offers Barrel of Fun," *Cedar Rapids Republican*, 26 February 1926.
31. "The Cherry Sisters Nice, Clean Act Is on the Stage Again," *The Des Moines Register*, 2 September 1928.
32. Effie Cherry, "The Autobiography of the Cherry Sisters," unpublished.
33. "Cherry Sisters Sign for Return to Vaudeville," *Des Moines Register*, 8 July 1926.
34. From a copy of an original speech, in Effie's handwriting, sent to Mrs. Gertrude Berry of Marion, Iowa. Part of the collection of the Marion Heritage Center and Museum, Iowa.
35. "Curfew for Young C.R. Sinners," *The Cedar Rapids Gazette*, 26 February 1950.

Chapter 13

1. Ward Morehouse, "Broadway After Dark," *New York Sun*, 6 September 1930.
2. "Cherry Sisters—They Never Say Die!," *The Des Moines Register*, 27 January 1929.
3. "Famed Cherry Sister Flays Stage Morals," *Cedar Valley Daily Times*, 26 January 1932.
4. Ibid.
5. "Boy Badly in Need of Camp Fears Earnings Can't Be Spared," *Cedar Rapids Evening Gazette and Republican*, 13 May 1931.
6. Letter from the Rev. Zavodsky to Lizzie Cherry, 3 June 1931. Orville Rennie and Jane Rennie Collection, 1875–1987. Ms. 178. Special

Collections, State Historical Society of Iowa, Iowa City.

7. "Cherry Sisters in Des Moines to Do Their Gypsy Act," *Cedar Rapids Evening Gazette and Republican*, 24 March 1929.

8. *Salamanca Inquirer*, 8 January 1932.

9. *Mason City Globe-Gazette*, 20 March 1934.

10. "The Cherry Sisters on the Stage Again in Burlesque," Keith Kerman, *St. Louis Post Dispatch*, 22 January 1933.

11. Letter from Lizzie Cherry to Addie and Effie, 25 December 1933. Orville Rennie and Jane Rennie Collection, 1875–1987. Ms. 178. Special Collections, State Historical Society of Iowa, Iowa City.

12. Ernest Nickel, "Cherry Sisters Turn Talents to Writing," *Cedar Rapids Tribune*, 9 February 1934.

13. "A Brief Sketch of the Life and Death of Ella Francis Cherry, Pioneer of Linn County," *Cedar Rapids Gazette*, 3 April 1934.

14. "Sues Cherry Sisters for $703 on Note," *Cedar Rapids Gazette*, 27 March 1934.

15. "Cherry Sisters Back on Stage," *Olean Times-Herald*, 28 September 1934.

16. "Cherry Sisters Return After Years" Absence," *Cedar Rapids Gazette*, 13 March 1934.

17. "Cherrys," *Cedar Valley Daily Times*, 31 July 1933.

18. Letter from Carl Whyte to the Probate Court, 23 May 1946. Orville Rennie and Jane Rennie Collection, 1875–1987. Ms. 178. Special Collections, State Historical Society of Iowa, Iowa City.

19. "Cherry Sisters, Toasted with Tomatoes, Reappear," *Mason City Globe*, 27 September 1934.

20. Letter to Lizzie Cherry from Addie and Effie, Covington, Ky., 28 October 1934. Orville Rennie and Jane Rennie Collection, 1875–1987. Ms. 178. Special Collections, State Historical Society of Iowa, Iowa City.

21. Letter from Effie to Cherry to Mrs. Gertie Berry, 4 December 1935. Part of the collection of the Marion Heritage Center and Museum, Iowa.

22. Letter from Mrs. I.E. Isham to Addie and Effie Cherry, 4 February 1936. Orville Rennie and Jane Rennie Collection, 1875–1987. Ms. 178. Special Collections, State Historical Society of Iowa, Iowa City.

23. "Cherry Sisters Pause in Sixth Street," *St. Louis Star and Times*, 19 February 1936.

24. Letter to Lizzie Cherry from Addie and Effie, 24 February 1936. Orville Rennie and Jane Rennie Collection, 1875–1987. Ms. 178. Special Collections, State Historical Society of Iowa, Iowa City.

25. Letter to Lizzie Cherry from Addie and Effie, 24 February 1936. Orville Rennie and Jane Rennie Collection, 1875–1987. Ms. 178. Special Collections, State Historical Society of Iowa, Iowa City.

26. *St. Louis Star and Times*, 21 February 1936.

27. "Cherry Sisters Pause in Sixth Street," *St. Louis Star and Times*, 19 February 1936.

28. Letter to Lizzie Cherrie from Addie, 28 March 1936. Orville Rennie and Jane Rennie Collection, 1875–1987. Ms178. Special Collections, State Historical Society of Iowa, Iowa City.

Chapter 14

1. Effie Cherry, "In Memory of Miss Elizabeth Cherry," *Tapestry* (April 1941). Orville Rennie and Jane Rennie Collection, 1875–1987. Ms. 178. Special Collections, State Historical Society of Iowa, Iowa City.

2. "Cherry Sisters Made Debut 40 Years Ago: Now Guard Homestead," *Cedar Rapids Gazette*, 28 November 1936.

3. *Manitowoc Sun-Messenger*, 16 April 1937.

4. "Cherry Sisters, Iowa's Famous Thespians, Still Believe Their Apple Knocking Drama Was Good," *The Lincoln Star*, 20 December 1936.

5. "Swing Music Arouses Indignation Of Addie and Effie, Famous Sisters," *Tonawanda Evening News*, 28 June 1938.

6. "Last of Cherry Sisters Fading," *Chicago Daily Tribune*, 13 December 1942.

7. "Death of Addie Cherry Recalls Vaude's Lousiest Act on Vegetable Circuit," *Variety*, 28 October 1942.

8. "Last of Cherry Sisters Fading," *Chicago Daily Tribune*, 13 December 1942.

9. "Postscript on the Fabulous Cherry Girls," *Cedar Rapids Gazette*, 17 September 1944.

10. "Fortune from Movie Based on Life of Cherry Sisters Eludes Grasp of Bar Pianist," *Waterloo Sunday Courier*, 4 March 1945.

11. "Film to Revive Cherry Sisters Fame," *The Salt Lake Tribune*, 18 January 1945.

12. Jim Healey, "Last of the Cherry Sisters Is Dead," *Albany Times Union*, 15 August 1944.

13. "The Cherry Sisters," *The Louisville Courier-Journal*, 23 August 1944.

14. "The Cherry Sisters," *The New York Sun*, 8 August 1944.

15. "Postscript on the Fabulous Cherry Girls," *Cedar Rapids Gazette*, 17 September 1944.

Chapter 15

1. Avery Hale, "So Bad they Were Good," *Coronet Magazine*, December 1944.

2. "Film to Revive Cherry Sisters Fame," *The Salt Lake Tribune*, 18 January 1945.

3. Letter from Harry Gourfain to Orville Rennie, 18 July 1945. Orville Rennie and Jane Rennie Collection, 1875–1987. Ms. 178. Special Collections, State Historical Society of Iowa, Iowa City.

4. "Louella Parsons' Hollywood," *Albany Times Union*, 13 January 1948.

5. Louella Parsons, "Warners Fancy New Story on Gay '90s," *Rochester Democrat and Chronicle*, 17 June 1938.

6. *The St. Louis Star and Times*, 22 May 1946.

7. Letter from Carl Whyte to E.V. Fuller, 13 November 1945. Orville Rennie and Jane Rennie Collection, 1875–1987. Ms. 178. Special Collections, State Historical Society of Iowa, Iowa City.

8. James L. Smith, "Tells Secret Romance of Effie Cherry," *The Des Moines Register*, 4 March 1945.

9. Effie Cherry, "The Autobiography of the Cherry Sisters," unpublished.

10. Van Etten, p. 308.

11. "Effie and Addie Fare Thee Well," *Cedar Rapids Daily Republican*, 20 February 1906.

12. *Iowa Recorder*, 1 October 1895.

13. "Cherry Sisters Seem Overripe," *The Des Moines Capital*, 24 March 1924.

14. Letter from Carl Whyte to the Probate Court, 23 May 1946. Orville Rennie and Jane Rennie Collection, 1875–1987. Ms. 178. Special Collections, State Historical Society of Iowa, Iowa City.

15. James L. Smith, "Tells Secret Romance of Effie Cherry," *The Des Moines Register*, 4 March 1945.

16. Letter from Carl Whyte to the Probate Court, 23 May 1946. Orville Rennie and Jane Rennie Collection, 1875–1987. Ms. 178. Special Collections, State Historical Society of Iowa, Iowa City.

17. Letter from Dixie Willson to Orville Rennie, 7 December 1962. Orville Rennie and Jane Rennie Collection, 1875–1987. Ms. 178. Special Collections, State Historical Society of Iowa, Iowa City.

18. Letter from Virginia Sale to Orville Rennie, 18 August 1960. Orville Rennie and Jane Rennie Collection, 1875–1987. Ms. 178. Special Collections, State Historical Society of Iowa, Iowa City.

19. Thomas Morrow, "Sisters Leave Farm to Give Vaudeville Quite a Shock," *Chicago Tribune*, 30 June 1955.

20. "Our Washington Letter," *Marion Register*, 19 May 1897.

21. "Split Skirt and Fight Movies Created Furore in Early Days," *Cedar Rapids Gazette*, 24 October 1937.

Bibliography

Lyon-Dalberg-Acton, Richard. *A Brit Among the Hawkeyes.* Ames: Iowa State University Press, 1998.

Allen, Fred. *Much Ado About Me.* Boston: Little, Brown, 1956.

Allston Brown, T. *A History of the New York Stage.* New York: Dodd, Mead, 1903.

Cherry, Effie. *The Autobiography of the Cherry Sisters* [unpublished]. Box 3, Folder 4. Orville Rennie and Jane Rennie Collection, 1875–1987. Ms. 178. Special Collections, State Historical Society of Iowa, Iowa City.

Cullen, Frank. *Vaudeville Old and New, Volume One.* New York: Routledge, 2006.

Keaton, Buster, with Charles Samuels. *My Wonderful World of Slapstick.* New York: Doubleday, 1956.

Sheehan, Vincent. *Oscar Hammerstein I: The Life and Exploits of an Impresario.* New York: Simon & Schuster, 1956.

Taubman, Howard. *The Making of the American Theatre.* London: Longmans, Green, 1965.

Van Etten, Winifred. *The Queens of Corn* (unpublished). Box 4, Folder 1. Orville Rennie and Jane Rennie Collection, 1875–1987. Ms. 178. Special Collections, State Historical Society of Iowa, Iowa City.

Wilson, Jennie L. *Legal Status of Women in Iowa.* Des Moines: Iowa Printing Company, 1894.

Index

Aarons, Alfred E. 50-1
Allen, Fred 45
Andrews, Helen 39

Ballard, James 61-2, 65-6, 77
Bara, Theda 121-2
Barnum. Phineas T. 34, 37
The Barrison Sisters 10, 57, 59
Braska, Mary 5, 98
Brock, Lou 139
Brookhart, Smith W. 132, 133

Cherry, Addie birth 20; death 151; performance 8, 47, 54, 67, 85-6; relationship with the press 9, 105-6, 129
Cherry, Alfred 20, 23
Cherry, Anna 20, 23
Cherry, Effie attitude toward the press 3, 9, 38; birth 20; death 152; health 97-8, 103-4, 106, 128, 151-2; performance 8, 15, 27, 47, 54; political campaigns 124-6, 129-30, 133-4; relationships with men 157-8; writings 4, 11, 15, 20, 21-22, 25, 46, 51, 102-3, 128-9, 135-6, 148, 157-8
Cherry, Ella attitude toward her sisters 21, 65, 75, 98, 99; birth 20; death 121, 141; difficulty with neighbors 12, 42, 107, 114-5, 122; life on the farm 36, 38-9, 87, 90-1, 96, 107, 140; performance 8, 22, 28, 70
Cherry, Inez 20, 23
Cherry, Jessie birth 20; death 97, 98-9; performance 8, 15, 41, 54, 100; recordings 100-2
Cherry, Laura 4, 18, 19, 22, 23, 25
Cherry, Lizzie attitude toward money 9, 13, 21, 23, 39, 69, 95, 97, 108; birth 20; death 148-9; leaves the act 68-70; performance 8, 15, 55, 107, 111
Cherry, Nathan 6, 20, 21, 23-4, 61, 95, 158
The Cherry Sisters court cases 12, 36, 38-9, 42, 66, 80, 82, 84-7, 89-90, 92, 93, 99, 107, 108, 114, 118-22, 141-2, 149; faith 3, 22, 26, 40, 96, 112, 125, 133, 152; property and investments 65, 75, 87, 89, 94, 99, 105-6, 115, 120-1, 149; political views 74, 78, 132; press reaction 1, 8, 10-11, 12, 15-6, 28-9, 30, 32-3, 43, 50-1, 53-5, 57-8, 63, 67, 72, 76, 80, 88, 95, 112-3, 127-8; temperance 3, 26, 96, 103-4, 129; using a net or screen 45-6, 52, 62, 111-2, 121-2, 127, 136, 139, 151
Cherry, Thomas 4, 17-21, 23-4, 25, 36
Chicago World's Fair 6, 28, 54, 142
Coates, Robert "Romeo" 3
Collins, Lottie 36-7
Cooper, Gary 133, 139
Crandall, E.C. 27, 32, 33

Daniels, Sam 9, 27
Davis, Fred P. 12-3, 14-5
Del Valle, Cezar 116, 150, 153
Downing, Bob 117, 153-4
Dressler, Marie 57, 64-5, 69
Dunham, Mary 47, 68, 162

Eulogy on the Cherry Sisters 36, 53, 61, 76, 107, 140, 146, 164

Fair Columbia 31, 41, 53, 62, 101, 163, 164
The Fanny Hill Company 11
Faulks, Fred W. 43
Floyd, Charlie 40
Ford, James L. 55, 57, 60
Fox, Della 31
Fretwell, D.S.M 13, 15, 27, 38

Grant, Sophronia 118-21, 142
Grinnell, Orlando 76, 78
The Gypsy's Warning 27-8, 53, 54-5, 62, 85, 107, 113, 132, 135, 142, 147, 151 164

Haas, William 70, 71, 72, 73
Hamilton, Billy 79, 84-5, 86, 87
Hammerstein, Arthur 52, 56
Hammerstein, Oscar 48-9, 51, 55, 56, 57, 58-9, 61, 65, 153
Hammerstein, Oscar II 48
Hammerstein, Willie 49-50, 52, 55-6, 109
Hardy, Bill 142, 143
Harris, Cal 92, 122-3
Houdini, Harry 82, 119

Irish Ballad (*The True Biddy Just from the Emerald Isle*) 35, 53, 69, 85, 163, 164

Jennish, William H. 101
Jones, George (Count Joannes) 2

Keaton, Buster 56
Kirby, J.J. 75
Koster, John, and Bial, Albert 49, 59, 116

Lanigan, John T. 82, 102

Macready, William Charles 2–3
McKinley, William 74

Nation, Carrie 2, 91

O'Brien, Dan 159–60
O'Connor, James Owen 3
Onken, Al 41
The Orphan Flower Girl (*Barefooted Iona, the Orphan Flower Girl*) 8, 15, 38, 53–4, 57, 163, 164,165
Owen, Carl 5, 7, 22, 60, 154

Parsons, Eugene 5
Patterson, James E. 89, 158
Patterson, Jennie 5, 25
Perham, Douglas 131
Pitts, Zasu 159
Pringle, Della 70

Rall, J.F. 126, 133
Rand, Sally 142
Rawson, Isabell 37, 163
Reilly, Pat 66, 67–8

Rennie, Orville 155–6, 158–9
Rice, Marshall 33–6
Riddell, F.P. 22
Rickel, Henry 120
The Ringling Brothers 45, 110
Roehl, William 31, 33, 34–5
Rogers, Will 109–10
Rosenthal, Jake 102–3
Russell, Lillian 31, 110, 135, 142, 156

St. Denis, Ruth 40
Sale, Virginia 159
Sargent, Epes W. "Chicot" 64
Sears, C.B 72–73
Swan, Ray 126–7

Talbot, Blanche 111, 119
Thayer, Frank D. 101
Trilby (*The Hypnotizing of Trilby*) 50, 60, 80, 86, 164, 165
Trousdale, Merle 126–7

Uncle Tom's Cabin 62, 64

Van Etten, Winifred 150, 159

Warner, Jack L. 156
West, Mae 117, 143, 153
Wheeler, A.J. 38
Whyte, Carl 142–3, 152, 155, 156–8
Willson, Dixie 156, 158
Wilson, Woodrow 57

Zanuck, Darryl F. 155–6
Zavodsky, Reverend F.J. 137–8

www.ingramcontent.com/pod-product-compliance
Lightning Source LLC
Chambersburg PA
CBHW032057300426
44116CB00007B/781